REINCARNATION

REINCARNATION

ANCIENT BELIEFS
AND MODERN EVIDENCE

DAVID CHRISTIE-MURRAY

PRISM · UNITY

Originally published in Great Britain by David & Charles (Publishers)
Limited 1981

This edition published in Great Britain 1988 by:
PRISM PRESS
2 South Street,
Bridport,
Dorset DT6 3NQ

and distributed in the USA by:
AVERY PUBLISHING GROUP INC.,
350 Thorens Avenue,
Garden City Park,
New York 11040

and published in Australia 1988 by:
UNITY PRESS
6a Ortona Road,
Lindfield,
NSW 2070

ISBN 1 85327 012 1

Printed and bound in the Channel Islands
by The Guernsey Press Limited.

CONTENTS

TO LIZ

FOREWORD

No author can ever fully acknowledge the debt he owes to those whose previous work has inspired and helped him. My interest in reincarnation was excited—the word is deliberately chosen—by the reading some five years ago of Head and Cranston's first anthology on the subject, and no surveyor of rebirth beliefs and evidence could fail to draw upon the treasuries they have collected from writings east and west and ancient and modern. Eva Martin's *The Ring of Return*, though less ambitious, is another valuable and inspiring source-book.

Dr Ian Stevenson and Dr Arthur Guirdham read the chapters devoted to their work and I am grateful to them for their kindly and constructive comments. I also owe thanks to those who allowed me to refer to and one of whom gave me unpublished work of theirs, notably Miss Dianne Barker, Mr Alastair I. McIntosh and Mr Homer Belk Sewell, whose dissertations are listed in the Bibliography.

To any I have omitted to thank, let this foreword be a general expression of gratitude and an apology for any oversight of which I have been—unintentionally—guilty.

DAVID CHRISTIE-MURRAY

INTRODUCTION

Belief in survival after death is as old as belief itself. Such evidence as exists also indicates that belief in reincarnation is as old as belief in survival. Even in western civilisation, where orthodox Christianity has rejected the doctrine for almost two millennia in favour of the teaching that man's eternal destiny is determined by a single earthly life, the idea of rebirth has never entirely disappeared. A surprising number of great thinkers throughout the Christian centuries have accepted it either openly or, when this meant ostracism and the stake, in secrecy.

In spite of occasional heretical ripples of dissent, Catholicism, Orthodoxy and the many varieties of Protestantism all taught that man's soul was created with his body; with a specific beginning in time, it was henceforth immortal, without end; and its eternal destiny was settled according to its beliefs and behaviour during the seven or eight decades or less of its existence. For most Protestants that destiny was a straight consignment to heaven or hell. The Orthodox theologians sometimes surmised a middle state but not one of purging, and were generally content to leave the souls of the departed to the mercies of God. Catholics, realising that even omnipotent and omniscient God might have difficulty in deciding borderline cases cut off suddenly in life without chance of making their peace with Him, added purgatory where the blemishes of this life might be suitably purged for a sufficient time. The addition was reasonable, though without foundation in Scripture, and left reflective Protestants in a difficulty when the evolution of thought made perennial hellfire unthinkable and eternal heavenly bliss an unprofitable and uninteresting pastime. Most Protestants retreated into a spiritual interpretation, arguing that hell was not necessarily even uncomfortable but meant eternal separation from God, while heaven was eternal companionship with Him. Some found refuge in conditional salvation and immortality, recalcitrant sinners simply being annihilated. Both solutions were unsatisfactory, because they meant that the irresistible love of God had been defeated in some cases, and that however fulfilled the faithful in their heaven, the loss of even a single soul would diminish *Him* for ever. Others preached universal salvation, that every soul would somehow, somewhere, find its way home to God. To an increasing number that way seems to be reincarnation.

With the breakdown everywhere in ecclesiastical dogmatism, even in the most monolithic churches, the way is open for a resurrection of the doctrine for Christians. Reincarnation has always been a fundamental tenet of several of the great faiths of the world and flirted with by at least sections of almost every other. This can be seen from the first three chapters in this book. In 1969 a twelve-nation Gallup poll inquiring into the prevalence of the belief in the West concluded that in Austria 20 per cent believed, in France 20 per cent, in Great Britain 18 per cent, in Greece 22 per cent, in the Netherlands 10 per cent, in Norway 14 per cent, in Sweden 12 per cent, in the United States 20 per cent, and in West Germany 25 per cent. It is probable that a similar census taken today would show an increase in the percentages; the belief is more alive than it was a decade ago.

This is due partly to the interest shown in eastern religions by pop-singers, hippies and the counter-culture. More permanent and more important is the change in attitude that a century of learning about other faiths has brought to western theologians and other thinkers. It is no longer true to say that 'there are comparative religions but Christianity is not one of them'. An increasing knowledge about other religions and their origins, together with a greater comprehension of the antecedents of Christianity itself, has brought an awareness that exotic doctrines rejected as superstitions by the first missionaries may need to be reconsidered seriously and with an open mind.

The difficulty for the ordinary inquiring man who does not have a theological or philosophical training, or who has no contact with the mysteries explored by psychical researchers, is that his main source of information, the media, is unsatisfactory. Newspapers are ephemeral, their articles limited by length and the needs of the marketplace; one stimulating report about, say, a case of hypnotic regression into past lives and the readers' letters that it inspires are the most that can be expected before the subject is swallowed up in a thousand others. There is the same ephemerality on radio and television; the clock seems to cut off every discussion just as it is 'getting interesting'. Courses of lectures on the subject are more satisfactory, but comparatively few can commit themselves to weeks of attendance. Books are even better because the reader can return to them as much as he needs to, and use their bibliographies to follow up lines of interest.

The media often present arguments fairly, for and against a subject under discussion. But time is against anything more than a superficial treatment, and the reader, listener or viewer is liable to have his prejudices reinforced by what he sees or hears. However hard a lecturer tries to be objective, he is almost certain to reveal his personal bias. It is only in a book, where an author can revise every word he has written before publication, that personal opinions can be eliminated with a view to giving a completely objective account.

A reader does not want to be proselytised in a subject about which he may know very little; if he does, he can go to a society or church that teaches the emphasis that attracts him. He wants information and, where possible, evidence upon which he can pass judgement. He wants to be informed about other interpretations of the data given by other honest thinkers so that he can draw his own conclusions from the differing views. If he can be stimulated and excited by what he reads, so much the better.

Reincarnation is an exciting concept. There can surely not exist an adult westerner who does not wonder on occasions what *really* happens when he dies, whatever the theologians, philosophers and spiritually minded speculate and the materialists affirm. To such a man, distrustful of old teachings about heaven and hell and frustrated with unrealised potentialities within himself and by the sense of unfinished business that haunts even the most fulfilled and fruitful life, the idea of rebirth can appeal with an almost euphoric optimism. The doctrine also seems to explain so much left unexplained by non-reincarnationist survival teachings.

Not that there is one simple doctrine of reincarnation. There are dozens; and part of the object of this book is to present a survey of the types of doctrine that exist so that a reader may be able to choose that which appears most reasonable to him and to measure it against other teachings that may have been given to him in youth. He may smile at the naïvety of some primitive views, though he may equally be surprised at the sophistication of others. Hinduism and Buddhism may offer him a choice between mutually exclusive beliefs and yet he may be able to reconcile them at a sufficiently deep level. If a Christian, he may discover that although the majority of Christian thinkers down the ages have rejected reincarnation, a number have accepted it, and an increasing number today seem able to contemplate doing so. If he is not a Christian and therefore untroubled with the need to reconcile, the reader will find that there are other modern faiths of which reincarnation is a fundamental tenet.

More important to the average person than speculation is evidence. Provided that he is careful to distinguish between evidence and proof, there is plenty of the former. It is equally true that the evidence can nearly always be explained other than by a reincarnationist interpretation; such alternative explanations will be presented wherever relevant so that he can choose between them. The evidence in this book includes the experience of children who, from the moment they know enough language to communicate, tell their parents of earlier lives in details which can be checked and confirmed; they recognise former relatives and spouses, picking them out from crowds, find their way to their old homes from the outskirts of towns which they have never visited before, point out alterations in buildings and landscapes made since they died and reveal places where they kept or hid valuables when they lived before. Such memories fade as the child grows and the present life fills more and more of his horizon. Adults, on the other hand, often tend to grow into a conviction that they were once some character or characters in the past, and with the years develop the 'far memory' that persuades them that their feelings are true. Revelations in dreams, instantaneous recall, the recollection of former existences that can be a by-product of training in meditation— all merely illusions to the disbeliever—are completely convincing to those who experience them.

The evidence further includes cases of *déjà vu*, the feeling 'I have been here before' when the subject 'knows' that he has not; of these a reincarnationist explanation seems the best of the several possible. More exotic still are revelations given in spiritualist seances or cases where several sensitives have independently disclosed the same past life to an individual. A special case of such a revelatory sensitive is Edgar Cayce (see Chapter 6), whose many hundreds of 'life readings' helped his subjects to obtain self-fulfilment by making known to them the experience of past lives.

The most startling evidence comes from hypnotic regression into alleged previous existences, a practice that began almost a century ago and sporadically causes a flutter of interest in the media. There are positive and negative approaches to this from a reincarnationist's point of view, and the clash of facts (anachronisms versus accuracies of historical minutiae which the subject could not possibly have known by normal means) makes for stimulating debate.

Allied to the altered states of consciousness which appear in hypnotic regression, though not apparently identical with them, is the psychological manipulation brought about by the 'Christos' experience. The process, induced by simple techniques of rhythmical massage and mental exercises, could almost be described as a 'do-it-yourself' reincarnation because many subjects, though not all, find themselves in what seem to be previous existences. Some of these have been verified at least to the satisfaction of those who experienced them. The Christos experience and hypnotic regression are two methods by which the ordinary man can perhaps 'experience reincarnation' for himself. But there are other explanations of most Christos encounters and, as always, some evidence but no proof of past lives.

Wherever reincarnation is debated by the knowledgeable, the work of Dr Ian Stevenson of the Department of Behavioural

Medicine and Psychiatry of the University of Virginia is known and respected. Under his inspiration the University of Virginia has recorded nearly two thousand cases of reincarnationist-type experiences from all over the world, a considerable number of which Dr Stevenson has investigated personally in places as far-flung as India, Ceylon, the Lebanon, Alaska, Great Britain. His objective scholarly approach and the vast quantity of material he has amassed and studied are examined and summarised in Chapter 9.

The possibility of individual rebirth is enthralling, but reincarnation takes on new meanings and wider dimensions when it is realised that a very large number of those who believe the doctrine accept also that group incarnation exists. Men and women who have had close relationships in past lives are reunited, for well or ill, in future existences. If the doctrine of karma—action that brings upon the doer inevitable results good or bad in this or future incarnations, an article of faith for all modern reincarnationists—is accepted, then there is a karma for races, nations, cities, societies, communities and groups of every kind. Close groups of friends, therefore, are likely to meet in the future, especially if their relationship has been in any way traumatic. Enemies, too, may reappear—only those whose relationships are neutral tend not to meet again. Reunion with friends has been the experience of Dr Arthur Guirdham (Chapter 10), who was led by a series of encounters and experiences to the conviction that he had been a Cathar in twelfth-century France, and that acquaintances and friends had been Cathars with him. They felt the same, and whatever explanations sceptics may find for the many coincidences and strange facts that appear in his books, the story of his experiences cannot be dismissed lightly. His is the most detailed group experience written about at length today.

The examination of doctrines and mustering of evidence is not the whole story in surveying reincarnation. The arguments for and against must be sifted and brought together so that the open-minded reader can make his choice between them, or enjoy the mental exercise and make no choice at all; this is the purpose of Chapter 11. Finally there are many differing views about the progress of the entity after death (the term 'soul' is unsuitable because it has implications that many reincarnationists would not accept) and about such items as the length of intermission (between death and the next rebirth); some effort needs to be made to summarise and, if possible, to reconcile them. Chapter 12, therefore, attempts to suggest a 'theology' of reincarnation which can be accepted by twentieth-century man.

1

REINCARNATION
IN WORLD CULTURES

Reincarnation may be one of the oldest beliefs in the world. It is thought by some archaeologists to be the reason for the placing of corpses of the New Stone Age period (*c* 10,000 to *c* 5000 BC) in the foetal position at burial, so that rebirth might be facilitated. This view, it is claimed, is reinforced by the myths of those peoples whose funeral customs are designed to bring about the rebirth of the deceased into a new life. The cleansing of the corpse is perhaps a magical, ritualistic equivalent of the cleansing of the newborn; the shroud may represent the covering of the foetus by membranes.

The preparation of a *corpse* for rebirth may indicate an almost physical idea of what is reborn. Where it is believed that a *spirit* or *soul* passes on into a new life, various ideas concerning the human entity may obtain. Among some tribes it is thought that a single soul is reincarnated, if conditions are right. Among others a man is believed to have a number of souls, one that rests with the body, a second that remains present with his family or tribe, a third that departs to a land far away and a fourth that seeks reincarnation. Before death one of the souls may be separate and go out through the mouth or nostrils, thus explaining out-of-the-body or clairvoyant experiences.

In advanced religions a distinction must be made between reincarnation and karmic *theory* or *doctrines* which have developed, sometimes during millennia, to suit particular theological and religious traditions. For example, peoples living so close to nature that they regard humankind as an integral part of creation may find no difficulty in picturing themselves as being reborn in animal or insect bodies. Members of advanced cultures, with developed philosophies, conscious of how far above the most evolved animal man's thought has raised him, find the idea of sinking into an animal body repugnant.

As a catalogue of tribes and their beliefs would be long and repetitious, selected examples of reincarnation theory will be described.

Europe

In ancient Europe a 'reincarnation belt' covered at least the north of the continent, with outposts in the south, such as the Lombards in Italy. Ancient English and Scottish ballads speak of the souls of men and women passing into animals, birds or plants, and according to British and Breton folklore the spirits of dead fishermen and sailors dwell in the bodies of white seagulls, and those of unbaptised children flutter through the air in the form of birds until Judgement Day. Teutons and even Romans (according to Pliny) carefully tended house-snakes as the incarnations of ancestors or as guardian genii of their homes; as late as 1870 housemaids at the vicarage of St Cleer, Cornwall, refused to kill spiders because they believed that their dead master, Parson Jupp, had been reborn in one.[1] There is a Welsh claim that the doctrine of reincarnation began with the Celts far back in prehistory and that it was from them that it found its way to the East to flower in Hinduism and Buddhism.[2]

Africa

Throughout Africa hundreds of tribes believe in reincarnation in one form or another. Theodore Besterman, summarising the beliefs of over a hundred peoples in all parts of the continent, found that thirty-six believed the dead returned as humans, forty-seven as animals, and twelve as other entities, the more civilised inclining to the first.[3]

Of the tribes who believe in reincarnation as men, the Zulus have one of the most advanced creeds. Within the body dwells a soul, within the soul a spark of the divine universal spirit, the I Tongo. Seven grades of men exist, of whom the highest, perfect men, reach a state after many reincarnations in which rebirth has ceased. They dwell on earth in physical forms of their own choosing and can retain or relinquish that form as they choose. The final destiny of humankind is reunion with the I Tongo.

Ancestors are favourite candidates for reincarnation, the soul entering sometimes at conception, sometimes at birth, and witch-doctors are usually called in to discern which ancestor is present in the infant. This is not an easy task as the several souls of an ancestor may be present in more than one child, and sex may change from birth to birth. There is the added complication that the spirit may not be that of a direct forebear, as an uncle on either side may enter a nephew, or an aunt a niece. The Yoruba inquire of their family god which of the ancestors has come back into the latest baby, and at his rebirth he is greeted with the words, 'Thou hast come.' They name a boy *babatunde* ('father has returned') and a girl *yetunde (iyantunde)* ('mother has returned'); in Ghana the word is *ababio* ('he is come again'). The Yoruba also believe that children mistreated by their parents are reborn over and over again within the same families, and among certain Kenyan and Ugandan tribes the child is solemnly named for its predecessor, now once more among the living. In other tribes dead children are reborn as their own brothers and sisters.

In Northern Nigeria the souls of the dead hover near their homes in the branches of trees, waiting for a chance to enter the wombs of women, and Ibibio women in Southern Nigeria believe similarly that spirit children make their way into their mothers from the nearest trees, rocks or water-pools where the spirits of the dead await rebirth. Sometimes an ancestor will reveal his desire for rebirth to a woman in a dream. Bereaved women bring curls clipped from the heads of their dead babies and dedicate them to 'the goddess of the face of love' or motherhood (the same word), praying that she will set the feet of the child back on the road to life. Among the BaGandas children were named after an ancestor with the hope that some part of the ancestral spirit would enter the child and help him, though this would be permanent possession rather than reincarnation.

Some tribes believe the soul will choose the body of a person of similar rank to its former self, and therefore bury the dead man near the houses of his relatives, enabling his soul to enter a newborn child of suitable status. Others think that spirits of dead men can live where they choose, in the corpse, in a hut, in a sacred object or in the body of a living being whose spirit it absorbs. In a Calabar tribe small children are shown objects belonging to former family members and the choice of any of the possessions indicates that their former owner has been reborn in the child. Among the Bagongo, children remember past lives (belief affects performance). The Bassongo think that when the body disintegrates at death the soul goes first to God in the centre of the earth; after between two months and two years it becomes homesick, asks to return to earth and resurrects in a child about to be born. Some common scar or mark proves that the baby is the deceased reborn. The sex may vary; and if a pregnant woman suffers much, it is because the former person died painfully.

Several African tribes believe that ancestral spirits return to their old homes as snakes; milk and sometimes meat are offered either because their presence shows that the ancestor is hungry or because it will protect those living in the kraal. (There is a similar Chinese belief that a snake's visit represents that of an ancestor. Prostrations are made to it, cash-paper and candles are burned, and when it leaves it is graciously escorted upon its way.) The Betsileo of Madagascar maintain that nobles are reborn as boa-constrictors, commoners in good standing as crocodiles, and the dregs of the tribe as eels. The souls of dead ancestors are also sometimes thought to dwell in the sacred fish with which holy pools and streams abound. If a pot-pourri is made of the beliefs of a large number of tribes, human souls may pass into bodies of animals of every kind, and in some societies a man may use magic to secure his rebirth as the animal of his choice. But only chiefs can become lions or, in some tribes, hippopotamuses. One's future fate may depend on one's lot in this life: the poor and neglected become chimpanzees; the spirit of a man for whom the due rites have not been performed may reincarnate in a solitary animal or a mad human being; if a man's family die out after his decease he becomes a frog; sometimes the good are born as babies and gentle animals and the bad as savage beasts. There is a good deal of overlapping here with beliefs in werewolves, were-tigers, bears, hyenas and lions, in cultures all over the world. Mothers in some Lower Congo and Cameroon tribes believe that the noises made by their infants are the speech of ancestors. (Some Red Indian tribes believe the same.) Linked with the idea of totem animals is the avoidance of the flesh of the animal an Ababu tribesman expects to become in the next life. Death in this life is birth into the next; death in the next world is birth into this. Rites ensuring rebirth may be found all over the world, of which a typical African example is the use of ochre (haematite resembling blood representing life) in Swaziland.

Africans, unlike Hindus and Buddhists, regard life as happy and reincarnation as a good destiny. They have little idea of any end to the process and regard childlessness as a curse because it blocks the channel of rebirth. Ancestors are generally believed to reappear only in their own families.

Asia

Vast areas of Asia are filled with the adherents of the great religions of Hinduism, Buddhism and Islam and some lesser ones, which are dealt with below. These have in the course of centuries wiped out or absorbed various local beliefs which were probably as diverse and numerous as those in Africa a century ago. There still remains a number of primitive ideas of rebirth in communities living in remote hills and forests and out of contact with the great movements of Asiatic thought.

Typical of several primitive Indian tribes and lower castes of Hinduism are the beliefs and practices of the Khonds of Orissa, in the north-east of India. A fowl is sacrificed to the spirit of an ancestor to ask him to enter a newborn child. Seven days later, when the birth is celebrated, a magician determines which ancestor has reappeared, and the child will be given that ancestor's name.

Reincarnation may have existed as an aspect of their fertility rites and ancestor-worship among the pre-Aryan peoples of India and been adapted by the invading Aryans. There was a stage during the development of Hinduism when a kind of natural cycle was used as a vehicle of rebirth. The souls of those who lived lives of austerity, charity and piety travelled to the world of fathers and thence to the moon, where they lived happily as a reward for their righteousness. Falling to the earth as rain, they passed into food consumed by men and entered into the wombs of women to be reborn. Evildoers returned as animals or insects. The process ended in the normal Hindu realisation of the identity of the self, the *atman*, with Brahman, the absolute (see page 35).

In Assam, the Angami Nagas believed the soul passed through a series of insects, the Chang Nagas that the souls of those who could sing became cicadas and of others dung-beetles, the Lushais that wasps and hornets were souls, and yet other tribes that, more specifically, those wood-boring wasps and hornets which took up their abode in the wooden soul-figures they made to commemorate the dead were the souls of those remembered. The Konyak Nagas performed ceremonies over phallic cists containing skulls of dead persons in order to secure birth of a sex corresponding to that of the skull. The skull and head were supposed to contain the semi-material 'soul matter' on which all life depends, often in diminutive form (whence perhaps the practice of head-shrinking); head-hunting was based on a belief in a cycle of life dependent on the possession of soul matter and the addition of more of it to the community's general stock. This soul matter increased the fertility of humans, cattle and crops. The Karens of Burma held that the soul was a kind of pupa that burst and spread its contents over fields, fertilising them and passing through eaten grain into the bodies of men and animals and into seminal fluid, propagating new life. Many other tribes believed variations of the same theme, that the soul goes into the crops; by preserving the smoke-dried corpse of recently dead persons, their funeral ceremonies could be delayed and accommodated to the cycle of the agricultural year when their soul matter could be used at its greatest potential. A Lushai doctrine was that the soul, settling in the form of dew, was reincarnated in the body on which it lay, and another idea was that the souls of lovers were to be found in intertwining trees and flowers growing on graves.

Among occultists there is frequently mentioned an esoteric eastern religion, closely associated with Tibet and possibly—if it exists at all—a refinement of Buddhism. This is taught by the great masters, the mahatmas, with whom certain advanced individuals throughout the world are allegedly in touch. The teaching is that man is composed of seven principles and evolves by a long series of lives in each of a number of worlds corresponding to the seven. After a circuit of lives has been completed it must be repeated on a higher plane until, after many successive cycles, each comprising hundreds of lives, the individual enters into the perfect fullness of experience.

An oriental tradition that does not seem to be attached to any particular religion is that the soul is allowed one 'comfortable' incarnation for every six lives of arduous development, and that lives grow correspondingly tougher as the soul breaks the ties that bind it to earth.

Pacific Ocean

In the vast stretches of Oceania—the Pacific Islands, Indonesia, Micronesia and Melanesia—the belief in transmigration of human souls into the animal world is as widespread and varied as its peoples and geography. The Sea Dyaks of Borneo believe that the soul dies several times and eventually becomes an insect or a jungle plant. A number of peoples in Eastern and Central Melanesia believe that spirits live in the next world for a while, die a second time, then turn into white ants, others that after the second death they become a variety of creatures. The inhabitants of Northern Guinea hold monkeys, snakes and crocodiles sacred, because they are animated by the spirits of the dead. Papuans and other New Guinea natives do not eat fish, pigs or cassowaries, for the same reason. Lifu natives and Solomon Islanders, when dying, tell their families what creatures their souls will animate so that their relatives will never kill or injure them. The Bakongs of Borneo believe that their dead will reincarnate as the bearcats that frequent their raised coffins, and in some parts of Melanesia fishermen assert that their grandparents and perhaps even earlier generations return in the form of birds to direct them to shoals of fish. In parts of Indonesia the soul may become the ferocious tiger, while in Semang and the

Malay Peninsula transmigration is confined to chiefs and magicians, whose souls inhabit rhinoceroses and elephants and in these shapes protect their kinsmen.

The Poso Alfures of Celebes believe in three souls, the vital principle (*inosa*), intellectual (*angga*) and divine element (*tanoana*), the last of which leaves the body during sleep, wanders in dreams and is of the same nature as many animals and plants. It must be small enough to leave by the mouth and is portrayed as a manikin, though it may be described as flying and represented as a butterfly or a bird. Similar ideas are found in farther India, where the soul leaves the mouth sometimes as a manikin, sometimes as an insect, and even in Germany of old, where it appeared as a snake, weasel or mouse.

In Bali, where Hinduism is the prevailing religion, the individual is believed to reincarnate over and over again in the same family. Perhaps the Okinawans have one of the most advanced theologies of rebirth in this part of the world. Human spirits leave their bodies at death, stay in their homes for forty-eight days and on the forty-ninth enter *gusho*, an 'after-present world' state. They cannot enter animals, and within seven generations return in the form of an individual closely resembling the former incarnation. Some spirits remain in *gusho* indefinitely and greet new arrivals. Not mind but spirit reincarnates, mind being received by the individual through ancestral descent.

The idea behind cannibalism, once rife in the Pacific, may have been the absorption of the soul matter of the dead man and the addition of it to one's own. In New Britain the heads of enemies were worn as masks so that the wearer could acquire the soul of the dead man, and the use of the hair of slain foemen for ornaments by the inhabitants of New Britain may have represented a similar belief.

Australia

Belief in the reincarnation of ancestors exists in every tribe of the northern clans of Central Australia, and it may be presumed that the doctrine was originally universal among the Australian aborigines. They believe that all living persons are reincarnations of the dead. After death the soul lingers on in the neighbourhood, haunting pools, gorges or trees, as in African beliefs, on the lookout for a woman into whom it may pass to be born again. It can be born only into its own clan, though some beliefs, such as that the spirit of a dead man enters into his slayer, contradict this idea. The reincarnation of grandfathers into their grandchildren is frequent.

Palaeolithic Australian aborigines, especially the Aranda, believed in continuous rebirth. They 'placed' the souls in stone plaques called *churinga*, whereupon the ancestors came alive, developed very large forms of animals and men and travelled round their tribal territory, leaving special marks. Then they disappeared but left souls behind which emerged from the *churinga* and became people.

The aborigines have complicated rituals that ensure their continued existence. These rituals and myths are their 'dreaming', as they call the spiritual dimension, and signify the continuity of life unlimited by space and time. Initiation into the cult, open to men only, is a ritual form of death and rebirth into life, a sharing of the burial ceremony which ensures that the spirit returns to its 'dreaming', from which it will be reborn.

A belief, shared by some American cultures is that spirits are reincarnated as white men. It is recorded of the late Sir George Grey, a nineteenth-century governor of South Australia, that he was identified by an old native woman as her dead son come to life again; while an aborigine just before his hanging for murder cheerfully faced death in his belief that he would 'jump up whitefella'.

The Americas

The Tlingit Indians of south-east Alaska believe that the soul reincarnates into a new body among its relatives, and used to cremate their dead. A pregnant woman dreaming often of a dead relative believes that he will be born as her child. If the baby is found to have a birthmark which had existed on the body of the deceased, it is considered that the same person has returned to earth, and the child is given his name. It is possible that the

Tlingits may have been influenced by Buddhism, and there are also certain superficial resemblances to Hinduism. They have a concept of karma, though not called by that name, with the expectation that misfortunes in one life may diminish in another. Like the religions of India, Burma and Ceylon, the Tlingit creed holds that children who remember past lives will die young.

Spread throughout the northern wastes from Alaska to Greenland are many tribes of Eskimos, some of whom are described as possessing reincarnation beliefs like those of India, but the similarities could easily be coincidental. Some tribes mummified their dead as late as the nineteenth century and believed also in rebirth into new bodies. Animal transmigration was accepted by others—an Eskimo widow refused to eat walrus after a magician had told her that her late husband had entered into one. Manley P. Hall mentions a custom whereby an aged Eskimo selects a newly married couple and asks them if he may be their first-born child. If he is a good and honourable man they will probably consent, whereupon the man departs some distance from the camp and kills himself so that his soul may pass into the chosen family.[4] Among the Behring Strait Eskimos, the first child to be born after someone's death will be given the name of the dead person and will represent him at festivals held in his honour. The western Eskimos of Alaska developed a system of five ascending heavens, each to be attained after an earthly incarnation with gradual progressive purification and eventual release from the cycle of rebirth.

At least some dozens of tribes of North American Indians held reincarnation beliefs, although it is said that only in the Northwest was a coherent theology formulated. Other authorities claim that the belief is especially deeply rooted among the tribes of the Eastern United States.[5] Both statements may be true, for a deep conviction may be intuitive rather than formalised and expressed in custom rather than dogma. In the Northwest, half the children in the five Gitksan Indian reserves in British Columbia are recognised as reincarnations of specific people.[6] Their identification is helped by the presence of birthmarks corresponding to wounds or other physical markings or deformities of the reborn ancestors or on the basis of dreams in which an ancestor announces his return.[7] A boy in Vancouver Island was revered by the Indians because he had a mark on his hip like the scar of a gunshot wound borne by a great chief four generations earlier.[8] Part of the funeral ceremonies of the Carrier Indians of British Columbia was that a medicine man would stand at the head of the corpse and look upon its breast through both his hands. He would then 'blow' the soul into one of the relatives, and the dead man would be reincarnated in the first child born of the recipient.

In the east of Canada, the Hurons believed that a man had two souls. One remained in the cemetery until the relatives held their periodic feast of the dead, and then took flight to the underworld, while the other stayed close to the decaying corpse, unless it was born again in some descendant. The Hurons also buried children by the roadside so that their souls might enter into women who passed by and be reborn. Several customs were connected with women and children. The Hopis of Arizona made a road from the grave of a little child to its old home so that its soul might live again in the next baby born to the family. Algonquin women who wanted children would sometimes gather round a dying man or a grave in the hope that his spirit would enter them.

Some Indians claimed to have full knowledge of former incarnations, though, according to the beliefs of the Lenape of Delaware and New Jersey, only the pure in heart might be able to remember their former lives. Among other snippets of reincarnation belief, Hiawatha, the legendary chief and hero, was expected one day to return. The Powhatans believed that their chiefs transmigrated into small wood-birds. The practice of scalping may indicate an idea that the soul was located in the hair (compare the beliefs held in parts of the Pacific and the story of Samson). In both North and South America there were Indian cultures which incorporated the belief that by offering themselves as human sacrifices to the gods the victims earned extra rewards in their next sojourn on earth. Common to the two Americas also was the belief that white men were ancient heroes who had been reborn to seize lands they had formerly owned, which largely explained the collapse of the Inca empire before a handful of Spaniards.

Transmigration into the animal world was widely accepted by South Americans. The ancient Mexicans believed that princes, nobles, fallen warriors and sacrificial victims, after a sojourn in the east paradise of the sun-god, were reborn as birds of brilliantly coloured plumage or as clouds or as precious stones. Commoners became weasels, foul-smelling beasts or beetles. Women who died in childbirth went to the west paradise of the sun and might return as moths. Other recipients of human souls were hawks and eagles, for the Caingue of Paraguay domestic pigs, and, for the Canados of Equador, jaguars, which they never attacked save in self-defence. New Mexican Indians believed that a dying baby would return and that if the body were buried beneath the home hearth the soul would find its way to the gates of rebirth and return to the same family.[9] The Incas made the return even more certain by mummifying the body so that the soul could return to its former receptacle.

A number of religions became more than tribal and some supranational, spreading over considerable areas of the world's surface. Of these Zoroastrianism, extant today among the Parsees of India, possibly has the longest continuous history.

Zoroaster is a title given to a series of teachers rather than the name of any one, and the man usually referred to as Zoroaster, the latest in the series, lived during the seventh millennium BC. He taught that human souls are immortal and infinite spirits who descend from on high for a succession of lives in mortal bodies to gain experience and return. The number of lives allocated to them is far fewer than those estimated by other eastern religions, although some Persian and Arabian mystics extend the total. During the intermission between earthly lives the soul has several abodes, one luminous, one dark, some a mixture. If it sinks into a body from a luminous abode, it tends to live a life distinguished for knowledge and sanctity. At the end of this it returns above, the positions of virtuous souls comforming with the degrees of their virtue. Perfect men attain a beatific vision.

A soul's sojourn in a dark abode leads to an evil life, thence to a darker place. It is separated from the primitive source of life, and may, unless purified, become an evil spirit. Mixed abodes lead to lives of imperfect goodness, and the souls who have lived them migrate from one body to another until the virtue of their behaviour emancipates them from matter and they move upwards in the spiritual scale. There is a primitive idea of karma, rewards and punishments being meted out for good and bad deeds in former lives.

Modern Parsees do not teach reincarnation as part of their creed, though many of them speculate about previous lives.

Other Persian religions advocating reincarnation were Mithraism, dating from several centuries BC, among whose *magi* it was an important doctrine; and probably Manichaeism, founded by the Persian, Mani, who was born about AD 215. The views of the Manichees have survived largely in the works of their Christian opponents and may have been misrepresented.

'Ancient Egypt' is often popularly referred to as if it were an unchanging unity, whereas its pre-Christian history stretches for over three millennia, with possibly another four millennia of prehistory to be added, when the nation was in the making. During that time Egyptian religion became bewilderingly complex because the Egyptians added new elements to the old in their creeds even when they contradicted each other.

To write, as Herodotus, Plato and Plutarch did, that reincarnation was the general belief of the Egyptians is an oversimplification. The Egyptians had a number of different views of what happened in the after-life. Reincarnation was certainly one of these, at least for royalty and aristocracy.

Kings whose names ended in -*cheres*, such as Mencheres of the Fifth Dynasty (*c* 2494–*c* 2345 BC), were said to be renewed incarnations of the Cheres; that is, they were all the same individual. The souls of men were composite beings, consisting of the *bai* or *ba*, represented as a bird or the shadow, the *ka*, or double, and the *akh*, which was a spiritual power obtained after death. The *ka*-names of certain of the pharaohs of the second millennium BC, Amonemhat I, Senusert I and Setekhy I, were respectively 'He who repeats births', 'He whose birth lives' and 'Repeater of births'. By the Eighteenth Dynasty (1567–1320 BC) it was believed that lesser folk could be reborn, and The Book of the Dead gives the spells to be recited in order to incarnate in various forms. Reincarnations were not always welcome—one reason for embalming the dead was to delay or even prevent their coming back to life on earth.

Return was sometimes thought to be inevitable, even after an intermission of happiness. The sensitive soul was said to pass after death by the Capricorn gate (of the gods) into the *amenthe*, a kind of heaven, where it dwelt in continuous pleasure until, descending by the Cancer gate (of men), it went to animate a new body.

Herodotus, the Greek historian living in the fifth century BC and an extensive traveller, reflected the Egyptian beliefs of his day. The Egyptians were the first, he wrote, to teach the immortality of the soul. At the death of the body it enters into some other living thing, comes to birth and, after living through all creatures of land, sea and air in a cycle lasting three thousand years, it enters a human body once more at birth. Twelve of these cycles, according to another ancient writer, Pierius, make a complete revolution after which all things are restored to their former state.

The faculty of transformation was, it seems, desirable, a principal privilege and power of the just in the Egyptian paradise. It allowed them to change into anything they liked anywhere in the universe. Egyptian ritual writings are full of allusions to the doctrine; and there are many inscriptions calling for a man to pass through transformations agreeable to himself. Extant funeral books show that the soul was reborn into a new being formed by the reunion of corporeal elements and passed through a succession of infancies, youthfulnesses and maturities in order to accomplish new terrestrial existences under many forms. The method of reincarnation conceived of was a purely materialistic one. Bodies changed themselves by exchanging their molecules, the dissolution of old bodies providing the material to form new.

The recorded views of humans reborn as animals are inconsistent. At times some Egyptians held that the entering of a human soul into a lower animal might be a punishment for sin.[10] Seemingly a more general teaching was that the soul ascended through all degrees until it became human. Then, guided by the spirits of beings of outstanding virtue, it progressed through thousands of degrees of higher intelligence to perfection. In each existence the soul forgets previous lives but keeps its *kerdar* (karma). When it arrives at the end of its incarnations and a sufficient degree of purity, it achieves a condition where, as an Egyptian text of 300 BC says, 'At the end all his different lives will be revealed to a man.'

The Hermetic Works, in their present form dating from some period during the first three centuries AD, summarise the doctrine of reincarnation probably held then by many cultured Egyptians. These works were supposed to have been compiled by Hermes Trismegistus or Thoth (Greek and Egyptian names of the god of wisdom). All souls, they taught, derived from the one soul of the universe. They developed from creeping things to watery to land creatures, from birds to human beings. 'The soul passeth from form to form and the mansions of her pilgrimage are manifold.'[11] The soul had to earn future immortality by piety, defined as knowing God and injuring no one. Such a soul became a holy power, pure intelligence, and passed into the sphere of the gods, thus obtaining its most perfect glory. The impious soul remained in its own proper essence, for although changes might be down as well as up, divine law preserved the human soul from the infamy of entering an animal. After death, souls' destinations were determined by their experiences in the body, the impious spirit being punished by having to seek another human body into which to enter (a 'vacant' body was perhaps hard to find). Souls were sexless, since sex was a feature of physical bodies only.

The most ancient of the surviving great religions is Hinduism. It originated at some time during the fourth millennium BC but does not seem to have adopted a belief in rebirth until about 600 BC. (The earliest known investigation among Hindus into a case of reincarnation took place in the eighteenth century.) There is no unambiguous text upholding the doctrine, for example, in the Rigveda, the earliest Hindu scripture, collected early in the first millennium BC. The Aryan invaders may have taken over and refined the idea of transmigration of souls from the indigenous inhabitants, and once adopted it became widespread by the time the Buddha was born, in the sixth century BC. In the century preceding his birth, Hindu scriptures are full of references to reincarnation; traditionally the belief was an esoteric secret belonging to the Brahmin warrior caste of which Buddha was a member.

All great religions develop different schools of thought. There are theological forms of a religion and popular forms, the former being normally purer, stricter and more dogmatic, the latter tolerated by the theologians as a concession to the spiritually illiterate majority. The following summary of Hindu doctrine is an approximation, therefore—just as a general statement of the teachings of Christianity written for a Hindu readership might be.

Hinduism begins with a conception of a timescale as vast as the extent of the universe of modern astronomy. Since the cycle of rebirth can last throughout the whole of this near-eternity, the effect on the ordinary man, for whom existence means struggle and suffering, is intense depression, and Hinduism has been accused of causing social stagnation, fatalism, callousness and pain. Behind the present universe, which has its own successive cycles, is another existence which is eternal and changeless, to penetrate to which is the greatest of all achievements.

Although it has many gods, of whom the chief may be conceived of almost monotheistically as God, there are nontheistic as well as theistic systems within the faith, and these lay different emphases on reincarnation and karma. There exists an absolute Brahman, which is timeless, non- or supra-personal, the ultimate spiritual reality in and behind the universe. With this, according to some schools of Hindu thought, the human soul is mystically identical, while others, who conceive of Brahman as in some sense a personality and, in fact, God, preach an I–Thou relationship with Him, maintaining that the highest spirit must be different from individual souls, else they could not communicate with Him. From the supreme being there emanated human souls, which became gradually immersed in matter, and will return to Him after many lives.

There exists an individual self for each soul, a *jive*, *jivatman* or *atman*, from which is projected into a vast series of incarnations illusory separate individuals consisting of psychophysical egos. The soul has existed eternally in the past though it will not, as a separate entity, continue eternally into the future. The ego exists only in the realm of illusion (*maya*) and is but a temporary expression of an eternal reality, usually unaware of its everlasting part or of the recording of all its experience of all its lives in the *atman*. At death there survives a 'subtle body', mental rather than physical, which registers all the emotional, aesthetic, intellectual and spiritual dispositions built up in the existence just ended and adds them to the total of its impressions (*samskaras*). It is a bundle of *samskaras* that is reborn. When the man dies, the soul 'becomes conscious and enters into Consciousness' and makes for itself another form, newer and fairer, like the forms of departed spirits, or of the seraphs, or of the gods. Intermission between lives may last for thousands of years, when the soul in one or other of the Hindu heavens (planes of existence) may both give and receive help and attention and be rewarded and punished. Karma may be partially paid for during the intermission, partly in a high or low condition of rebirth in the next existence. Even if rewarded in heaven for its goodness, the soul may have to return to earth later for its ancient sins, and its state of rebirth will depend on which of the three cosmic qualities— goodness, passion and darkness—is uppermost within it. Souls of the first quality become deities, those of the second men, those of the third beasts. The man enters whatever form his heart desires, wishes being expressed through will in works; whatever work he does, he grows into the likeness of it.

In Hinduism, gods, men, animals, plants and minerals all reincarnate, and the Laws of Manu, a Sanskrit document written between 200 BC and AD 200, allocate various animal, vegetable and mineral incarnations to humans who have committed appropriate sins. This doctrine was encouraged by brahmin priests who could enforce caste practices by teaching that the penalty for breaking them would be rebirth in an unclean animal, an insect or a stone.

The doctrine is in some measure still held. Although it is acknowledged that the essential characteristics of humanity cannot possibly exist in an animal form, *physical* atoms can 'enter into organic combinations according to their affinities, and when released from one individual system they retain a tendency to be attracted by other systems, not necessarily human, with similar characteristics'.[12] For example, those atoms which are the vehicle of a gluttonous appetite may reincarnate as a pig, but only the appetite, not the whole human. This conception is aided by the belief that not all the *samskaras* are re-embodied on each occasion but only those most dominant and demanding of further activity and expression.

There is a development in ideas from the earliest *upanishads* (scriptures) to modern doctrine. The Brihad-Aranyaka Upanishad taught that the soul leaves the body by one of its apertures and returns to a new and more beautiful form in another life. In others of the earliest *upanishads* some souls come down in rain and cloud, are born on earth as plants, may be eaten as food, emitted as semen and start a new life in the womb. Good souls will be born of women of the priestly, princely or merchant classes, evil ones of bitches, sows or outcaste women. The Bhagavad-Gita likens the 'dwellers in the body' to a man who throws away old clothes at death and puts on new when he is born again. Later it was believed that the subtle body joins the physical embryo provided by the parents. The soul enters the body, pervading it, yet imperceptible and unattached to it, and supports the body with the mind. The self is not to be grasped by any of the senses. Only by the mind is the great self perceived.

It is only in an earthly existence that the soul is able to exercise its freedom responsibly to develop further towards the ultimate self-awareness of liberation (*moksha*). Between AD 300 and 600 six philosophical schools arose with different emphases but all devoted to the achievement of this aim. They taught that morality and religious observance were conducive to favourable rebirths on the lower stages of spiritual progress and that the higher demanded asceticism and mystical gnosis.

Some of these schools were nontheistic, some theistic. For the nontheistic division of Hindu thought, karma is not a consciously directed process but one of automatic retribution, an expression of moral and psychic law parallel to natural law, from which there is no escape. The theist Hindu believes that karma is a *spiritual* necessity, an embodiment of the mind and will of

God. He presides over the rebirth process, continuously monitoring the course of each individual's career and the complex interaction of the plethora of karmic destinies. What is more, God sometimes intervenes personally and directly; the Bhagavad-Gita relates that the god Krishna, in a dialogue with his disciple Arjuna, teaches that he incarnates 'for the preservation of the just, the destruction of the wicked, and the establishment of righteousness'.[13]

For both theistic and nontheistic Hinduism the machinery of karmic reward and retribution is the caste system, part of an ordered universe in which animate creatures were arranged in an hierarchical order with humanity above all other forms and orthodox brahmins above all other humans. Every man reaps what he has sown by being born into a higher or lower caste. Since the status of a caste can never be advanced in a single lifetime, the position of a man for his whole life on earth is irretrievably fixed by the status of the group into which he is born. Each caste has its duties and prohibitions. Observation of the former gives its members purity, failure to obey the latter pollutes him. A man's status in his next life is determined partly by the faithfulness with which he follows his caste duties, partly by the quality of his life as an individual, and it is in the latter that advance in successive incarnations is made; for the *individual* status finishing point of one life is the *group* status starting-point of the next. Some group behaviour to which a man must adhere may include acts usually regarded by mankind as immoral, such as the ritual murders of *thuggee*, and one cannot but sympathise with an individual whose personal moral conscience might conflict with his group's conventions—like the cannibal in the song who felt that 'it was wrong to eat people'. (Now the practice of *thuggee*, is extinct.)

Where children claim to remember a previous life—about one in 450 do so in Northern India[14]—they tend to recall lives as unrelated members of a higher caste who lived in or near the subject's village. I know of no case where a caste lower than the present one was chosen.

It is possible for the wicked to be lost eternally, sinking in birth after birth into ever more demonic wombs and never attaining to God or the equivalent nontheistic fulfilment of nirvana. Another unhappy fate is that of the man at whose death the proper rites are not performed, for his soul may become a ghost and haunt the living. If the ceremonies and libations are observed properly, the spirit attains a subtle body which can incarnate anew. Through this grace, God can be a saviour lifting His worshippers out of the ruck into the theistic concept of nirvana, an eternally secure and timeless state of blissful communion with the Godhead. Such salvation may be earned by worship of and devotion to the gods, by unremitting attention to the appropriate ceremonies and festivals, by benevolence expressing itself in the building of shrines, temples, schools and hospitals and the digging of wells, and by pilgrimages to Hindu holy places, and is open to all, even 'women, artisans and serfs'. It may also be won by a withdrawal from social life into asceticism or solitary meditation; this earns merit enough to release the ascetic from several reincarnations and is the quickest way to eventual release. The object of meditation is, through mystical experience, to attain gnosis, the esoteric realisation that man's apparent separate personality is an illusion and that the extinction of his separateness is only a loss of ignorance. He attains bliss by recognising that he *is* the absolute Brahman, such recognition resulting in the highest and most perfect consciousness, the ecstasy of true being. Patanjali, ancient founder of the school of yoga philosophy, described the process in his Aphorisms.

A knowledge of the former incarnations arises in the ascetic from holding in his mind the trains of self-reproductive thought . . . By concentrating his mind upon the true nature of the soul as being entirely distinct from any experiences, and disconnected from all material things . . . a Knowledge of the true nature of the soul itself arises . . . When the mind no longer conceives itself to be the knower or experiencer, and has become one with the soul—the real knower and experiencer . . . the soul is emancipated.[15]

One who has achieved this state of complete disinterestedness about the process of change and becoming, though no longer subject to reincarnation, may continue to live upon earth. His soul is in no way subject to his body, he completely transcends his mental, physical, temporal existence.

The modern Hindu reincarnationist has to meet challenges to his beliefs, as all men of a faith do. If human souls are progressing, why does the whole human race not advance? He may argue that it *is* advancing—we are at least theoretically more aware of and concerned with world welfare, undeveloped nations and socio-economic problems than we were a century ago; or that there has not been time—if souls produce a phenomenal self only once in, perhaps, some thousands of years; or, if he is a Vedantist, that there can never be discernible spiritual progress in the realm of illusion represented by this world. On the positive side he can claim that there do exist on this earth enlightened souls who have attained release and enlightenment, pointing to recognised gurus and yogis as examples. The Hindu reincarnationist believes his holy writings reveal the truth of reincarnation: inherited behaviour, such as suckling, must have been learned in previous lives (this may be a case of evolution of a survival instinct); the universal human fear of death presupposes a knowledge of previous deaths (the modern view suggests death is a joyful experience, so what is there to be afraid of?); love at first sight, friendships, antipathies, reflect relationships in a previous life (all these are balanced by the equal mysteries of *developing* love, friendship and antipathy). The frequent arguments that infant geniuses must have carried over their talents from a previous life and that the differences between children of the same parents must be due to different previous incarnations are answered by the counter-claims of fortunate genetic combinations and the many different possible permutations of genetic elements in a pair of parents. Hindu thinkers contend that every individual, while the product of his parents' genes, is also heir to the incalculable factor of karma.

Under Hinduism, although it is also used by Jains and Tibetan Buddhists, may be mentioned Tantrism, a system of esoteric practice whose adherents believe in rebirth but also that they can win salvation in one life.

In the study of Judaism the most familiar collection of Jewish documents is the Old Testament. As might be expected from a religion developing over many centuries, this contains a number of views of man's destiny after death, but rebirth is not among them. Reincarnationists quote a number of isolated texts as upholding or suggesting the doctrine but to an objective reader they appear extraordinarily weak and sometimes founded upon lack of understanding of the original.

The texts are Joshua 24: 3; Job 14: 14; Psalms 90: 3–6; Proverbs 8: 22–31; Ecclesiastes 1: 9–11; Jeremiah 1: 4–5; Malachi 4: 4–5; and, in the Apocrypha, Wisdom 8: 19–20 and Ecclesiasticus 41: 11–12. It is hard to see how the Joshua verse, a perfectly straightforward statement of how Abraham emigrated to Canaan from the other side of the flood—that is, the river Jordan—can be interpreted as upholding rebirth.

Job cries:

> If only you would hide me in Sheol [the underworld of the departed] and shelter me there until your anger is past, fixing a certain day for calling me to mind—for once a man is dead, can he come back to life? Day after day of my service I would wait for my relief to come. Then you would call, and I should answer, you would want to see the work of your hands once more.

Psalm 90: 3 in the Authorised Version reads, 'Thou turnest men to destruction; and sayest, Return, ye children of men', but in the more accurate Jerusalem Bible version, 'You can turn men back into dust by saying, "Back to what you were, you sons of men!"' The passage in Proverbs is a personalised description of Wisdom, sometimes considered by Christian theologians to be a harbinger of the doctrine of the Holy Spirit, not a description by Solomon of his incarnations since the beginning of time. The Ecclesiastes verses may be summarised in the single sentence contained within them, 'There is nothing new under the sun.' Yahweh's words to Jeremiah, 'Before I formed you in the womb I knew you; before you came to birth I consecrated you', speak of the foreknowledge or foreplanning of God and, at the most, upholds the idea of pre-existence. Yahweh promised through Malachi, 'Behold I will send you Elijah the prophet before the coming of the great and dreadful day of the Lord.' Elijah had never died and his reappearance would therefore be on a par with those great heroes of history, such as Frederick Barbarossa, who are traditionally supposed to return when their country is in danger. Ecclesiasticus states that godless men 'were born to be accursed, and when you die, that curse will be your portion ... but a good reputation lasts for ever', and Solomon said in Wisdom, 'I had received a good soul as my lot, or, rather, being good, I had entered an undefiled body.'

Only the Job and Wisdom passages can possibly be given a reincarnationist meaning, and even in them the doctrine is anything but explicit. Considering the prevalence of the belief from the earliest times throughout the world, and the size of the Old Testament corpus of writings, such neglect amounts to a rejection.

Yet Josephus, the Jewish historian, maintains that both the Essenes (c 200 BC to AD 200) and the Pharisees (from 200 BC until their doctrines came to be accepted as orthodox Judaism) accepted reincarnation.[16] The former cheerfully gave up their lives in the struggle against the Romans, as men who expected to receive them again. They believed that souls are immortal; that they come out of the most subtle air and are united to bodies as to prisons into which they are drawn by a natural enticement, but when they are set free from the bonds of the flesh they fly upwards rejoicing, as released from a long bondage. The Essenes are said to have studied the return of individuals, and may have been influenced by Pythagorean thought, as was the little-known Jewish sect of Therapeutae in Egypt in the first century AD.

The Pharisees also believed that souls have 'immortal vigour' in them and that the virtuous have power to revive and live again on earth. All souls are indestructible but whereas the souls of good men are removed into other bodies, those of evil men are subject to eternal punishment.

The Talmud, a collection of Jewish law and tradition compiled from before the time of Christ for the next two centuries, taught that God created a limited number of souls whose destiny it was to reincarnate until purified for the Day of Judgement. The righteous would then be assured of a reward in a future world. The Talmud taught specifically that Abel's soul passed into the body of Seth and thence into that of Moses. Edgar Cayce

(Chapter 7) promulgated the same idea even of Christ himself as the culmination of a series of Biblical incarnations.

The Cabala, written in its present form in about AD 1000, supposedly dated to the beginning of the Christian era. It was traditionally far older, believed by those who accepted its authority to be the hidden wisdom behind the Old Testament, orally transmitted in uninterrupted course from Moses onwards. It seems to have assumed reincarnation as a doctrine so widely accepted that it scarcely needed expounding, but it does contain some explicit teaching. No man is perfect who has not kept the 613 precepts of the law, and he who fails to do this is doomed to undergo transmigration as many times as is necessary, until he has observed everything he neglected in his former existence. During the lengthy intermissions men are brought to judgement both before they enter the world and after they leave it, and are ignorant of the many transmigrations and testings they have to undergo. But this forgetfulness is a blessing. Repeated lives are also a blessing because they give a man opportunities to develop all the perfections of which the germ was planted in them to fit them for re-entry into the absolute substance from which they came and for reunion with God.

The Talmudic idea of Biblical 'incarnation series' is repeated in the Cabala, although sometimes apparently confusedly. Adam's soul passed into Moses into David and will inhabit the Messiah; Japhet's into Samson; and Terah's into Job. Cain's 'essential soul' passed into Jethro, his 'spirit' into Korah and his 'animal soul' into the Egyptian killed by Moses. An idea of karma is suggested by the tale that since Cain had robbed Abel's twin sister and reincarnated as Jethro, the latter gave his daughter to Moses who had received his soul from Abel (did Abel and Adam share a soul?).

Eve became Sarah became Hannah became the Shunammite woman became the widow of Zarepta. Hannah was also the receptacle of Rahab's soul via Heber the Keenite, whose heroine wife, Jael, slayer of Sisera, became the not-so-heroic high priest Eli.

A man niggardly in either a financial or spiritual sense was punished by transmigration into a woman. Sometimes the souls of pious Jews passed into gentiles in order that they might plead on behalf of Israelites and treat them kindly.

Jewish sects later than the Pharisees, Essenes and Therapeutae revived the idea of transmigration in Judaism. The Karaites, founded in Bagdad in AD 765 and still surviving, mainly in southern Russia, rejected rabbinism and Talmudism and based their tenets on their interpretation of scripture. The title Hassidim, the name of the forerunners of the Pharisees and of other sects at various periods in Jewish history, was adopted by a movement among Polish Jews of the eighteenth century. It had considerable influence, spreading to the Ukraine, Galicia and Lithuania, and still persists; among these Hassidim reincarnation is a universal belief. The philosopher Martin Buber (1878–1965) was a Hassid and spread the beliefs.

Rabbi Isaac Luria (1534–72) taught not only metempsychosis but also the possible impregnation of two souls into one body, thus explaining the apparent confusion in the Cabala. Rabbi Manasseh Ben Israel (1604–57) wrote in his *Nishmath Hayem'*:

> ... the doctrine of the transmigration of souls is a firm and infallible dogma accepted by the whole assemblage of our church with one accord ... We are therefore in duty bound to accept this dogma with acclamation ... as the truth of it has been incontestably demonstrated by the Zohar [the Book of Light, the definitive work of the Cabala] and all the books of the Cabalists. [17]

If men sin, God sends their indestructible souls back into the world to be purified by metempsychosis. S. Ansky, alias Solomon Judah Rapoport (1863–1920), author of *The Dybbuk*, believed that 'through many transmigrations, the human soul is drawn by pain and grief ... to the source of its being, the Exalted Throne above.'[18] Sholem Asch (1880–1957), famous for his *The Nazarene* (1939), wrote:

> If the law of the transmigration of souls is a true one, then these, between their exchange of bodies, must pass through the sea of forgetfulness. According to the Jewish view we make the transition under the overlordship of the Angel of Forgetfulness. But it sometimes happens that the Angel of Forgetfulness himself forgets to

remove from our memories the records of the former world; and then our senses are haunted by fragmentary recollections of another life.[19]

The great eastern faith Buddhism differs basically from Hinduism in that whereas the latter postulates an eternal individual self, the *atman*, to which the illusory separate individuals that are incarnated relate, the former denies the existence of a permanent self or soul that transmigrates from life to life. There is only an illusory ego in continuous process of change, which incarnates because of its desires and attachments and, once incarnated, takes part in a process through which it changes from second to transitory second, a human personality being only a 'stream of psychophysical events'. The 'I' who has just completed that sentence is not the same 'I' who began it, and present is related to past only as effect is continuous with cause. The illusion that there is a permanent unchanging self or substantial soul keeps karma and the wheel of rebirth, *samsara*, moving. The object of the Buddhist is to escape *samsara* by extinguishing the three fires of craving, ill-will and ignorance. History is thus a meaningless jumble of events through which human streams of psychophysical events meander until at last they are sufficiently enlightened to attain nirvana.

In Buddhist psychology the individual consists of five sections: the physical body; feelings and sensations; perceptions (awareness, recognitions); mental formations (impulses, emotions, moral law and its accumulated character dispositions); consciousness. At death these fall apart, leaving a 'germ of consciousness' to be reincarnated. The nature of the new individual depends on the quality of the potencies contained in the germ.

An individual's last thoughts before death determine the nature of rebirth by causing the first moment of thought in the new life. (Therefore meditation on death can contribute notably to the enlightenment that leads to nirvana.) The 'fundamental thought' at death becomes the 'emigrating thought' becomes the 'rebirth thought', nucleus of the new existence. Whether the fundamental thought is the very last thought in the life or the total quality of life's endeavour, regarded as conditioning the final thought, is debatable. In Buddhism a common metaphor of rebirth is the lighting of a new candle from one burned out. Nothing remains of the first candle but the flame.

The germ of consciousness is a life-craving set of character dispositions and latent memories which becomes attached to a new embryo to form a fresh empirical self. This system of dispositions corresponds roughly to the western concept of a 'psychic factor' and is, in eastern thought, *vinnana*, 'that which rebecomes', not consciousness but rather an unconscious dispositional state, the karmic deposit of the past. Its craving for life gives it a grasping force which grapples it to a new point of entry in the stream of biological life. There may be some law of affinity that automatically attracts a particular bundle of dispositions to an appropriate embryo and determines the nature of the next birth.

Only a minority of births are into human life. Rebirth may occur in many worlds, *kama* worlds of sense which include our earth, purgatory and the nearer *deva* (angel) worlds; *rupa* worlds of visible form though not sense, the further Brahma and supra-Brahma spheres; and the *arupa* worlds, incorporeal worlds of thought. The best men (bundles of dispositions?) meet in heaven and commune with resplendent gods. Others are reborn as men. Yet others, especially the covetous and mean, reappear as *pretas* (ghosts), creatures rejoicing in evil and always ready to do harm. Some less wicked appear as animals, though intelligent leaders of oriental thought do not hold with the transmigration of humans into animals, a concept simply for popular consumption. The worst criminals go to hell. None of these conditions, however, is eternal. The Tibetans believe that some human beings, the highest lamas, are always immediately reborn as humans. These include the Dalai Lama, who is a reincarnating *bodhisattva* (an enlightened being who has attained nirvana but postpones his entry into it in order to help mankind), the Panchen or Teshu (Tashu) Lama, the spiritual head of state, who is an embodiment of a buddha, Amitabha, and several hundred others, normally principals of monasteries. They also accept the existence of *tulkus*, individuals of great spiritual achievement who can control the time and place of their rebirths. It was estimated that in 1950 there were about a thousand *tulkus* in a population of about four million. They were identified when young on the basis of omens and the similarity of their behaviour to that of abbots of Buddhist monasteries.

The Buddha himself willed to be reborn into every order of life so as to accomplish the liberation of all creatures from the bondage of the law of rebirth. He passed through hundreds of existences, all of which he remembered—from four hundred in one account to as many as there are plants in the universe in others. Some 550 narratives of his births in various animals and human forms appear in the Jatakas (birth stories); for the ardent Buddhist, there is not a particle of earth anywhere which the Buddha has not sanctified by some form of existence on or in it.

Yet it is maintained by some schools of Buddhist thought that Buddha did teach the existence in man of an immortal reincarnating individuality that could move up and down for almost eternity until it was finally redeemed. He said in his last moments, 'The spiritual body is immortal.' Northern Buddhism, the Mahayana school, taught the doctrine of a permanent identity which unites all the incarnations of a single individual—indeed, the doctrine of karma becomes almost senseless if divorced from the idea of a reincarnating ego of some sort. If there is no unchanging centre, memory of past lives with their sense of connection and continuity becomes an almost insuperable difficulty. Buddha himself gives some support to this view by his metaphor of a pearl necklace, every life a pearl and the string upon which they are strung the connecting link.

Although memory of past lives is denied to most ordinary men, it does exist as a mark of Buddhist achievement:

Him I call a Brahman who knows the mystery of death and rebirth of all human beings, who is free from attachment, who is happy with himself and enlightened . . . him I call the Brahman who knows his former lives, who knows heaven and hell, who has reached the ends of birth . . .[20]

With his heart thus serene, made pure, translucent, cultured, devoid of evil, supple, ready to act, firm and imperturbable, he [the saint]

directs and bends down his mind to the knowledge of the memory of
his previous temporary state. He recalls to his mind . . . one birth, or
two . . . or three or a thousand or a hundred thousand births . . .[21]

Memory of past lives is a by-product of the life of contemplation
that leads a man along the road to nirvana, in spite of the fact that
he has no permanent soul to be the agent of remembering; and as
it is every man's destiny eventually to attain nirvana, every man
will eventually recover memories of all his innumerable lives.
This is part of enlightenment. He will scarcely look upon these
objectively, as the death of one person followed by the birth of
another. In spite of the development of the 'germ of consciousness' from life to life, one feels that the entity that has become a
bodhisattva is essentially the same as that which has passed
through a thousand lives of spiritual babyhood, childhood, ado-
lescence and ever-maturing adulthood. Even when Buddhism
denies the existence of the empirical self, it must at heart acknowledge some abiding consciousness, memory and, above all,
responsibility of the ego that finally achieves nirvana.

Karma, for the Buddhist, is universal causality, each act
bringing its inevitable result, right resulting in right, wrong in
wrong. This fact provides beings with opportunities for moral
advancement. Yet the generation of even right karma keeps the
wheel of life turning, and extinction of karma is necessary for the
attainment of nirvana. There is also a common karma of humanity, made up of the karma of the societies, classes and nations to
which we belong, for our actions affect others, and Buddha certainly taught the existence of collective, rather than individual,
karma.

Nirvana, the goal of all existences, is not extinction and
nothingness—this misconception is a western parody of
Buddha's teaching that the state is indescribable and inexpressible, beyond existence and nonexistence. It is a transcendent
condition of ultimate truth, complete passionlessness and blissful enlightenment, free from all craving for individual satisfaction, suffering and sorrow. It is absolute immortality through
the absorption of the soul into itself.

Like all great religions Buddhism has its 'theological' side, with many schools of thought debating and disagreeing about the inner meaning of some of Buddha's teaching, and its popular aspect. There is no need here to discuss the relative merits of the Hinayana (Theravada or Southern) and Mahayana (Northern) forms of teaching. But the pure Buddhist road to nirvana is too hard for many to follow or even to contemplate. Some laity, monks and even buddhas (enlightened ones) prefer heaven or rebirth to nirvana, and rebirth itself to cessation. By taking a great vow and performing good deeds to others through a long series of incarnations, the priest Honen (1132–1212) claimed to have brought about the existence of a blissful realm for all who called upon his name in faith, thus founding the Jodo, or Pure Realm sect. Moral discipline and meditation could also act as short cuts to nirvana, while in Tibet the recitation of certain mantras could wipe out the karma of a hundred years. It is not only in the West that indulgences are known.

Almost contemporary with Buddhism is Jainism, historically dating back to about 600 BC, though it claims to be much older. It drew its original inspiration from Hinduism, of which it may be regarded as a successful heresy. 'Jain' is from Sanskrit *jina*, a victor or vanquisher, and implies conquest of the bondage of pleasure, pain, life and death which is imposed by the phenomenal world upon the soul of man. This soul is a spiritual, immaterial, eternal entity running through the various stages of births and deaths. It possesses a collection of habits and attitudes, but the soul does not consist of these; it is not these *personal* attributes that are immortal, though there is an *individuality* that is. The soul of man was originally pure, and the destiny and duty of the Jain is to develop his nature and those of his fellows to highest perfection. Jainism has no god, most of a deity's functions being appropriated to the perfected soul of man.

The cause of the bondage of mankind and the process of transmigration is karma, for the Jain an almost material substance. It is a subtle invisible essence of various kinds that flows into and clogs the individual, one type inhibiting knowledge, another giving pleasure, another imposing pain. All activity produces karma, but evil deeds result in especially dense karmic matter.

Jains believe in countless souls in human beings, animals and plants, and regard injury of other living creatures as particularly heinous.

The burden of old karma and acquisition of new keep the soul in an endless process of rebirth. At death the soul with its covering of karma or matter is born into a new body, the nature of which is determined by the quality of the karma. But the past can be atoned for and the inflow of new karma stopped by many lives of religious austerity and penance and of disciplined non-injury to others. Salvation is the liberation of the soul from matter and its ascent into the bliss at the top of the universe, where it will continue in eternal joyful omniscience and inactivity.

First found documented in the fourth century BC but probably some centuries older is Taoism. *Tao* means 'way', and the way of life of Taoism is a practical, philosophical and religious system, complementing Confucianism and Chinese Buddhism, holding that the *tao* itself is something that existed before heaven and earth: it is still, formless, solitary, unchanging, reaching everywhere without suffering harm, eternal, the mother of the universe. All else is in continuous flux. Unlike Buddhists, Taoists have a positive attitude towards reincarnation. Chuang Tzu (*c* 300 BC), one of their early philosophers, exclaimed:

> To have attained to the human form must always be a source of joy, and then to undergo countless transitions, with only the infinite to look forward to—what incomparable bliss is that![22]

In Chinese Taoism, Yenlo-Wang (Yama), king of the underworld has ten courts under him of which the tenth is occupied by a staff of administrators who organise transmigration. There a type of rebirth for every soul is determined, the soul is led to the hall of oblivion, given a magic broth of forgetfulness by an old hag called Granny Meng and flung into a torrent of foaming red waters which precipitates it into its new existence.

Mohammedans are, in the main, not reincarnationists. A text from the Koran, much quoted by those who believe in rebirth, runs, 'God generates beings and hence they return over and over again, until they return to him.' No great doctrine should be based on a single text, and it is more than countered by other views of the after-life taught in the Koran and held by orthodox Moslems. In the early days of Islam, however, there was widespread belief in reincarnation in each of three forms. There was *hulul*, the periodic incarnation of the perfect man or deity; *rij'at*, the return of an imam or spiritual leader after death; and *tanasukh*, reincarnation of the souls of ordinary men. As with other faiths, rebirth was said to have been taught by the leaders of Islam who succeeded the Prophet to select inner circles, but not to the masses—though no ordinary Moslem who accepted the belief in it or favoured it would be regarded as heretical.

The alleged esoteric doctrine of Islam was preserved, so they asserted, by the Sufis, who went even further in claiming that they anticipated Mohammed by several thousands of years. They linked rebirth with a teaching of the conscious evolution and limitless perfectibility of man. Some Islamic sects were credited with rebirth doctrines. The Shi'a Moslems believed that the twelfth and last imam, a divinely inspired spiritual leader, Mohammed al Muntazar, who 'disappeared' in 878, is still alive and will appear before the last day to save the world. This, however, is not reincarnation in a general or full sense. The Isma'ils, an offshoot of the Shi'ites, were affected by neo-Platonism and developed a form of rebirth belief, and the Druses, who split off from the Isma'ils, and to whom reincarnation is a fundamental tenet, believe that the souls of the righteous immediately pass at death into progressively more perfect embodiments, till they reach the stage of reabsorption into the Godhead. The wicked are reborn in a lower condition. If an interval between lives apparently exists, it must have been filled by another, forgotten, incarnation. The only time an interval is allowed is during war, when the release of too many Druse souls may choke the pipeline. The Druse culture encourages claims to remember previous lives but considerable scepticism may exist about individual claims. The atmosphere encourages children to talk, and it is perhaps for these reasons that the incidence of reincarnation cases among Druses is perhaps the highest in the world.

A doctrine almost exactly similar to that of the Druses was taught by Jalal-ud-din Rumi (1207–73) one of Persia's great mystical poets, a heterodox Mohammedan and founder of the Mevlevi order of dancing dervishes.

His greatest work was the *Mathnawi-i Ma'nawi*, some 30,000 couplets in six books, in which he taught that souls advanced from inorganic to plant to animal to man to angel to 'what no man can conceive; we shall merge in Infinity as in the beginning. Have we not been told, "All of us shall return unto Him"?' 'I am,' he wrote, 'but one soul but I have a hundred thousand bodies . . . Two thousand men have I seen who were I; but none as good as I am now.'[23]

The Bektashees, a Turkish Moslem sect much influenced by alien cultures, believe that human souls may enter into animals, for which reason they are unwilling to kill any living creature, lest it contain the spirit of a man. A Mohammedan sect in Hindustan, the Bohras, also believe in reincarnation.

Finally, Sikhism, a religion combining elements from Hinduism and Mohammedanism, was founded by Nânak (1469–1593), who said that he had been born many times as tree, bird and animal, and had in many lives performed both good and evil deeds. Beings are caught in the whirling wheel of *samsara*, involuntary births and deaths, because of self-identification with the body and its environment. Karma explains the differing conditions of men's lives, but it is not the inevitable process that Buddhism believes it to be. Above all is God; his divine grace, allied with the leading of good lives by men in obedience to God's commands and with a life of prayer, brings about liberation and salvation.

There is an 'other-worldly' aspect of Sikhism and a 'this-worldly'.

The other-worldly aspect is the ultimate union of every man's soul with God after he had passed through various existences by transmigration.

Of the 'this-worldly' aspect Radhakrishnan wrote:

The aim of liberation is to escape from the world of space and time but to be enlightened, wherever we may be . . . for those who are no longer bound to the wheel of *samsara*, life on earth is central to the bliss of eternity. Their life is joy and where joy is, there is creation. They have no other country here below except the world itself. They owe their loyalty and love to the whole of humanity.[24]

2

REINCARNATION
IN WESTERN THOUGHT

Almost every writer on reincarnation begins with the half-truth that the doctrine (there are in fact several doctrines) of rebirth is an eastern concept that has had little currency in the West. The statement is statistically true in that reincarnation is accepted by well over four hundred million Buddhists, Hindus, Jains and Sikhs, whereas orthodox Christianity has on the whole rejected it; it is not true in that the belief in various forms has been widespread in the ancient cultures of Europe, both among its primitive peoples and in the more advanced cultures of Greece and Rome. Early Christianity flirted with it, many powerful heretical sects embraced it, and the names of those intellectuals, philosophers and poets in the last couple of centuries who accepted it as a possible form of human survival read like a roll of honour. Before them there were sometimes bold individual thinkers who braved charges of heresy and possible death at the stake for the belief, sometimes movements of thought embracing it, surprising in the geographical distribution and number of their adherents.

More a group teaching than a movement, the concept of transmigration of souls began in Greece with the Orphics, who flourished from about the sixth century BC. Herodotus[25] states that they derived their doctrine from Egypt, although the Greeks may have brought it from the East themselves. Orphism began with a doctrine of the fall: men were born of soot from the bodies of Titans immolated by Zeus's thunderbolts after they had devoured his son, Zagreus. In man's gross, earthy Titanic body, therefore, there was a divine Zagrean particle, his soul, which must be freed. The soul, aspiring to freedom, obtained true life when death released it; but only to be reimprisoned in flesh, either animal or human, throughout long ages of expiation and purification. During these aeons lives alternated in earthly bodies and in Hades. Ultimate release from the cycle was gained by conscious living according to ascetic Orphic discipline and observance of Orphic rites. The divine powers would then recognise the human soul as numbered among the pure, a 'Son of Earth and starry Heaven' who shall be 'god instead of mortal'. Thereafter he would dwell beneath the earth in the world of souls, communing with the gods.

Later Greek mystery religions inculcated similar doctrines to initiates. The Eleusinian mysteries, in portraying the story of Demeter and Persephone, represented the heavenly state of bliss after death by Persephone's six months in the upper world, and earthly incarnation by the half-year's sojourn in Hades. At her loom Persephone wove new bodies for old souls. It was recognised then that some people remembered past lives by the instructions buried with some bodies directing the souls to ask for the water of remembrance from the spring in Hades; this would enable them later to recall what had happened to them in their previous life.

Perhaps the first known individual teacher of reincarnation in Greece was Pherecydes (c 550 BC). He taught in his *Theologia*, generally known as the *Seven Adyta*, doctrines of metempsychosis and the soul's immortality which he learned from the secret books of the Phoenicians and from Chaldaean and Egyptian teachers. He taught the far more famous Pythagoras.

Pythagoras (c 582–c 500 BC) did not, as Shakespeare stated, teach that the soul of our grandam might inhabit a woodcock, although there is an apocryphal story that he recognised the soul of a dead friend gazing mournfully through the eyes of a dog that was being beaten. He claimed to have been Aethelides, son of the god Mercury, who gave him the gift of remembering his former incarnations and discerning those of others. He recalled having been Euphorbus, fatally wounded by Menelaus at Troy; Hermotimus, who in a temple of Apollo recognised Euphorbus' shield, dedicated there by Menelaus, as his own; and Pyrrus, a Delian fisherman, before he was reborn as Pythagoras. There was also ascribed to him a female life as a beautiful courtesan.

Pythagoras is reported to have travelled in the East, perhaps as far as India, and to have belonged to a brotherhood at Cortona which had much in common with the Orphics. Scholars differ as to exactly what he taught, and it is probably on the alleged similarity of the brotherhood to the Orphics that he is said to have preached the immortality of the human soul, its imprisonment in the body, its life below as a long purgatory, now in Hades, now on earth as man or animal, and its ultimate immortal salvation gained through sacred knowledge and asceticism. If all his disciples were like Empedocles (c 490–30 BC), whom he bound by oath not to reveal his esoteric teaching, it is no wonder that all that can be certainly ascribed to him is the doctrine of metempsychosis. Empedocles himself in *The Purification* stated that he had been girl, thicket, bird and fish, and that the worthiest human souls were reborn as lions or bay-trees.

A late contemporary of Pythagoras, Pindar (c 518–c 438 BC), the Greek choral lyrist, in his *Olympians* ii represents this world and the next as each places of temporary rewards or punishments for conduct in the other. Those who live righteously three times on either side of the grave pass to a state of eternal bliss. In another fragment he portrays Persephone, mother of the murdered Zagreus, accepting 'satisfaction for her ancient grief' from some of the dead who were reincarnated after eight years to distinguished lives on earth.

Because of Plato's (427–347 BC) enormous influence on European thought throughout the centuries, he is probably the most important thinker to be considered in the history of western reincarnationism. Influenced himself by Orphic and Pythagorean views, he expressed his theories of rebirth in his *Republic, Phaedo, Phaedrus, Menos, Timaeus* and *Laws*. He taught the immortality of the soul which belongs, in its perfection, to the upper air, the universe of being, the transcendental world of ideas (truth, beauty and goodness). There existed a fixed number of souls, which were a kind of substance whose essential quality was life. The substance, though immortal, changed its forms, being subject to constant re-embodiment in the universe of becoming, alternating with escape from its physical bodies back into the realm of being. This process obeyed the cyclical process of nature. Some forms, such as heat and cold, are incompatible, and, since life is the essential quality of the soul, it must retire at the approach of death, to its former abode, into communion with itself, to assimilate its earthly experiences and memories. Meanwhile its physical individuality disappears with its former body, whose elements go to constitute other bodies and individualities. The human soul is reborn in one of nine states of probation, according to the degree of vision of the truth which it has attained in its previous life. The sensuous man, for example, reincarnates more quickly and in worse conditions. The righteous improve their lot, the unrighteous deteriorate and may pass into the body of a beast and again from the beast into a man, although the soul of one who has never seen the truth ('never beheld true being') will not pass into the human form. A fallen soul cannot recover its pristine state for ten thousand years unless it has belonged to a guileless lover of philosophy, and a philosopher's life should be spent in trying to liberate the soul from dependence on the body.

After their sojourns in the realm of being, souls, reinvigorated, desire again further trials of their strength, further knowledge of the universe and the companionship of former friends. They are allowed to choose, but the myth of Er in the tenth book of the *Republic* suggests that the choice is determined by their former wisdom or folly and is therefore not free. Er, left for dead on a battlefield and returning to life after ten days, related how he had seen the souls of men choosing one or another variety of human or animal life.

The soul makes its own bodies, but since it cannot do so without expending energy, there will come a time when it cannot make a fresh body, when it will disappear—presumably permanently into the realm of being. Reincarnation is therefore not endless. Nor is there personal immortality, which implies some form of memory and continuity of consciousness. Yet, having seen all things that exist, the soul will eventually have all knowledge, which would logically include its own memories and past consciousness together with those of everybody else.

Aristotle (384–22 BC) began by accepting pre-existence and

reincarnation but later rejected the latter. He taught that the whole soul was immortal, that its normal state was life without a body and that its sojourn in the body was a severe illness.

Neither in Greece nor Rome did reincarnation seize the imagination of the people and it remained within the province of the intellectuals. Rome followed the Greeks in the doctrine of rebirth as she did in so many other aspects of religion and culture. The Calabrian poet Ennius (239?–169 BC), who flattered himself that he was the reincarnation of Homer—their soul had previously inhabited a peacock—and was mocked for his view, may have been the first to introduce it into Italy. Of the various Roman philosophies, the Stoics believed the universe to be governed by cycles, but reincarnation was not part of orthodox Stoicism. After the destruction of each world the individual soul returned to the soul of the world from which it had originally emanated. Cosmic life was believed to be an infinite series of exactly similar cycles, so in the new world the same soul, endowed with the same qualities, found itself in the same existence—a belief that certainly needed stoical qualities. Posidonius (c 135–51 BC) taught reincarnation and was extremely influential, while Lucretius (c 94–c 50 BC), sceptical about life after death, was possibly the first to ask, 'Why don't we remember past lives?'

Philosophers concern themselves with what they believe to be the facts of existence. Poets deal in fantasies which may or may not reflect their beliefs but at least present what is usually acceptable to their readers. Virgil's Pythagorean vision of the after-life in Book VI of the *Aeneid*, in which the dead Anchises gave his son Aeneas a guided tour of the underworld, included the purification of souls. A god then summoned them to drink of Lethe, the river of forgetfulness, and they were ready to enter earthly bodies once more. Ovid taught that the soul passes both from beasts into humans and from humans into beasts, and used the metaphor of pliable wax moulded into different shapes yet ever the same. Sallust argued that transmigration could be proved from the congenital afflictions of many men, a view allegedly confirmed by some of the evidence presented by modern reincarnationists.

For the philosopher Philo Judaeus of Alexandria (20 BC–AD 54), the air was full of souls of a twofold origin, higher and lower, creatures of God and creatures of sense, sin and evil, those nearest the earth desiring and descending to live in a series of human bodies. Those possessed of a diviner structure were freed from bonds of earth, and all urged their way back to the heavenly region, their true home. Deliverance from the world was won by mortification of all the senses; failing this, reincarnation followed. Another Jew, Josephus the historian, reported that there was a teaching that 'all souls are incorruptible, but that the souls of good men are only removed into other bodies, with the further detail that the faithful obtain a most holy place in heaven, whence in time they return into pure bodies. Suicides, however, sink to the darkest region in Hades.[26]

Apollonius of Tyana (first century AD), who recalled a former life as pilot of an Egyptian vessel, heard from Iarchus, a wise man of Kashmir, of his own previous incarnation as an Indian king, and had pointed out to him a stripling who, though highly gifted, detested philosophy because he had been Palamedes of Troy, ambushed and slain by Odysseus and denied a place by Homer in his epic.

There is disagreement among theologians as to whether early Christianity tolerated or even taught reincarnation. Relevant passages from the Bible are discussed in Chapters 2 and 4 but the church fathers, who contributed much to western thought, should be mentioned here. Justin Martyr (AD 100?–165), in his *Dialogue with Trypho*, speaks of the soul inhabiting a human body more than once but being unable to remember previous existences. Souls who become unworthy to see God are joined to the bodies of wild beasts. Trypho, a Jew whom he meets on his travels, opposes Justin's view; it is not clear whether Justin accepts his arguments.[27]

The teaching of Clement of Alexandria (AD 150?–220?) is ambiguous. He seems in his *Exhortation to the Heathen* to hint at the pre-existence of souls, an opinion later condemned as heretical by orthodox Catholics yet necessary if reincarnation is accepted. 'Before the beginning of the world,' he writes, 'were we rational creatures of the Word of God',[28] but adds in another work, 'God created us when we did not exist before.'[29] Else-where[30] he postpones discussion as to whether the soul changes to another body, an indication that he may have been uncertain, and he is reputed to have written many tales, not extant, of metempsychoses and worlds before Adam. Clement is interesting in that he says he does not write down everything he knows—his esoteric Christianity is not for everyone. This was the claim also of Christian varieties of Gnosticism, of which there were many. They taught that they were the custodians of the secret teaching that included reincarnation, handed down verbally by Christ to his disciples. Not much in the way of gnostic writing has survived, but the *Pistis Sophia*, a gnostic gospel, probably of the third century, although supposed to be the esoteric teaching of Jesus to Mary Magdalene, teaches that souls are 'poured from one into another of different kinds of bodies of the world', that sinful bodies are 'cast into a body which is suitable to the sins which it hath committed', the curser into a body 'continually troubled in its heart', the thief into 'a lame, halt and blind body' and the arrogant man into 'a lame and deformed body, so that all despise it persistently'. The ignorant doer of good is given a disposition to seek and find the truth, to discover 'the mysteries of the Light'. Some who have received the mysteries may still transgress, die unrepentant and suffer eternal annihilation as a punishment.[31]

Origen (AD 185–c 254), possibly the greatest of the Greek patristic thinkers, taught the pre-existence of the soul or spirit, which being immaterial has neither beginning nor end of life. All spirits were created blameless; all will, after full purification continuing in successive worlds, at last return to their original perfection and enter heaven. They animate several bodies successively, these transmigrations being determined by their merits or faults in previous lives:

> Everyone therefore of those who descend to the earth is, according to his deserts or the position that he had there, ordained to be born in this world either in a different place or in a different nation, or in a different occupation, or with different infirmities or to be descended from religious or at least pious parents . . .[32]

If it can be shown, Origen also wrote, that souls exist independently of bodies and that their condition is worse in the body than out of it, then bodies are of secondary importance and clothe souls from time to time to meet their varying requirements. When fallen souls have raised themselves to higher things, their bodies are annihilated. They are thus ever vanishing and ever reappearing until the return to original perfection is achieved. Whether Origen taught pre-existence on the earth or in other spheres is disputed, but not that he taught the two ideas themselves, rejected in the main by orthodox Christianity. For him they explained certain scriptural narratives, among others the struggle of Jacob and Esau before their birth and the reference to Jeremiah when still in his mother's womb.

One of Origen's teachers was Ammonius Saccas, who in AD 193 founded the Alexandrian school of neo-Platonism. With it the doctrine of reincarnation remained in prominence and was taught by Saccas' successors for over three hundred years, influencing many prominent thinkers. The murder of the virgin philosopher Hypatia caused the school to be moved to Athens in 414. Hierocles (*fl c* 430), an alumnus of the school, commented on Pythagoras' *Golden Verses* that only metaphorically, through virtue, could a human soul become that of a god; or of a beast, through vice. The school was closed in AD 529 by the Christian emperor Justinian, after nearly a millennium of Platonism.

Plotinus (*c* 205–70), another pupil of Ammonius Saccas and regarded as the founder of neo-Platonism, was among those philosophers who saw successive incarnations under the analogy of an actor changing roles, the same actor wearing different *personae* or masks, different personalities, while remaining the same individual beneath. The whole of each soul did not enter into bodies; something belonging to it always abode in the 'intelligible world' of abstract forms. This superior part of the soul is never influenced by fraudulent delights and lives a life uniform and divine, a conception which, as will be seen, comes close to the Hindu idea of the *atman*. That part of the soul that falls becomes merged with matter through a desire to be something independent in itself; but the soul that fights its way back into the intelligible world, by carrying back the experience of what it has known in the fallen state, learns how blessed it is to abide in that upper realm. Plotinus did believe, however, that men 'who have used only their senses' become transmigrated into animal or vegetable according to their natures. The irrationally angry became ferocious animals, the lustful and greedy pass into the bodies of lascivious or gluttonous creatures, the lazy degenerate into plants.

Porphyry (233–c 304), Plotinus' pupil and literary executor, in his *On Abstinence from Animal Flesh* taught that 'in the choice of life [that man] is the more accurate judge who has obtained an experience of both [the better and the worse kinds of life] than he who has only experienced one of them ... He who lives according to intellect ... has passed through the irrational life.'

Iamblichus (250–330) was one of the first thinkers to solve the problem of the apparent injustice of existence by asserting that the gods see the whole panorama of lives that every soul has lived. With these in view they reward or punish, unjustly to the man who observes only the present life but deservedly in the eyes of those who know all. An individual example of such punishment is suggested by Sallu(i)stius (c 370) who surmised that atheism was a punishment for neglect of the gods in a former life. The same writer wrote, in his treatise *Concerning the Gods* 'If transmigration takes place into a rational being, the soul becomes that body's soul; if into an irrational creature, the soul accompanies it from the outside ... A rational soul could never inhabit an irrational creature.' Thus the soul 'accompanies' babies and idiots, a belief that is found in later varieties of reincarnationist faith where it is stated that the soul does not fully enter a child until he is about seven years old.

St Gregory of Nazianzus (329?–389) asserted that the difference between Christians and pagans was that the former believed that the resurrection body, composed of the same atoms, was compacted around the soul while the latter supposed that the soul alighted in other bodies.[33] The Emperor Julian the Apostate believed himself to be a reincarnation of Alexander the Great.

St Jerome (c 347–c 420) is said to have supported reincarnation in his 'Letter to Avitus' and that the doctrine was propounded among the early Christians as an esoteric doctrine. Jerome was also an admirer and translator of Origen. He lists several alternative theories of the origin of souls which can scarcely be bettered as a summary of the various views that have been and still are held in various quarters: souls have either fallen from heaven, as Pythagoras, Plato and Origen believe; or they are of the proper substance of God, as the Stoics, Manichees and Priscillian heretics of Spain believe; or are kept in a repository formerly built by God, as some ecclesiastics foolishly believe; or are daily made by God and sent into bodies; or come into existence by traduction (souls derive from souls, bodies are from bodies), as Tertullian, Apollinaris and the greater part of the western church believe.

St Augustine of Hippo (354–430), with his enormous breadth of mind and surmise, is claimed as an authority by both sides on the question of reincarnation. Some of his texts suggest a doctrine of rebirth, others deny it. Chalcidius (early fourth century) wrote that 'souls who have failed to unite themselves with God are compelled . . . to begin a new kind of life, entirely different from their former, until they repent of their sins',[34] while Synesius (c 370–430) in his *Treatise on Providence* is quoted on the periodical incarnation among men of wise benefactors and heroes. Nemesius (late fourth century), the bishop of Emesa, taught that human souls migrate only into human bodies. Other early fathers opposed reincarnation, considering that the belief entailed men becoming 'flies, gnats and bushes'; an imposing list of thinkers who condemned the doctrine can be assembled.

Macrobius (fourth to fifth centuries) accounted for the memories some men have of former lives by the incomplete intoxication of a soul descending to earth and made drunk through the new draught of 'matter's impetuous flood'. Like other philosophers, Macrobius envisages the soul descending from a realm of purity and light and eventually returning to its original perfection purified from the contagion of vice.

Proclus (410–85) envisaged a manifold of souls descending from a unified primal soul and eventually becoming reunited with it. Every soul can descend into and ascend from a temporal process an infinite number of times. It can reincarnate in a brutal life but not in a brute. An eternal life cannot start from or finish at a point in time and, while self-will causes some human souls to descend more often than is necessary, the cosmic law requires that each shall descend at least once in every world-period. Such descent is not sinful but is a necessary part of the soul's education or a necessary cosmic service.

Neo-Platonists were not unanimous on whether souls could attain final release from the circle of birth, though Porphyry conceded that the souls of philosophers would finally be released for ever.

Alongside the classical tradition of reincarnation with its ancestry probably in the East was a native European strain. The early Teutonic peoples of Europe are said to have held the belief that heroes and heroines were reborn in other people, and the East Goths, Germans, Norwegians, Icelanders and Irish Gaels all acceded to reincarnation in various forms. The Celts inhabiting Europe west of the Rhine held rebirth beliefs that were pre-Roman—according to one writer,[35] derived from Atlantis. Druidic teaching, noted by several Roman authors of whom the best known is Julius Caesar, was that souls were immortal and passed some years after death into other bodies. The Celts were reported to lend each other money on promise of repayment in a future life, and Caesar wrote that their warriors were much encouraged to valour through disregarding death, since they knew they would live again.

Celtic beliefs found literary expression in the work of the sixth-century bard of Wales, Taliesin, who had been in turn a sword blade, raindrop, word in a book, book itself, a light in a lantern, bridge, eagle—'There is nothing that I have not been'—and foretold that he would continue to be until doomsday. Likewise, in the eleventh century *The Book of the Dun Cow*, incorporating far earlier material, Tuan, son of King Cairell, tells of his successive incarnations as man, stag, boar, hawk and salmon which, being eaten by Cairell's wife, passed into her womb and was born as Tuan. How far these works are poetic hyperbole, how far they reflect genuine reincarnationist belief, is arguable.

The relationship of modern Wicca—the 'old religion' of

witchcraft—to any ancient form of worship is uncertain (the original faith may be as old as the Stone Age), but it too accepts reincarnation as a tenet of belief:

> We tend to identify with one or two [of the twelve archetypes of human consciousness] . . . the Enchantress and Mother Nature . . . therefore are in tune with the endless cycle of nature and the tides of the sea, believing us to be subject to the same laws. So an endless cycle of birth-death is part of the belief. I quote from the Book of Shadows, '. . . and upon Death, peace unutterable, and the promise that you will return again'.[36]

Until the Renaissance liberated the minds of men, reincarnation, though never explicitly condemned by any papal encyclical, was killed in western European thought by three weapons. The first was its condemnation by a Council of Constantinople in AD 543. Its edicts were powerful and included the decrees that whoever taught the pre-existence of the soul and the monstrous doctrine of its return to earth should be anathema; Origen and six others were condemned for their heretical opinions. The second weapon was the implicit condemnation of metempsychosis by the Council of Lyons (AD 1274) and the Council of Florence (1439) which affirmed that departing souls go immediately to heaven, purgatory, or hell. The third weapon was persecution, especially that of the Inquisition, and suppression by force of arms, of which the cruellest example was the Albigensian so-called crusade (1209).

Sects of Christian gnostics, numbering some seventy-two in the Middle Ages, spread from Syrian Armenia, through Asia Minor, into Bulgaria, and reached Italy before AD 1000 and France by 1022, where they flourished mightily in the south under the names of Cathari or Albigenses. Their teaching was spread by troubadours affected by Arabic and Sufi influences, whose songs of apparent human love were allegories of spiritual healing. They believed that human souls were fallen spirits passing through probation, and held a belief in transmigration not unlike that of Buddhism though modified by the belief that Christ's earthly mission was the redemption of fallen spirits. Good lives were rewarded by reincarnation in bodies suitable for further spiritual development, evil ones by rebirth in bodies full of flaws and hereditary vices. They and their culture, in some ways far superior to that of their orthodox contemporaries, were annihilated in blood, flame and rapine by an army of savages to whom loot meant everything and the honour of Christ nothing.

Not only heterodox Christians, however, accepted reincarnation. St Francis of Assisi (1181/2–1226) is claimed by some scholars as an adherent to the doctrine, and before him Johannes Scotus Erigena (c 810–77), the schoolman and philosopher, and after him Bonaventura (1221–74). Such was the general opposition of the orthodox that it is surprising that there should have been a revival of neo-Platonism as early as there was. But there was never a crusade to wipe out Gnosticism in Italy, and some families were too powerful to be touched even by the Inquisition. Dante's *Divine Comedy* was influenced by Albigensian allegory and Canto XX of the *Paradiso* is explicit in saying, 'he from Hell came back into his bones . . . the glorious soul returning to flesh where it abode awhile'.

The revival of neo-Platonism began in Florence under the protection of the de Medici family. Marsilio Ficino, son of Cosimo de Medici's chief physician, translated Plotinus, Iamblichus, Proclus and Synesius. As tutor to Lorenzo de Medici, Cosimo's grandson, he influenced the prince who, allied with Giovanni Pico, son of the prince of Mirandola, accelerated the movement. George Gemistus (1355–1450), who attended the 1439 Council of Florence as an emissary of the Greek Church, wrote that 'our soul . . . is sent by the gods now into one body, now into another'. Giordano Bruno (1548–1600) in *The Expulsion of the Triumphant* agreed that 'since the soul is not found without body, and yet is not body, it may be in one body or in another, and pass from body to body'.[37] After a lifetime of wandering through Europe, which included a season of lecturing at Oxford on immortality and reincarnation, he was burned at the stake by the Inquisition in Venice in 1600. His teaching included the idea that missed opportunities in one life could result in incarnation in a worse body in a succeeding existence, or that there could be progress with each succeeding life, rising to perfection.

From Italy neo-Platonism travelled to France under the patronage of François I (1515–47), where Guillaume Pastel, an Oriental scholar, studied the Cabala and wrote of reincarnation. Cardinal Nicolas de Cusa revived it in Germany in the fifteenth century, followed by the Benedictine abbot Trithemius and John Reuchlin, both Cabalists, and Cornelius Agrippa. Colet, Erasmus, Grocyn and Linacre, of whom the last two studied at the Florentine Platonic academy, brought Platonism to England, and in time gave rise to the Cambridge Platonists and their Oxford allies.

Part of Edmund Spenser's *Faerie Queene* (Book III, Canto VI, stanzas 30–33) show a marked neo-Platonic influence; the philosophy was powerfully in the air at that period, though Shakespeare's two references to Pythagoras and his one reference to reincarnation in Sonnet 59 show no more than his nodding acquaintance with the doctrine. John Donne's 'I launch at Paradise and I sail towards home' from his poem 'The Progress of the Soul' is Platonism, even Gnosticism. The group of scholars known as the Cambridge Platonists included Henry More, Ralph Cudworth and John Smith and had their counterparts, John Norris and Joseph Glanvil, at Oxford. They studied classical writers on reincarnation such as Plotinus and Philo, tried to reconcile Christian and Platonic doctrines and studied the Cabala and similar esoteric writings. Cudworth in *The True Intellectual System of the Universe* (1678) dismissed Platonic doctrines of pre-existence and reincarnation but drew attention to them. More, however, upheld them in *The Immortality of the Soul*: 'The pre-existence of souls is a necessary result of the wisdom and goodness of God.' Present troubles, he wrote, result from past lives of sin.

Glanvil, chaplain to Charles II and therefore a man of authority, also made a Christian claim for pre-existence. It was 'the constant opinion of the Jews and therefore accepted by Christ and his apostles'. 'The soul came prejudiced into this body with some implicit notions that it learned in another'[38].

Almost contemporary with the English Platonists, the Count of St Germain at the court of Louis XIV was one of the few Europeans who remembered past lives and events in them. In what is now Belgium the naturalist and philosopher Franciscus Mercurius van Helmont (1618–99) wrote *De Revolutione Animarum*, published in London in 1684, as 'Two Hundred Queries Moderately Propounded Concerning the Doctrine of Human Souls', said to be one of the first two volumes in western literature specifically devoted to reincarnation. In spite of the 'moderately', Helmont was imprisoned in Rome in 1662 for teaching pantheism and reincarnation. Among other seventeenth-century writers who touched on rebirth were Dryden (1631–1700) whose 'Ode to the Memory of Mrs Anne Killigrew' visualised her 'pre-existing soul' as reincarnated in all the classical poets including Sappho. Benedict Spinoza (1632–77) answered the question as to why we do not remember past lives by writing, 'It is impossible for us to remember that we had existence prior to the body, since the body can have no vestige of it, and eternity cannot be defined in terms of time or have any relation to time. Yet we perceive that our mind is eternal.'[39] Leibniz (1646–1716) the German philosopher and mathematician, believed 'that all souls have pre-existed always in a sort of organised body'.[40] The continuity of an individual's life is no more completely broken by death than by sleep. The Chevalier Ramsay (1686–1743) admitted that the doctrine of pre-existence was nowhere revealed but that it was evidently supposed, as without it original sin became not only inexplicable but absurd.[41]

The mystic Emanuel Swedenborg (1688–1772) believed that animal-like men became animals and virtuous men pure spirits in the after-death world, but he did not teach reincarnation on this earth. Voltaire found the doctrine 'neither absurd nor useless . . . it is no more surprising to be born twice than once; everything in nature is resurrection'[42], while the intensely sceptical David Hume (1711–76) agreed with other philosophers in asserting that pre-existence was 'the natural correlative of a belief in immortality', while metempsychosis was 'the only system of this kind that philosophy can hearken to'.[43]

By the 1700s men were no longer burned for heresy, and controversy, including religious polemic, was political rather than doctrinal. Popular Catholicism and Protestantism agreed in preaching a Christianity that taught that men were given a single life and awarded heaven, purgatory or hell (if Catholic), heaven or hell (if Protestant), on their life's record. Every individual had a new soul created by God and joined to the baby possibly at conception, possibly at birth, a soul which began and grew with the physical body and survived its death, being immortal for the future only. Popular interest in pre-existence and reincarnation died—there were no gnostics or Cathari to keep it alive among the men and women in the pews.

It did not die among the scholars and philosophers, and there were, during the eighteenth and nineteenth centuries, schools of thought as well as a number of prominent individuals contributing their own surmises. Soame Jenyns (1704–87), the British writer and politician saw that transmigration explains the injustices of life. He argued that sexual intercourse could not create an immortal soul, which to be immortal must have existed eternally before the formation of the body if it was to exist for ever after its dissolution.[44] Benjamin Franklin (1706–90), a printer by trade, wrote quaintly that in spite of all the inconveniences of human life he would not object to a second edition of himself, hoping that the errata of the first might be corrected.[45] Among eighteenth century men of action Frederick the Great believed in reincarnation. Napoleon claimed on several occasions to be Charlemagne reborn. Among philosophers, the Swiss Johann Georg Sulzer (1720–79) echoed Voltaire in asking why, if there are laws that unite the soul to a physical body, might there not be similar laws governing a second union with another.[46]

Philosophy in its reincarnationist aspect in the eighteenth century belonged especially to Germany, where 'during the classical period of German literature metempsychosis attracted such attention that the period may almost be styled the flourishing epoch of the doctrine'.[47] The German transcendentalists included Immanuel Kant (1724–1804), who believed that souls had pre-existence and would travel to other planets after their incarnation(s) here. G. E. Lessing (1729–81) pleaded passionately in *The Divine Education of the Human Race*:

> Is this hypothesis [of reincarnation] ridiculous merely because it is the oldest, because the human intellect adopted it without demur, before men's minds had been distracted and weakened by the sophistry of the schools? On the contrary, the first and earliest opinion in matters of speculation is invariably the most probable, because it was immediately accepted by the sound understanding of mankind. Why should I not return as often as I am capable of acquiring fresh knowledge and further power? Do I achieve so much in one sojourning as to make it not worth my while to return? Never! . . . Is not the whole of eternity mine?[48]

J. G. von Herder (1744–1803) argued that great and rare men cannot have become what they were in a single existence; that memories of past lives held by some men meant that they really discerned further vistas than the average; that children sometimes utter ideas which must have come after long preparation; that *déjà vu* confirms pre-existence; and that animals will ascend to a higher grade of being.[49] J. G. Fichte (1762–1814) suggested in *The Destiny of Man* that there were two systems within mankind, the sensuous which might consist of an innumerable series of particular lives, and the purely spiritual which alone gave the sensuous meaning and value. Man was not a product of the world of sense, and the purpose of his existence lay beyond time, space and the senses.[50] Friedrich Schleiermacher (1768–1834), theologian and philosopher, taught that 'excellent individuals' return recognised only by 'the Seers' and show by their greater advance how much the climate of mankind has improved and is better adapted to the nourishing of noble growths.[51]

It was the opinion of Friedrich von Schlegel (1772–1829) that man, too imperfect and material, needed to evolve into a far more refined form to partake of the 'higher kind of immortality'. Metempsychosis he viewed as 'continuance of spirit, alternately using organic forms'.[52] Arthur Schopenhauer (1788–1860) also accepted evolution through reincarnation into new and better bodies and was one of the first western writers to express the idea of group rebirth: 'In the succession of births . . . the persons who now stand in close connection or contact with us will also be born along with us at the next birth; and will have the same or analagous relations and sentiments towards us as now, whether these are of a friendly or hostile description.'[53] He also suggested that what survived was our character, that is our will, not our intellect, which was mental, and that 'palingenesis' was a better word to use for this theory of survival than 'metempsychosis'. The latter term suggested that the whole psyche was reborn whereas it was only the will that is born again. It was to him an incredible delusion that man was created out of nothing and that his present birth was his first entrance into life.[54]

The German philosophers were supported by their writers. Goethe's (1749–1832) view, as interpreted by George Santayana,[55] was that 'a deep mind has deep roots in nature—it will bloom many times over. But what a deep mind carries over into its next incarnation—perhaps in some remote sphere—is not its conventional merits and demerits... What remains is only what was deep in that deep mind, so deep that new situations may again imply and admit it.' Goethe could explain Charlotte von Stein's influence over him only by metempsychosis and believed that they must have been man and wife in a former existence.[56] In a conversation with Johannes Falk in 1832 he said:

> I am certain that I have been here as I am now a thousand times before and I hope to return a thousand times ... When one reflects upon the eternity of the universe one can conceive of no other destiny than that the Monads [souls] should eventually participate in the bliss of the Gods as joyfully co-operating forces. The work of creation will be entrusted to them.[57]

Johann Peter Hebel (1780–1826), the German poet and prelate, in notes for a sermon on 'We have lived before' regretted that since wisdom is the fruit of experience, how little has one life to offer: 'Having finished with many wanderings, preserved my "I" through so many forms and conditions, become acquainted with joys and sorrows and purified through both; what memories, what bliss, what gain!'[58]

In England the poets Blake (1757–1827), Wordsworth (1770–1850), Coleridge (1772–1834) and Southey (1774–1843) were associated with belief in reincarnation, and there are hints of it in

Thomas Carlisle (1795–1881). Wordsworth may have affirmed only pre-existence in his 'Ode on the Intimations of Immortality', and Southey was cautious in his statement that 'The system of progressive existence seems, of all others, the most benevolent . . . the most probable.'[59] But Shelley (1792–1822) fainted with emotion aroused by a *déjà vu* experience. Sir Humphrey Davy (1778–1829), the chemist, surmised that 'conscience . . . may bear relations to a former state of being'.[60] But probably the clearest eighteenth-century voice in England came from Thomas Taylor (1758–1835), the Platonist: 'every soul must perform periods, both of ascensions from generation and of descensions into generation . . . these will never fail through an infinite time . . . It follows that the soul, while an inhabitant of earth, is in a fallen condition, an apostate from deity, an exile from the orb of life.'[61]

Eighteenth-century France added its voice in the person of Charles François Fourier (1772–1837), the founder of Socialism. One of the reincarnationist optimists, he believed that many lives await us, 'some in this world, and the rest in a higher sphere, with a finer body and more delicate senses'.[62] He believed that when earth came to an end there would be a transmigration of humanity *en masse* to another planet, and he agreed that some exceptional individuals remembered their past experiences. Pierre Leroux (1797–1871) explained evil and suffering as being necessary phases through which creatures must pass in successive lives to reach a state of happiness which God sees. Forgetfulness of previous existences did not matter. Each existence was a link in a chain. When reincarnated 'we are the exact sequel of what we were; still the same being but grown larger'.[63]

Born at the end of the century, the French novelist Honoré de Balzac (1799–1850) was a convinced reincarnationist. Humans live through many lives, first to learn the worthlessness of worldly treasures, then to weary themselves of erring science and of human language, to exhaust matter and allow the entry of spirit: 'Then follow other existences—all to be lived to reach the place where Light effulgent shines. Death is the post-house of the journey. A lifetime may be needed merely to gain the virtues which annul the errors of man's preceding life.' The final life is that of prayer, which separates matter from spirit and brings the seeker to God.[64]

In the nineteenth century, transcendentalism and reincarnation, while not neglected by the thinkers and Romantics of Europe (for romanticism it had a particular appeal), crossed the Atlantic. American transcendentalism was influenced by Greek, German, English and oriental thought, with a reincarnationist streak running through each strain. Scarcely an American writer of note was untouched. Emerson (1803–82), much influenced by the Bhagavadgita, likened successive lives to going upstairs. Longfellow (1807–82) owned a copy of the Bhagavadgita and was also interested in hermetic philosophy, his last poem being in honour of Hermes Trismegistus. Whittier (1807–92) paraphrased part of the Bhagavadgita which treats of the periodic return of souls, and Edgar Allen Poe (1809–88), like his English contemporary Tennyson (1809–92), may have accepted rebirth. The doctrine has also been linked with the names of Thoreau (1817–62), who believed that he had lived in Judaea at the time of Christ, Herman Melville (1819–91) and Walt Whitman (1819–91). This last writer distinguished between mere personality and the deeper self. We are all involved in a process of spiritual evolution that parallels natural evolution. Rocks, trees and planets have an identity or *eidolon* that persists as they rise to a higher state of being. All men are divine and will eventually become gods. Later in the century, Kahlil Gibran (1883–1931) the Lebanese-born American poet declared that the human spirit has lived and will live timelessly, that the bonds of love, devotion and friendship *and* hostility and hatred have the same effect of reassembling groups of entities from one cycle to another. Indifference separates—souls who neither love nor hate one another meet only once in the pattern of the ages. Eugene O'Neill (1888–1953) has a reincarnation theme in his play *The Great God Brown*, but there is always a question whether novelists and playwrights express their own beliefs or those of their characters.

The American writers were paralleled by the philosophers and theologians. William R. Alger, a Unitarian minister and scholar, began by wholeheartedly rejecting rebirth but was converted by his further study into a complete reversal of his first position in his *Reincarnation, A Study of Forgotten Truth*. James Freeman Clarke (1810–88), another Unitarian minister and a transcendentalist, wrote a chapter on 'The Soul and Its Transmigrations in All Religions' and argued that as physically we have reached our present state by a very long and gradual evolution from the lowest animal organisms, so have our souls evolved.

Professor Francis Bowen (1811–90) the Harvard University philosopher in a celebrated article on 'Christian Metempsychosis' in the *Princeton Review*, May 1881, argued that the inequalities of life were inconsistent with the wisdom and goodness of God and made nonsense of the idea that a new soul was created for each body. The difficulty disappeared if 'metempsychosis is included in the scheme of the divine government of the world'. Any memory of our past lives would unfit us for the new part we have to play. Bowen pointed out that many long passages of any one life are completely lost to memory, even though they may have contributed largely to build up the heart and the intellect that distinguish one man from another. Our responsibility is not lessened by such forgetfulness. He adopted Kant's idea of the 'intelligible character' (with which we are born) and the 'empirical' or 'acquired character' (which we make): 'Kant would make us responsible not for the particular crime, which we could not help committing, but for being such a person as to be capable of that crime. We are accountable not for what we do, but for what we are.' Bowen's view that even in this life we live in a succession of bodies is supported by the estimate that approximately 98 per cent of the atoms in a human body are replaced by others from our air, food and drink in a year, and 100 per cent in fifty-three weeks. A man of seventy-five has had at least seventy new brains and bodies; it is a problem for physiologists as well as philosophers as to where memories and the sense of individuality are stored.

Better known than Bowen because of his Gifford Lectures, *The Varieties of Religious Experience*, was William James (1842–1910), philosopher and psychologist. In *The Will to*

Believe and Human Immortality he surmised that 'the sphere of being that supplied the consciousness [in life] might, in ways unknown to us, continue still [after death].' To the objection that this was a pantheistic idea of immortality, not a Christian, which teaches survival in a strictly personal form, James replied:

> *one may conceive a mental world behind the veil in as individualistic a form as one pleases, without any detriment to the general scheme by which the brain is represented as a transmissive organ* ... the reader would be in accord with everything that the text of my lecture intended to say, were he to assert that every memory and affection of his present life is to be preserved, and that he shall never *in saecula saeculorum* cease to be able to say to himself, 'I am the same personal being who in old times upon the earth had these experiences.'[65]

Gustave Stromberg (1882–1962), the Swedish–American astronomer-physicist, supports the view of the individuality of the human soul which is 'a perceiving, feeling, willing, knowing and remembering entity ... *indestructible and immortal, it carries an indelible record of all its activities*'.[66] Herbert Fingarette (b 1921), the American philosopher and psychologist, adopts a Buddhist tenet when he writes, 'In the course of spiritual progress towards freedom from the round of births and rebirths one eventually achieves the power of remembering past lives. One then sees their connection with the present life.' In achieving this 'superknowledge' one is concurrently achieving liberation from karmic bonds.[67]

More practical Americans inclined to similar views. Henry Ford (1863–1947) became a reincarnationist at the age of twenty-six, believing that 'genius was the fruit of long experience in many lives. Some are older souls than others and they know more.'[68] Thomas Edison (1847–1931) held the interesting theory that our bodies are composed of infinitesimally small individuals, each one an immortal unit of life. When we die, swarms of units, like bees, disperse and go on functioning in some other form or environment.[69]

Many of the great names in nineteenth-century European literature were at least favourable to reincarnation and not a few actively believed it. Victor Hugo (1802–85) wrote, 'Each time we die we gain more of life. Souls pass from one sphere to another without loss of personality, become more and more bright . . .' and again, 'The whole creation is a perpetual ascension from brute to man, from man to God. To divest ourselves more and more of matter, to be clothed more and more with spirit, such is the law.'[70] 'The I which persists after death is the I anterior and external to life.'[70] For all his achievements, Hugo felt that he had lives yet in which to achieve more: 'when I go down to the grave I can say like many others, "I have finished my day's work" but I cannot say, "I have finished my life." My day's work will begin again the next morning.'[71]

Gustave Flaubert (1821–80), though nowhere as explicit as Hugo, is another French writer associated with reincarnation.

A host of British writers in the nineteenth and twentieth centuries have touched on reincarnation, and in some cases have stated it baldly as their faith: Matthew Arnold, Clifford Bax, Arnold Bennett, A. C. Benson, Algernon Blackwood, Robert Browning, Samuel Butler, Thomas Carlyle, Marie Corelli, Francis Cornford, G. Lowes Dickinson, Austen Dobson, Conan Doyle, John Drinkwater, George Eliot, Rider Haggard, James Joyce, Rudyard Kipling, Jack London, Bulwer Lytton, Rose Macaulay, John Masefield, Alice Meynell, Thomas Moore, Arthur O'Shaughnessy, Walter Pater, D. G. Rossetti, George Russell ('AE'), Walter Scott, William Sharp ('Fiona McLeod'), Percy Bysshe Shelley, Francis Thompson, Martin Tupper, H. A. Vachell, Oscar Wilde and W. B. Yeats. Arnold Bennett's character Morice Loring in *The Glimpse* saw 'the endless series of [his] lives'. A. C. Benson in *The Thread of Gold*, gave a fictional account of the period of intermission between lives. Blackwood's *Julius Le Vallon* saw the working out of karma in successive 'sections' of eternal life. Browning's poem 'Evelyn Hope' looked forward to reunion with her though 'delayed it may be for more lives yet'. Marie Corelli in *Ardath: The Story of a Dead Self*, produced an argument against remembering past lives: 'Never to lose sight of one's own bygone wilful sins—this would be an immortal destiny too terrible to endure.' Lowes Dickinson wrote that what mattered most in his present experience was the sense he had of something in him making for more and better life. Conan Doyle's *History of Spiritualism* contained the sentiment

> that it is inconceivable that we have been born in time for eternity. Existence afterwards seems to postulate existence before ... such existences may well form a cycle which is all clear to us when we come to the end of it, when perhaps we may see a whole rosary of lives threaded upon one personality.[72]

Rider Haggard believed each man to be immeasurably ancient, forged in many fires, and believed that in previous lives he himself had been Norseman, Zulu and Egyptian. Jack London in 'The Jacket' wrote, 'I have been growing, developing, through incalculable myriads of millenniums ... I am this spirit compounded of the memories of my endless incarnations. I am man born of woman ... I have been woman born of woman.'[73] John Masefield in his poem 'A Creed' makes the most explicit statement of belief in reincarnation culminating in final glory, while Rossetti is almost as explicit in 'Sudden Light' when he cries, 'I have been here before ... You have been mine before.'[74]

George Russell (AE), to whom reincarnation was a faith as strong as Masefield's, wrote in 'The Memory of the Spirit' from *The Candle of Spirit*, 'I see breaking in upon the images of this world forms of I know not what antiquity. Endlessly the procession of varying forms goes back into remote yesterdays of the world ... Were not [these] ... I ask myself memories of the spirit incarnated many times?'[75] In conversations with friends Russell recounted how fragmentary glimpses of former lives had been disclosed to him in certain meditations—'Druidic times in Ireland; Spanish life, riding into the gates of a walled town, the most remote that he had caught, life in India'. 'I came at long last,' he added, 'almost to believe that, like Ulysses in the Platonic myth, I had chosen before birth a life in which I was primarily to be mystic.'

'Fiona McLeod', like Rossetti, recognised in 'her' love the loved one of a past life—'Where have I known thee, dear, in what strange place'—and in 'A Record' wrote, 'Each death is but a birth, a change, Each soul through myriad by-ways strange,

Through birth and death, doth upward range.' H. A. Vachell in *The Other Side* declared, 'I could not have been really happy had I not believed in reincarnation . . . To me it explains adequately the mysteries of sin and suffering; and the apparent injustice involved in lives widely and cruelly differentiated.'[76]

Included among writers, though he was as much philosopher and explorer of the human mind and spirit, should be Aldous Huxley (1894–1963). He wrote:

> The eschatologists of the Orient affirm that there are certain posthumous conditions in which meritorious souls are capable of advancing from a heaven of happy personal survival to genuine immortality in union with the timeless eternal Godhead . . . In the Vedantic cosmology there is something in the nature of a soul that reincarnates in a gross or subtle body, or manifests itself in some incorporeal state.[77]

Also a writer-philosopher, Raynor C. Johnson (b 1901), friend of AE, is an upholder of reincarnation;

> The permanent soul which stores the wisdom, goodness, artistic sensitivity, interest and skills of the past, surely influences in some degree the new personality which it is sending forth into the world . . . Plato has a theory that the kind of knowledge which comes easily is 'old' knowledge, in the sense that we have laid foundations for it in prior lives . . . On this view the child prodigy would be the reincarnation of a soul of very specialised development.[78]

Of other European writers, Tolstoy (1828–1910) wrote in a letter, 'The dreams of our present life are the environment in which we work out the impressions, thoughts, feelings, of a former life . . . our life is but one of the dreams of the more real life, and so it is endlessly, until the very last one, a very real one— the life of God.'[79] Of his fellow-Slavs in Poland it has been written, 'In no other country is the unanimity in [professing belief in reincarnation] so complete as in Poland. All the greatest poets of Poland such as Mickiewicz, Slowacki, Krasinski, Norwid, Wyspianski [all of the nineteenth century] mention their past lives as a matter of course.'[80] The poets were seconded in their belief by the philosopher Cieszkowski and the mystic Towianski.

Not a few European philosopers and theologians discovered reincarnation in the nineteenth and twentieth centuries. Jean Reynaud (1806–63) of France challenged, 'Who dares affirm that in the depths of our being our soul will not some day be able to shed light on these successive journeyings? ... Let us try to conceive of the infinite treasures of a memory enriched by the recollections of a long series of incarnations—each different, yet all linked together.'[81] Charles Renouvier (1815–1903) had a theory of monads (indestructible germs): 'But it is not once only that each person must live again on earth owing to the actualisation of one of those seminal potencies; it is a certain number of times, we do not know how many...' Speaking of the several individuals which are the several lives of one person, he writes:

> These individuals, whom memory does not tie together, also have no memory of the person whom each of them comes to continue on earth ... a person, reintegrated in the world of ends, recovers the memory of its state in the world of origins, and of the diverse lives which it has gone through, in the course of which it has received and undergone the trials of the life of pain.[82]

Denmark is represented by the religious philosopher Soren Kierkegaard (1813–55), who expressed his conviction thus; '"Write," said that voice, and the prophet answered, "For whom?" The voice said, "For the dead, for those you have loved in antiquity." "Will they read me?" "Yes, for they will come back as posterity."'[83] In Italy, Archbishop Passavalli (1820–97) declared that reincarnation was not condemned by the Roman Catholic Church and was not at all in conflict with any Catholic dogma.[84]

Germany produced a number of philosophers who upheld reincarnation. Carl du Prel (1839–99) affirmed that 'the hypothesis of a transcendental consciousness, which many followers of Darwin might repudiate, is ... completely compatible with Darwinism... The law of the Conservation of Energy ... avails also for the psychical world.'[85] Friedrich Nietzsche (1844–1900) wrote on *Eternal Recurrence*. Richard Wilhelm (1873–1930), theologian, missionary, Sinologue and collaborator with

C. G. Jung, declared that reincarnation is absolutely feasible for the Christian.

Jung (1875–1961) himself said of metempsychosis that

> one's life is prolonged in time by passing through different bodily existences; or, from another point of view, it is a life-sequence interrupted by different reincarnations ... It is by no means certain whether continuity of personality is guaranteed or not: there may be only a continuity of *karma*. Reincarnation, however, necessarily implies the continuity of personality ... one is able, at least potentially, to know that one has lived through previous existences and that these were one's own, ie that they had the same ego-form as the present life. Reincarnation means rebirth in a human body.[86]

In *Memories, Dreams, Reflections*, Jung proposed:

> Somewhere 'out there' there must be a determinant, a necessity conditioning the world, which seeks to put an end to the after-death state. This creative determinant—so I imagine it—must decide what souls will plunge again into birth ... perhaps that depends upon how much of completeness or incompleteness they have taken across with them from their human existence.[87]

Britain has several philosophers-theologians-psychologists to contribute. James Ward (1843–1925), philosopher and psychologist, argues against the objection to reincarnation on the grounds of personal discontinuity between lives by suggesting that the discontinuity is only temporary and that continuous but latent memories are revived after death or perhaps when all our existences are over. 'Between one active life and another,' he adds, 'there may well be ... an intermediate state of mental rumination and reflection ... a domain of recollection ... [which] may be a preparation for a new life [on earth], providing the change in character is notwithstanding still somehow retained.'[88] Bernard Bosanquet (1848–1923), Gifford lecturer in 1913, pointed out the difficulty, first mentioned by Aristotle, in the conception of an identical soul animating wholly different bodies in succession. The 'soul-thing' exists without any content of personality and 'we are offered chains of personalities linked together by impersonal transitions'.[89]

John McTaggart Ellis McTaggart (1866–1925) was possibly the best of the British pro-reincarnation philosophers. In his *Human Immortality and Pre-Existence* he suggested that gradual progress in a series of lives was the most likely of any scheme of survival. He answered the criticism that our hope of improvement would be destroyed if memory periodically ceased by pointing out, firstly, that memory makes us wiser; secondly, that memory helps us to resist temptation; thirdly, that memory tells us that the people with whom we are now related are the people whom we have loved in the past, and this may enter as an element into our present love for them. In *The Nature of Existence* he warned that 'if there is a plurality [of lives] extending over a long future, our prospects after leaving our present bodies have possibilities of evil much greater than those generally admitted by theories of immortality which reject . . . the possibility of an endless hell'.[90]

Frances M. Cornford (1874–1943) returns to the idea of human reincarnation in other creatures:

Caught in the wheel of Time, the soul, preserving its individual identity, passes through all shapes of life. This implies that man's soul is not 'human'; human life is only one of the shapes it passes through. Its substance is divine and immutable, and it is the same substance as all other souls in the world . . . each soul is an atomic individual, which persists throughout its . . . cycle of reincarnation.[91]

Arthur P. Shepherd (b 1885), Canon of Worcester Cathedral, in the second Maurice Elliott Memorial Lecture, 1961, said, 'The picture of reincarnation as the process of human evolution [gives] the answer to the problem of the new world situation . . . a universe of spirit beings, in infinite creative relationships to one another and to man.'[92] Another notable ecclesiastic, Leslie D. Weatherhead, has written favourably of reincarnation: 'We do not want to keep all our past identities, only that "true identity" which will not be lost; the pure gold of the ego will be maintained, purified and strengthened.'[93] Eva Gore-Booth confirms this thought in her belief that 'every false vibration dies out. The whole self is like a plant cut down to its roots to grow again next year.'[94] Last of the British thinkers—though many others could be added—is Hugh Roscoe, whose *Occultism and Christianity* states:

> the Immortal Ego in man, that part which is divine, seeks experience in a succession of mortal physical bodies, with intervals of varying length spent on other planes of being, between its incarnations . . . some [Egos] may be much older than others . . . at the start of their evolution all souls had equal opportunities . . . their present positions represent exactly the use they have made of the time and opportunities they have had so far.[95]

Nicholas Berdyaev (1874–1948), the Russian Christian philosopher, saw an advantage of belief in reincarnation in that man stops comparing his destiny with the fates of others and accepts it.[96] Two Swiss made contributions. Albert Schweitzer (1875–1965) wrote, 'If we assume that we have but one existence there arises the insoluble problem of what becomes of the spiritual Ego which has lost all contact with the Eternal. Those who hold the doctrine of reincarnation are faced by no such problem.'[97] Paul Tillich (1886-1965) called nirvana a 'symbol of eternal life [indicating] a life of absolute fulness, not the death of absolute nothingness'.[98] The Frenchman, Edouard Schuré, made the point that for the soul who had been emancipated from one incarnation but is due to return to earth, 'terrestrial birth is death . . . and death is a celestial resurrection'. He foresaw the destination of the triumphant soul as complete union with the divine intelligence, but 'the soul which has become pure spirit does not lose its individuality, but rather perfects it as it rejoins its archetype in God'.[99] The amen to this comes from the eastern philosopher Sarvepalli Radhakrishnan (b 1888), who sees the consummation of the world process being achieved when every man knows himself to be an immortal spirit.[100]

Three musicians join the chorus of support for reincarnation. Richard Wagner (1813–83), in a letter to Mathilde Wesendonck, wrote that 'in contrast to reincarnation and karma all other views appear petty and narrow'.[101] Gustav Mahler (1860–1911) affirmed that 'we all return; it is this certainty that gives meaning to life, and it does not make the slightest difference whether or not in a later incarnation we remember the former life'.[102] And Jean Sibelius (1865–1957) spoke openly with intimate friends of his belief and what appeared to him to be remembrances of previous lives.[103] The artist Salvador Dali (b 1904) believes himself to be the reincarnation of St John of the Cross.

Among statesmen and diplomats, Guiseppe Mazzini (1805–72) accepted the advance of the soul through a series of purifying incarnations, and that collective man progresses through the human generations; David Lloyd George (1863–1945) believed in reincarnation, expecting hereafter to suffer or benefit in accordance with what he had done in this world (perhaps the old song 'Lloyd George knew my father' should be revised to 'Lloyd George will know my grandson'). Gandhi (1869–1948) implicitly accepted rebirth when he wrote in a letter to a disciple, 'It is nature's kindness that we do not remember past births.'[104] Sir Francis Younghusband, (1863–1942) soldier, explorer and mystic, throws further light on the nothingness of nirvana when he wrote, 'One who has attained the state of Nirvana may indeed be motionless and regardless of all sights and sounds. Yet inwardly his soul may be in a condition of intensest activity. This is the goal of Buddhism . . . superlative activity.'[105]

Lord Hugh Dowding (1882–1970), British Air Chief Marshall, was convinced of the fact of reincarnation. Dr Gustave Geley (1868–1924) put forward the thesis that

individual consciousness is an integral part of that which is essential in the universe . . . Above the cerebral memory is the subconscious memory . . . In this essential memory there are engraved permanently all the events of the present life, and all the remembrances and conscious acquisitions of the vast series of antecedent lives.[106]

The long list of authorities may be closed with two psychical researchers, of whom the former was a brilliant scientist outside the realm of psychical research and the second may be said to have done more than any other man to bring that branch of knowledge within the recognised boundaries of scientific method. Sir Oliver Lodge (1851–1940) in *Man and the Universe* argues that

No science maintains that the whole of our personality is incarnate here or now; it is, in fact, beginning to surmise the contrary, and to suspect the existence of a larger transcendental individuality, with which men of genius are in touch more than ordinary men. We may be all partial incarnations of a larger self.[107]

J. B. Rhine (1895–1980) writes that proof of reincarnation is not to be discovered in hypnotic regression. Science must first try to discover whether there is a spirit personality which can exist apart from the body.[108]

Many other thinkers could be quoted and it could be asked why no mention has been made of Madame Blavatsky, Annie Besant, Rudolf Steiner, and many others. They will be found in Chapter 3, where the history of faiths incorporating reincarnation, such as theosophy and anthroposophy, is given. Nor is a list of authorities, however imposing, to be taken as an authority to believe. Many very intelligent and eminent men have held religious faiths that appear to common sense or to adherents of other forms of creed to be excessively silly. For every list of famous believers in a particular faith there can be compiled a list of equally famous believers in others or in none at all. In addition, the views quoted above and outlined in subsequent chapters are in many respects contradictory to each other; there is not one theory of rebirth but many. To believe in reincarnation is one thing; what kind of reincarnation to believe in is quite another. Yet the principle of rebirth, accepted by so huge a proportion of the human race and seriously considered by so many, is one which is difficult to ignore.

3

PRESENT-DAY
BELIEFS

It is not easy to assess the position generally of belief in any spiritual concept today. A religious map of the modern world would show vast areas that are officially and governmentally atheist—the whole of the communist bloc, for example—yet where millions adhere staunchly to their traditional faiths. In the nominally Christian West the church-going elements in most countries have been statistically on the decline, though they may by now have levelled out to a more or less constant percentage of the population. The spread of education has undermined 'superstition', as primitive or minor religions are often called, among less-developed peoples. Despite large pockets where traditional belief and religious practice are strong, the increase in literacy and media influence are, in many parts of the world, undermining the conventions of centuries.

Differences in emphasis lead to differences of knowledge. While radio, television and the press bring into the home Christian and other teaching which would in former times have been confined to a minority of the public, it is not easy to know their impact when a switch of a knob can silence them or an unreceptive reader glance them by. Three generations ago most educated people and the chapel-going among the uneducated would have 'known their Bibles' and the fundamental doctrines of their branch of the Christian faith, whereas today such knowledge is confined to theological students and a few lay enthusiasts. It is easy to be parochial. The current revival of fundamentalist Islam, for example, may belie what has been written. Nevertheless, ideas have more access to the world population than they have ever had before. In the West there is a freedom of thought even in the most monolithic churches that would have been un-

81

thinkable a century ago. In the less monolithic, where many old dogmas such as heaven, hell and the resurrection of the body are rejected even by those who recite the creed Sunday by Sunday, heterodox ideas of many varieties are the norm as the men and women in the pew pick and choose what they believe. Among them is a growing acceptance of the possibility of reincarnation. A Gallup poll has shown that in a representative sample of 918 adults in Great Britain, belief in reincarnation has increased from 18 per cent in 1968 to 28 per cent in 1979, the largest percentage being in the 25–34 age group; another poll declares that 25 per cent of all Americans accept it.

A number of strands, thin individually but strong collectively, have contributed to this increasing acceptance. One of them, Rosicrucianism, 'The Ancient Mystical Order Rosae Crucis', refounded in 1909 after many centuries—though there is some doubt as to whether it had previously existed except in fantasy—held that human souls were not individualised and separated from God but were the consciousness of God that illuminated each living human body. The body corresponded to an electric light bulb, the soul to the current flowing through it and lighting it. This current was also part of the larger source of electricity, the 'oversoul'. The death of the body was analagous to the bulb's going out when the flow of electricity to it was interrupted. By extension of the metaphor, the same electricity that had lit the dead bulb could light another, and would not be diminished by the breakdown of the single bulb. This idea was not specifically reincarnationist, but susceptible of a reincarnationist interpretation.

Rebirth was, however, taught more specifically in Rosicrucianism. Jesus is the focal point of enlightenment concerning the ultimate destiny of human souls. He attained Christhood through perfection of consciousness, his soul ascending into heaven to be absorbed into the consciousness of God and thereby to become one of the divine elements of the Godhead. This example we have to follow, being reincarnated again and again until we are perfected, accepted into God and also become part of the Godhead. Intermissions between births average 144 years.

A second strand, the spiritualists, are sharply divided between those who believe in reincarnation and those who do not. French spiritualists on the whole accept the idea, owing to the emphasis laid on it by Allan Kardec, their founder. English spiritualists reject it. Those who do not believe ascribe all other-life memories to spirit influence. Kardec claimed that the information in his *The Spirits' Book*[109] was based on information received from spirit entities speaking through mesmerised subjects. The purpose of reincarnation was expiation and progressive amelioration. Purification results in bliss, and rebirth then ceases. The different embodiments may take place on varying heavenly bodies, but we can return to earth, a planet far from perfect. Once an entity has become a human, no return to an animal body is possible. Some heavenly spheres are on a similar level to earth and there is therefore no need to reincarnate on them. Spirits may be reborn on a plane at a lower stage of evolution to act as guides. They are sexless—whether one incarnates as a man or woman depends on the trials ahead, although several incarnations following will usually be in the same sex. Heredity's role is limited to the animal part of life. Moral character may be similar from one life to the next, but repentance and other conditions may change it. Knowledge acquired in previous lives may produce innate concepts such as the idea of God or survival. Two successive lives are often not closely related because the spirit may progress in the beyond; material conditions in the next existence may be very different. Some talents may 'sleep' to allow others to find expression. Reincarnation sometimes occurs immediately following death, but usually after a time varying between a day and thousands of years. This may be due to what the spirit wills. During the intermission the 'itinerant' spirit, can temporarily visit higher spheres, which inspire in it the wish to evolve further and to reincarnate, hence its choice of the trials it will have to undergo in its coming earthly life. It may be allowed to choose its body. (One of the most terribly deformed people I have met told me that she had chosen her body, though not the reason for her choice.) After death our bad actions may be punished by their revelation to other spirits until they are expiated either in the spirit world or in a new incarnation.

If we wrong a person in this life without redress, the spirit of the injured party may be allowed to revenge itself on us in a future life. Two beings who knew and loved each other in one existence may be similarly attracted in subsequent incarnations. Kardec allowed that some people remembered past lives and that dreams informed others. He taught that reincarnation was not compulsory except perhaps for some very dull or lazy souls, or because of karmic necessity. What brought it about was the entity's desire for spiritual growth, or the entanglement in earthly desires which rendered the average human being unfit for the eternal life of the spirit and drew him back to earth. The spirits' path of progressive purification culminated when, having divested themselves of all materiality and blemishes, they entered the eternal felicity of fully cleansed beings in the presence of God.[110]

There may be differences of reincarnation doctrine among spiritualists; there is none among theosophists. 'Reincarnation is an ancient and universal doctrine, continuously taught in every culture and age, even though at times it has been excluded from the official statements of a faith', a leaflet issued by the Theosophical Society states. Humanity is a stage in evolution:

> the gradual transformation of the possible into the actual . . . Each individual . . . has behind him an immeasurably long past . . . no matter how short and apparently worthless, no life is wasted. For the doctrine of reincarnation cannot be understood apart from that of *karma* . . . karma makes man master of his destiny. In each today he chooses his tomorrow.

Theosophy does not try to define a final goal, maintaining that such a concept should give way to a 'limitless horizon'. 'Enough for us to know the direction and so to harmonise our lives with the great universal scheme.'

Such is the simple rebirth gospel of the Theosophical Movement, founded by Madame Blavatsky, Henry Olcott and William Judge in 1875 in New York city. It soon became worldwide. Its object was 'to reconcile all religions, sects and notions under a common system of ethics, based on eternal verities'. Theosophy has been described as 'Hinduism at its best' and 'pure Mahayana Buddhism', and Madame Blavatsky brought Christianity into her system by explaining Christian symbols as an esoteric revelation, thus following those who have distinguished between a secret Christian doctrine known to the inner circle of Christ and His apostles and transmitted orally to their successors, and the open teaching communicated to the uninitiated: 'the mysteries of the kingdom of heaven are revealed to you, but they are not revealed to them [the ordinary people].'[111] Judge called reincarnation 'the lost chord of Christianity'.

The 'Bible' of theosophy was the writings of Madame Blavatsky, notably *Isis Unveiled* and *The Secret Doctrine*. The latter was in two volumes, the first, entitled *Cosmogenesis*, dealing with the rebirth of worlds, notably our own universe, the second, *Anthropogenesis*, having to do with the evolution of the human form, the illumination of mind by the incarnation of human monads from prior worlds, the subsequent evolution by reincarnation of the early races of man up to the present, and mankind's future development. The tool by which the universe is shaped, its ineluctable law, is karma; karma and reincarnation have been called the abc of theosophy.

Blavatsky's theory of the cosmos was that it is eternally being created and destroyed. Our present universe is one of an infinite series which has no beginning and will have no end. There exists a supreme source, a universal oversoul, from which all individual souls emanate, being reabsorbed into it at the end of their cycle. Reabsorption is absolute existence, an unconditional unity, beyond all powers of human description. Such unity, however, while resulting in the disappearance of personal existence, does not destroy individuality, which is the eternal part of man. The monad that is absorbed retains its *paramartha* (selfconsciousness) and emerges as a still higher being on a higher plane, to recommence its circle of perfected activity.

Life is therefore a continuum, and re-embodiment a universal law of evolutionary progress; in an infinite universe there must be infinite possibilities for growth and development. There is no limit to the experience and ever-widening cycles of incarnations open to the individual, although both lives and world-cycles may alternate with periods of revitalising reunion with the oversoul.

Theosophy accepts that incarnation begins with mineral forms and progresses through plant, animal, human and divine, each human being becoming a microcosm of the universe. Consciousness evolves within a chemical atom as within a man or a group of men. One theosophist has defined reincarnation as 'a plan whereby imperishable conscious beings are supplied with physical bodies appropriate to their stage of growth, and through which they can come in contact with physical life'. The purpose of the process is education. The human stream of consciousness, once attained, never reverts to the animal.

Behind the personality in all its stages of development there is a self or individuality, the monad, an invisible spiritual entity outside time that dips down into time and incarnates in the series of personalities that fulfils the demands of evolution. The composition of each human is a sevenfold one of body (*rupa*), vitality (*prana-jiva*), astral body (*linga-sarika*), animal soul (*kama-rupa*), human soul (*manas*), spiritual soul (*buddhi*) and spirit (*atman*). The *manas* (mind and thinker), *buddhi* (highest power of intellection) and *atman* are the essential 'real' man, who is immortal. An alternate, simpler division is the four 'bodies', physical, etheric, emotional and mental. The rational but earthly or physical intellect of man is encased in and bound by matter. The *manas*, *buddhi* and *atman* reincarnate and these also constitute the permanent individuality of every man, the feeling of being himself and not some other.

The entity projecting a personality selects an environment that will allow its physical, emotional, intellectual and spiritual requirements to be fulfilled and which will enable that part of its karmic debts to be worked off in the coming life to be repaid. These will determine every kind of condition—race, physical refinement or deformity, temperament, health, sickness, conditions of comfort or stress, accidents, sanity or weakness of mind, even madness. Alteration of sexes is necessary for spiritual completeness although there are usually runs of lives in the same sex, not more than ten.

The inequalities of life are for the theosophist a source of hope rather than of despair; karma, which brings them about, is a law of absolute justice to which everything and everyone in the universe, even the supreme oversoul, is subject. This concept is a principal difference between theosophy and other beliefs. Here karma works independently of God whereas in the Unity Movement (see below) it is wholly a tool which God uses to fashion what is His will. Not only Unity but the whole of orthodox Christianity which shares the article of faith in the creed 'I believe in the forgiveness of sins' clashes head-on with theosophy in this; more than one theosophist has said that there never were two more pernicious doctrines than those of vicarious atonement and the forgiveness of sins. The Christian Church is accused of deliberately distorting the words of its Founder and laying stress upon these teachings to gain worldly power.

The cycle of life is described in different ways by different theosophical writers, the emphasis being sometimes on the individual, sometimes on the group. Thus, Olcott taught that though personalities shift, the one line of life along which they are strung like beads remains unbroken. It is always *that* line, never any other, an individual vital undulation which begins in nirvana and leads through many cyclic changes back to nirvana. Blavatsky saw that the goal of the struggle to achieve wisdom which leads to self-actualisation is nirvana, when the lower self or selves are absorbed and the true self liberated. Judge felt the need to reach complete self-consciousness through perfecting, after transformation, the whole mass of matter as well as soul. H. K. Challoner conceived the object of reincarnation to be the creation by the true self of a vehicle of consciousness through which it might mirror forth every aspect of its divinity in perfect equilibrium—like polishing a mighty diamond with a thousand facets through the vast cycle of lives; at its best the human manifestation could never be more than partial because of the body's restrictions.

The personalities as drops of experience endure as part of the entity but not as individualities. Personalities are merely units of experience which enrich the entity as it meditates the ages away. Hundreds of personalities bestow their part and bring their offerings of accomplishment. Thus enriched, the entity finally emits one personality in which all the virtues of past lives are embodied. This is the supreme incarnation, the world teacher.

Having manifested this final sublime embodiment, the entity returns this personality to itself and human evolution is finished. We are each part of this plan.

On earth men appear to be separate units but each is part of a group of souls, each specific group attuned to its own note or wavelength and destined to play a specific part in the final unity to be represented by the complete body of mankind. The members go forward at different paces according to the use they make of their measure of free will, but until every member has reached a certain stage of development, the group as such cannot do the work intended for it. The first requirement of each individual is to understand and control his own personality. The second is the uniting of the lower to the higher self which results in contact with the group. Conscious union between all members of the group both in and out of the body is the next achievement. Those gaining the power to sound the group 'note' clearly on the physical plane attract the others who are incarnated at the same time and, using them as a focus, those on the inner planes, that is, those not incarnated—the members of one group seldom incarnate at the same time—direct their united energies. Group combines with group, their notes forming chords and their chords harmonies.

Yet each individual has to lead his life individually, normally without memories of past existences. Theosophists find no difficulty in this forgetfulness. Even in this life details of the most vivid experiences become blurred, leaving in the mind the principles of things, not their minutiae. It is undesirable to remember every detailed hour of our childhood which taught us to walk, wash, read, write, calculate, all those experiences that have made us what we are; if we were cluttered with such details, we should be swamped by them. It is only by forgetting nonessentials that we can make room for new knowledge. If a man's mind were filled with all the mistakes, tragedies, losses and crimes—and all the ecstacies and triumphs—of his past existences, he would spend his present life brooding upon them or so dissipated in nostalgia that he would fail to fulfil the advance he was born to make. And the conditions of past lives might be so different as to be quite irrelevant to the present.

The young soul is influenced by the subconscious mind where the lessons of past existences are stored. The more mature spirit attunes itself to the superconscious. There are dangers in the subconscious since it contains not only undesirable elements as well as desirable carried over from previous lives but the bad elements in the present life which have not yet been absorbed and influenced for good by man's higher consciousness. But the desirable elements are strong—conscience, which is a summarised memory of past experience, and good taste, which Walter Pater said was the memory of a culture once known.

Human entities must pass through every experience, beautiful and terrible, creative and destructive, spiritual and physical, through myriads of millennia of rebirths, so as to gain that infinite breadth of experience that will enable full personalities to be emanated, and will also give them understanding of the struggles of all the other units developing towards the same ideal. The result is adeptship and liberation from the wheel of personality rebirth.

Entry into nirvana is a misnomer. It is the *return* of the final personality to the unconditional conciousness of the entity itself. Even nirvana is not eternal but will end, leaving the permanent entity, *adi-buddha*, sitting in profound contemplation above nothingness, until a new cycle of existence begins.

Karma is not a moral force, rewarding and punishing; but a constant impersonal balancing of the forces between personalities, determining their environment and being determined by it, 'a dynamic, cybernetic or self-adjusting system'. Its working binds us to the wheel of causality and continuity in time but also gives us the key to liberation, which is knowledge of the right way to accept or refuse experience from moment to moment. Ignorance is the root of all suffering and misery, but the man who knows is free; his knowledge teaches him to work out his past karma without setting new karmic forces in motion. There is a time-lag in the operation of karmic law and a man may be faced with a difficult situation now which is the result of a past life's karma.

The cycle of rebirth can be broken by one who has learned to do it at the present moment; from this dynamic point in life the individual can step off in another dimension, that of eternity. Buddha himself likened the process to a man climbing a ladder, who when he reaches the top, continues by stepping upwards and on and does not fall.

The many difficulties of attaining such a state have resulted in charges against theosophy as against Hinduism and Buddhism that such a belief must result in indolence, indifference, procrastination, evasion and wishful thinking. These charges are met by the answer that future existence depends on present integrity—but integrity itself may become an ideal only after a certain stage of progress has been reached. Theosophy's way of salvation remains overwhelmingly difficult for the ordinary person.

At death all the forces of body and mind rush through the brain, and the whole of the ending life down to the smallest detail—the personality's attitudes, opinions, ideas, convictions, experiences and conclusions—impresses itself indelibly on the inner man. The physical body dies, the astral body detaches itself from the physical and, life energy having departed, the remaining five elements find themselves on the plane of *kama loca*, perhaps the equivalent of paradise, possibly purgatory or Hades, the astral region penetrating and surrounding the earth. On this plane the ruling force is desire divorced from intelligence, and here the personality lives, entering into the activities of that world, getting into touch with its friends, physically incarnate or not, sloughing off impurities of character and elements of emotional experience that have no place in the next plane. These are, however, transferred to the permanent entity to become a permanent record. Blavatsky estimates the period of sojourn here as 150 to 300 years of earth-time, other theosophists as 25 years.

The astral body then dies and the being is born into the next stage, *devachan*, the mental world, equivalent of the Christian heaven. Here those parts of the entity's being which could not bloom on earth are enabled to flower. He is in touch with the *minds* of those he loves and admires, seeing them completely and objectively as in life but with their potentialities fully developed, great, good and wise. Entities in this state can sometimes help those on earth. It is the longest and happiest period of the post-mortem state, lasting for about five hundred years, a time of assimilation and development, during which the individuality gradually ceases to exist and the mental records are transferred to the permanent entity which alone remains, preparing to project another personality.

The new incarnation begins at a higher level than the last because it has absorbed the experience of the former. The soul body draws round itself automatically a cloud of mental and astral matter, out of which it fashions its mental and emotional body. Each personality from its formation to its extinction lasts one to two thousand years. Just before birth the new being sees all the causes that led it to *devachan*, thence back to life, and the justice of the procedure. It will understand then, if not while it is incarnate, that the inequalities of life are the fair result of past karmic inheritance.

The new personality is linked to the physical body formed by our parents between conception and birth. It does not choose its parents, their selection for karmic purposes being the business of unspecified spiritual intelligences.

The length of intermissions varies enormously. Blavatsky taught that sensualists and materialists return more quickly because life after death is governed by aspirations, and if there are no higher longings or beliefs, the soul is a blank and reincarnates almost immediately without regaining consciousness in the next world. Altruists can return quickly because of their ardent desire to benefit mankind. A primitive savage or undeveloped man may have a total cycle of physical and after-life of a few decades, of which the post-mortem period may be as little as five years. The attunement between an advanced personality and the permanent entity dictates the length of the life cycle. A long earth-life generally means a long sojourn in the unseen world. Intensity of living may lead to a lengthy intermission, for the wider and deeper the quantity and quality of experience, the longer the interval between incarnations. The more advanced the personality, the longer the time needed to assimilate its experience. A genius could have a personality cycle of ten millennia; he may find it difficult to find an appropriate environment on earth for his next personality. Indeed, he may never return to this world if he has advanced as far as he can in it. Annie Besant taught that the soul progresses through many worlds and is continually reborn in each of these until it has completed the evolution possible in every sphere of existence. Manley P. Hall estimates that there are approximately 800 lives in each human cycle. The length of these varies from five years for the less developed human types to 2,300 for the most developed, according to Irving S. Cooper, who claims that investigations into the past lives of some 250 people showed periods which averaged 500 years in the cases of intelligent men and women. None of these authorities provides data for these estimates, nor is it easy to see how acceptable criteria for such statements can be provided. They can only be a matter of belief.

Hence the difficulty with theosophy and all faiths founded on occult tradition. The surmises are majestic, terrifying in their immensities and eternities and as cold and impersonal as the illimitable darknesses of space. But statistically and experientially they are guesswork, with no more authority than any other faith and with rather less, the upholders of other creeds would say, than some.

It is in this respect that anthroposophy has an advantage over theosophy, for it maintains that spiritual matters can be researched in a manner analogous to empirical investigation into the material aspects of life. Its founder, Rudolf Steiner (1861–1925), an Austrian Roman Catholic, lectured within the Theosophical Society until the theosophists declared Krishnamurti, an Indian boy, to be a present-day incarnation of Christ, after which he severed all connections with them. Steiner was a mystic who claimed to be able to see back into previous lives of people he met casually. He came to believe that this perception was a natural property of human beings, not unique to a few like himself, but normally wholly submerged in the subconscious mind. By exercises which he described the faculty could be brought into the conscious mind and used for research into the spiritual dimension. Steiner had had some mathematical and scientific training and he believed that the scientific method combined with trained psychic perception could form a bridge between science and religion. This he called anthroposophy.

The Anthroposophical Society was founded in 1913 with headquarters in Switzerland. It is organised round sections for education, the arts, medicine and science, with an administratively parallel but independent 'Christian community' that is strongly reminiscent of Catholicism in its sacramentalism. Steiner's view of Christ was that of the orthodox Catholic, that he was God incarnate. But he added the doctrine that Christ had, from the beginning of time, guided human evolution by reincarnating human souls again and again on earth. Karma was the instrument by which he shaped them. God's purpose in this process was so to educate pure spirit by a descent into matter that it would eventually achieve a total liberation of a self-consciousness that would be morally perfect and completely differentiated from matter.

Since anthroposophy is as Christocentric as any orthodox Christian church and yet emphatically reincarnationist and karmic, it would seem on the surface that there is no reason why Christianity should not be the same. Is it possible for a 'true' Christian to believe in reincarnation?

Since the beginning of its era Christianity has been faced with a dilemma in determining to what supreme authority its Founder had entrusted the transmission of his message down the ages. His teaching was embodied in a number of writings and developed in a number of others, a selection of which came to be regarded as inspired by the Holy Spirit in a special way. Eventually, after some trial and error in which some books now admitted were excluded and others suffered the opposite fate, the canon of the New Testament was formed. This was the authority for the Church's belief and practice, by which its members were to be guided. The canon had an authority, therefore, greater than that of the Church. But it was the Church that had established the canon and the Church that interpreted its meaning in doubtful matters, and therefore the Church's authority was the greater. The situation has been neatly expressed in the saying that the Catholics promulgated the doctrine of an infallible Church to which the Protestants replied with the doctrine of an infallible Book. Sects like the Quakers made things even more difficult by affirming that both Church and Book should be tested by the inner light of God-guided conscience, which was the supreme authority.

So the question—can a true Christian be a reincarnationist?—depends on the individual Christian's attitude towards his authorities (which will also determine what a 'true' Christian is). Does the New Testament teach it or allow it? (The Old, which is part of the Christian Bible, has already been considered.) Does the Church teach it or allow it or, at the very least, not forbid it? Does the inner light uphold it?

Fourteen proof-texts from the New Testament are offered by reincarnationists, of which few need be considered seriously. Taking the books in their traditional order (chronology is not relevant here) we can list them as Matthew 11: 13, 16: 13–14, 17: 10–13; Mark 6: 14–16, 8: 27–8, 9: 9–13, 10: 28–31; Luke 9: 7–9, 18–19; John 9: 2; Romans 9: 10–13; Galatians 4: 19; and Revelation 3: 2 and 12.

The first Matthaean text reports Christ's saying in a sermon to the crowds, 'And if ye will receive it, this is Elias, which was to come.' As Elias (Elijah) had been taken up into heaven without dying, his coming again is not reincarnation. This was realised as early as Tertullian's time (160?–230), for he describes John the Baptist as Elias making a return visit to earth. The two were 'really and truly the same man, both in respect of his name and designation as well as of his unchanged humanity'. The tradition of Elijah's return was similar to those myths in many cultures which tell of a great national hero waiting until his country is in danger when he will return to its aid, not in another body but as himself. The Jewish tradition was that before the coming of the Messiah, Elijah would appear as his forerunner, and whether Elijah was literally meant or 'an Elijah' in the sense of a great prophet is debatable. In Matthew 16, Mark 8: 27–8, and Luke 9: 7–8 and 19, the disciples answer Jesus' question, 'Who do men say that I am?' 'Some say that thou art John the Baptist: some Elias, and others Jeremias, or one of the prophets.' Christ could not have been John the Baptist or his reincarnation because, until his beheading, John had been his almost exact contemporary for some thirty years. 'Jeremias, or one of the prophets' could indicate a popular belief in reincarnation, but could equally mean that the people were saying, 'He's a prophet just like those of the olden days, a regular Jeremiah.' Chapter 17 of Matthew again speaks of John the Baptist as Elias, and echoes Mark 9: 11–13, and Luke 9: 9.

In Mark 6, and Luke 9: 9, it is Herod who thinks Christ is John the Baptist risen from the dead, to which the same reply can be made as to Matthew 16. Chapter 10 promises that disciples of Jesus who have sacrificed everything for him 'shall receive an hundredfold now in this time, houses and brethren and sisters, and mothers, and children, and lands, with persecutions; and in the world to come eternal life'. Reincarnationists argue that those who have given up everything in this life will receive it back an hundredfold, it must be in another life that this will happen, when the positions of top dog and underdog will be reversed. To this the reply can be made that the joining of the Christian community will supply a man with all the friends and relations he needs, and spiritual wealth worth all the material he has surrendered. That the 'first shall be last; and the last first' was a continual theme with Jesus in his ministry to the poor and dispossessed: 'he hath put down the mighty from their seats and exalted them of low degree. He hath filled the hungry with good things: and the rich he hath sent empty away.'[112]

John 9: 2 is one passage that strongly suggests reincarnation. Jesus, passing a beggar born blind, is asked by his disciples, 'Master, who did sin, this man, or his parents, that he was born blind?' It is argued that if it was the man, he must have sinned in a previous life to have been born blind in this one. By failing to deny the implication of reincarnation in his reply, 'Neither hath this man sinned, nor his parents: but that the works of God should be made manifest in him', Jesus is believed by reincarnationists to have supported rebirth. But the punishment might be for sin in the future, known by an omniscient deity, as is possibly indicated by a modern translation, 'Rabbi, who sinned, this man or his parents, for him *to have been born* blind?' Even if this interpretation is not accepted, anti-reincarnationists can argue that to ignore a marginal doctrine is not necessarily to accept it, that nowhere did Christ specifically and positively preach rebirth, and that to found a theology of Christian reincarnation upon a single doubtful text is not legitimate.

Romans 9: 10–13 reads:

> Even more to the point is what was said to Rebecca when she was pregnant by our ancestor Isaac, but before her twin children were born and before either had done good or evil . . . Rebecca was told: *the older shall serve the younger*, or, as scripture says elsewhere: *I showed my love for Jacob and my hatred for Esau*.

It is difficult to see how a passage that in its context speaks of the plan and promise of God and his foreknowledge in carrying it out can possibly refer to reincarnation; nevertheless it is a passage cited by reincarnationists. Even more tenuous is Galatians 4: 19, where Paul writes, 'My little children, of whom I travail in birth again until Christ be formed in you', meaning that his Galatian converts and therefore his spiritual children, seduced from his Gospel by the Judaisers, had to be spiritually born into the truth all over again.

Revelation 3: 12 runs, 'Him that overcometh will I make a pillar in the temple of my God, and he shall go no more out', translated in the Jerusalem Bible as 'stay there for ever'. The reincarnationist sense 'no more go out [into the flesh]' is just possible, but it is again a flimsy basis for the doctrine.

There is no direct conflict between reincarnation and karma and the Bible. The examination of the texts above and in the case of the Old Testament (pages 37–8) show, on the other hand, that there is neither direct proclamation of the two doctrines nor implication. The Church of England position is that the Bible 'contains all things necessary for salvation'; it follows that for Anglican reincarnationists, their belief, even if permissible, would be officially regarded as superfluous.

There is a tradition that Jesus spent some of the years of his early manhood among the Essenes, since modern scholarship suggests that much of his teaching parallels theirs. As the Essenes seem to have been reincarnationists, it may be significant that Christ did not explicitly teach the belief. It could be argued that he rejected it outright; or that he avoided it in his public preaching, reserving it for that alleged occult doctrine revealed only to his inner circle; or that it is inherent in the spirit of his teaching.

Is the spirit of the New Testament, rather than the letter, favourable to rebirth? The usual answer to such a question would be no. First, the Christian view of immortality is that it must be personal:

> Man is seen throughout the Bible as a psychosomatic unity, so that the only way that eternal life can be pictured is not as the survival of the soul without the body but as the resurrection of the whole undivided personality . . .[113]

To this somewhat materialistic though orthodox view, the Rev Marcus Knight adds a larger dimension:

> Reincarnationist theory with its laws of the sense of value of the individual person, would weaken the sense of persons working together in community, for unless men can realise a value in each other which is the result of their value to God, they will lack concern for them as persons with whom they are to find bonds of brotherhood . . . Reincarnation depends on a view of God which reduces him to a principle of law, to an underlying impersonal force.[114]

The justice of this criticism must be left to the reader to decide. Reincarnationists who believe in the type of doctrine on page 88 might have grounds for disputing the argument, and they might justly contend that the power to make moral decisions presupposes a knowledge of morality. On the other hand, their emphasis on often esoteric knowledge does make it hard for the common man to find his way to God, while Christianity proclaims continuously that its gospel is for the poor, the weak and the dispossessed and, after all, to call sinners to repentance and consequently unity with God. Nevertheless, if believers in different creeds looked to reconcile their differences instead of exacerbating them, considerable underlying agreement might be found.

Since the New Testament gives so minimal an authority for reincarnation, the would-be Christian must turn to the Church, recognizing that, whether the Bible is superior or not in authority, there is no denomination that has not interpreted and de-

veloped scripture teaching to fit its own preconceptions. Much
stress is laid by Catholic theologians on the development of
Christian doctrine in the first five centuries by the patristic
writers; if upholders of the authority of the Church as para-
mount wish to be reincarnationists, they must find support in
the works of those fathers who specifically dealt with the subject.

Reincarnationists quote Justin Martyr (100?–165) as upholding the doctrine but, as has been seen (page 55), his support is at
best ambiguous, and theologians regard him as anti-rebirth.
There is no doubt that Irenaeus (c 130–c 200) was such; in his
treatise *Against Heresies* he attacks Carpocrates' doctrine of the
transmigration of souls. The Christian belief, however, that we
stand or fall by this one life, seems to be utterly unjust and is
opposed by the Irenaean concept that sees the 'divine creation of
personal life as taking place through a long and slow process
which extends far beyond this present earthly scene'.[115] Clement
of Alexandria's (150?–250?) teaching is summarised on page 55.
Tertullian (c 155–after 220) attacked Platonic doctrines of the
soul's pre-existence and the Pythagorean doctrine of transmigration.[116] Hippolytus (c 165–c 235) joined Irenaeus in his attack on
Carpocrates and rebirth.[117]

Origen (see page 56) wrote, 'Every soul comes into this world
strengthened by the victories or weakened by the defeats of this
[its] previous life. Its place in this world is determined by its previous merits or demerits. Its work in this world determines its
place in the world which is to follow this.'[118] But this pre-
existence of souls took place in the heavens, not in a series of previous lives, and against Celsus, Origen repudiates the idea of
human souls' passage into animals. The Emperor Justinian condemned Origen by an imperial edict which was later confirmed
by Pope Vergilius, and some of his teachings were also condemned in fifteen anathemas passed by a synod of Constantinople in 543. Justinian's condemnation was of Origen's alleged
doctrine that perfect spirits who had already reached heaven
could fall (it left untouched an equally questionable tradition
according to which reincarnation corresponded to the Christian
conception of purgatory). It must be noticed that reincarnation
was not so much as mentioned, let alone condemned, by any

general council of Constantinople or by any other, though in the first of the fifteen anathemas pre-existence was denounced.

Most of the other early fathers were hostile to various forms of the doctrine. Minucius Felix (second or third century) attacked the idea of humans passing into animals, and Lactantius (third century) opposed Pythagorean doctrine in *The Divine Institutes*. St Gregory of Nyssa (*c* 330–95?) wrote that 'It is absolutely necessary that the soul should be healed and purified, and if this does not take place during its life on earth, it must be accomplished in further lives.' This might hint at life in some future state; its *prima facie* interpretation that reincarnation might be meant is contradicted by Gregory's rejection of pre-existence and 'successive incorporation'.[119]

St Jerome's possibly favourable views are to be found on page 58. St Augustine's (354–430) cry, 'Did I not live in another body, or somewhere else, before entering my mother's womb?'[120] is countered by his assault on reincarnation and the Platonists in his *City of God*, Book X, Chapter 30. Synesius (*c* 370–430), Bishop of Ptolemais, suggests rebirth doctrine in a prayer he wrote—'Father, grant that my soul may merge into the light, and be no more thrust back into the illusion of earth'—and in a thesis on *Dreams* in which he said, 'It is possible by labour and time, and a transition into other lives, for the imaginative soul to emerge from this dark abode.' Another possible supporter is St Anastatius (d 401) who, although an opponent of Origen's views, according to Ruffinus, stated a belief in pre-existence and intimated an acceptance of reincarnation, while Nemesius (*fl c* 390), Bishop of Emissa, says that the Greek Christians of his time accepted metempsychosis. Arnobius (*fl c* 460), a Numidian apologist for Christianity, is quoted by both sides, Manley P. Hall saying that in his *Against the Heathen* he wrote that 'We die many times, and often do we rise from the dead' (but only perhaps like Shakespeare's cowards who 'die a thousand times'?), and left a record that Clement of Alexandria had written a most important account of metempsychosis (for or against?). He joins the throng of those who reject the human-into-animal thesis.[121]

Such are the gleanings for and against reincarnation of the

Christian fathers of the first five centuries—a meagre gathering. In an issue of the *Christian Parapsychologist* already quoted, wholly given over to articles on reincarnation, Tom Strong, following a statement that there is not condemnation of reincarnation in the Bible, only indications of support, continues, 'For 500 years, pre-existence and reincarnation were respected, permitted fields of Christian speculation', to which John Hick, a leading modern theologian, asserts flatly that reincarnation was *not* taught in that half-millennium.

During these centuries Christianity was a minority sect, one among a thousand religions and philosophies asserting claims to uniqueness of revelation. It had to contend against the high ideals of neo-Platonism, which taught that the multiplicity of souls had emanated from the eternal intelligence of the world-soul. Individual souls, deluded by pride and a desire for false independence, descended into the lower stage of existence, matter, which was nevertheless fundamentally good, and this process might be many times repeated. This was in order to gain further experience and be fitted for a higher exaltation. The neo-Platonists enticed men 'to bring the divine within them into that which is divine in the universe'. Then the Church had to make its way against the dualists, who believed in powers of good and evil, light and darkness. The Manichees and some gnostic sects were clear-cut foes, for he who served Mani could not also worship Christ.

Christian gnostics, however, were a different matter. They despised what came to be orthodox Christianity as food for the unsophisticated masses, seeking to provide the young Christian Church with a philosophical creed. They ranked themselves as initiates into a mystical system of Christian truth, secretly imparted by Christ to his innermost circle, never committed to writing. They taught that the world had been created by some fallen spirit or principle, and it was this evil creator that continually enticed the souls of men from a pre-existence higher stage into the slavery of material bodies. From this process Christian gnosis alone could deliver them.

Since reincarnation was a principal tenet of the gnostics' faith, it was possible that orthodox Christianity might have accepted it, had it not had some alternative viable doctrine. The alternative was there, shared by no other religion, the unique concept of the saving event for all men, both ignorant and knowledgeable, of Christ's atoning death. And whether the Church attacked Gnosticism in polemical writings which have disappeared except for such remnants as are mentioned above, or whether she ignored it, Gnosticism temporarily disappeared from the scene except for heretic sects on the outskirts, often geographical as well as spiritual, of orthodoxy, sects like the Bogomils, Paulicians, Priscillians and Cathari.

None the less, reincarnation continued to rear its head, ugly or beautiful, and such worthies as Duns Scotus (c 810–77), whose opponents gave 'Dunce' its pejorative meaning, St Francis of Assisi (1182–1226) and St Bonaventura (1221–74) are quoted as upholders of the doctrine. Once the Renaissance and Reformation had come and gone and men were free to think for themselves without risk of 'the thumbscrew and the stake', there were individual Christians of many denominations who accepted rebirth, as the last chapter shows. In the modern age, although no official decree has been passed, there have been and are outstanding personalities who continue to believe. The Roman Catholic archbishop Passavalli (1820–97) was unshaken till his death from the conviction that he had lived many times on earth and was likely to return. Cardinal Mercier, known for his defence of the rights of the Belgian people against the German occupiers in the First World War, stated that reincarnation did not in any way conflict with Roman Catholic dogma. Andre Pezzani, in *The Plurality of the Soul's Lives*, tried to reconcile reincarnation with the Roman Catholic idea of expiation. Pius XII (pope 1939–58) is said to have seriously contemplated the official recognition of the doctrine. Against these, it was rejected as heretical in a reply of the Holy Office of 24 April 1917, and in the aforementioned issue of the *Christian Parapyschologist*, Father Crehan SJ writes, 'For a Catholic it should be clear that our faith has no room for theories of reincarnation.'

Since it is argued that the New Testament neither condemns nor upholds reincarnation; that the absence of the doctrine in Holy Writ is no grounds for not accepting it today, as we hold many doctrines that have as little foundation; that the early Church wrote against only unsophisticated reincarnation teaching; and that the actual doctrine of rebirth as a proper means of ultimately accomplishing unity with God has never been anathematised or declared heretical in any ecumenical council—it is for the inner light to give the verdict. Tom Strong says as much when he writes, 'Christians ought to consider whether arguments from scripture, the fathers, or General Councils are any more relevant than they were in the case of Copernicus, Galileo and Darwin.'[122] The discussion centres on whether reincarnation can be accommodated to Christian theology.

The very centre of Christianity is the cross of Christ. His dying for mankind and his victory over sin, evil and death by his resurrection, and his winning for the whole of humanity the destiny of eternity in his presence is the dogma that has to be balanced against or reconciled with a faith in reincarnation. To reconcile the two is not difficult; for, if any faith be the true one, and if reincarnation be a process of education in which the gospel of progress tends steadily upwards, there must come a time when every entity arrives at a knowledge of the true faith. If Christianity be the true faith, every soul will come to a life in which it will become a genuine Christian and attain the goal at which the process of rebirth aims and which brings it to an end.

One of the strongest Protestant arguments against reincarnation is that if man is unable to come to conciliation in one life, it minimises the saving role of Jesus, for it implies that the penalty Christ paid on the cross was insufficient if men need several lives to be cleansed of sin. Provided that he has made the first faltering steps towards Christ in faith, even if man has fallen short of his goal at the end of his life, Christ will clothe him with the wedding-garment of his own righteousness and present him perfect before God. Yet this argument requires that faltering faith in Christ be there, and all sorts of devious stratagems are used to solve the problem of the fate of those countless millions who have never heard and will never hear of Christ. Reincarnation does seem to offer a better solution to the difficulty than orthodox Christian answers.

There remain certain official doctrines which cannot be

reconciled with reincarnation. Soul creation is one. The resurrection of the body is another. Eternal hell is a third. Purgatory—unless it is to be found in the discipline imposed by a succession of lives—is a fourth. Of these, whether they are official or not, the second in its literal sense is believed by increasingly fewer Christians and more and more are unhappy about the third.

Some Christians condemn popular reincarnation teaching because it is loveless and self-centred, concerned with repayment of past debts, settling old scores and failing to realise that although to err is human, to forgive is divine (much karmic doctrine has no room for forgiveness). It is said to boost separate personality at the expense of corporate units, and it is also alleged that people heavily addicted to alleged reincarnation memories are seldom satisfactory in their personal relationships with others, with a poor degree of spiritual development in the present life (I do not like *ad hominem* arguments of this type which can be levelled against some adherents of any faith). Perhaps their so-called memories are a system of delusion built up by an inadequate personality. Against this harsh judgement, other Christians argue that provided the personal punitive aspect of rebirth is rejected and the growth of the soul into fulness of being is seen to be the overriding factor, a scheme of rebirth into this or some other world of limitation is just and merciful. The growth of the soul implies also social growth into an ever-deepening awareness of what is meant by 'the communion of saints'. Such growth comes by experience whose fruit is the wisdom that leads man to an understanding of the nature of eternal life and the Love of God (which are the same thing) and to his realisation of his own identity with all creation and with God himself.

The Christian reincarnationist can claim that his faith answers problems that orthodox belief does not. These are primarily the appalling inequalities of human existence and the fact that between my beginning and ending this sentence some hundreds of human beings who have never had a physical or spiritual chance in life will have died and there is nothing that anyone can now do for them except pray in the most utterly inadequate terms. If all these dead have carried over anything that is positive in their often wretched lives into other existences, perhaps in other worlds, then maybe there is reason for their sufferings. But if their eternal fate depends on the quality of their one life lasting from a few minutes to a few decades, and if orthodox Christianity has to fall back on such arguments as 'God judges them by the way they tried to live up to the truth as they understood it' or 'God knows how they would have lived if they had existed in other circumstances', the weakness of the belief that God is love is at once manifest. The gnostic idea of a demiurge creator who is fundamentally evil much better fits the facts.

Tom Strong believes that reincarnation can explain for Christians how an inadequate human can evolve to the likeness of Christ and all the evolutionary gradations between the beast of Belsen and St Francis. He sees in it a reconciling of the spiritual traditions of East and West and the liberating knowledge that will be released when the laws of karma bow to the law of grace. He believes that the resulting insights into God's purpose and methods would be greater and could reverse the western plunge into materialism and agnostic humanism.[123]

It must be concluded that reincarnation has never been an orthodox Christian belief. Though it is spreading, it is still held only by a tiny minority of Church members. But there is no reason why it should not become an orthodox survival belief among Christians. Everlasting damnation in hell would have to be surrendered, but apart from reincarnation there are good philosophical reasons why this belief has no place in an evolving Christianity. An eternally punished sinner would mean an eternally failed love of God which would mean that the Supreme Being would be less than supreme which—if God exists at all—is an impossibility. Nor can finite man sin the infinite sin, even in a succession of lives, that alone could attract an infinite punishment. The purposes of purgatory, which are educational for life in the presence of God, can be achieved by reincarnation in this and other worlds (indeed, purgatory, though a spiritual state, has always been depicted in Christian imagery as another world where the dross of sin is purged away by the fires of the experi-

ence of penance). Heaven, eternal life of the whole of his fulfilled
creation in the presence of God, an utterly unimaginable
concept which can only be defined, not understood, is perhaps
further away than the believer's life's end than it is in orthodox
Christian thought, but it is far more certain. And the final
stumbling-block, salvation through Christ's atoning death on
the cross, is removed if the understanding and acceptance of this
is the final step in man's spiritual history, resulting perhaps in
the restoration of heaven at the believer's life's end after all. It
could be that, seeing that there are many unsatisfactory Christians, a number of Christian incarnations may be needed before
the believer can really grasp the meaning of the love of God and
of Christ's atonement sufficiently to enter heaven. This,
however, is precisely what other reincarnationists say, that
man's ultimate spiritual destination, or nirvana, is open to us all
the time, but can only be attained by a final act of faith, when the
individual has achieved enlightenment, and this may take many
lives.

Orthodox Christianity can accommodate reincarnation and
karma with its own teachings, as follows.

God's ultimate purpose for his entire universe is its salvation,
though what is meant by this we cannot know. His purpose for
mankind is that it may become morally perfect in order to enter
into a state of communion with himself, its Creator. Some would
say that all souls are born into the world in a fallen state due to the
cosmic effect of original sin; but the fall may be a 'fall upwards', a
growth into moral awareness from a state of 'innocence' which
will make men seek moral perfection.

Moral perfection implies opportunities for moral growth.
These are provided in a world containing both good and evil,
between which choice has to be made. Such perfection cannot be
attained by a human being starting from scratch—it can only be
reached by one who has climbed to a certain level of spiritual
achievement from which to launch himself. The soul has to experience life in the world countless times to acquire the
maximum measure of moral growth the world has been designed
to provide.

Morally significant actions, good and bad, produce respectively good and bad entail which, if not worked out in the present life, will be experienced in a future, either as initial conditions or as developments in the life; hence the appearance of inequity in human affairs. Awareness of entail exists normally only in the subconscious mind, but can work as effectively there as in the conscious. Karma is an instrument used by God, wholly under his control, to induce moral growth, but co-operates with and is subservient to grace. It may be that the way of salvation is the same for every soul, a coming to a life in which it is sufficiently far advanced to realise fully in experience the love of God expressed in Christ's atoning death and to avail itself of its benefits.

Whatever the position of orthodox Christianity, there are Christian movements of whose platform reincarnation is a principal plank. Charles Fillmore, born in 1854 in a log cabin in Minnesota and brought up in primitive conditions among hunters and trappers, with practically no formal education, was introduced to classical English and American literature by Mrs Caroline Taylor, a graduate of a New Hampshire college. His appetite for learning thus awakened, he never stopped studying till his death at ninety-four and he voraciously read philosophy and comparative religion on a vast scale. He was encouraged in this by his wife, Myrtle, who had been a schoolteacher. Charles, crippled in his youth, and Myrtle, having contracted a serious liver complaint a few years after their marriage, were miraculously cured. She also experienced a religious conversion and became one of the best-known faith-healers in the American Midwest.

In 1889, the Fillmores published a magazine called *Modern Thought*, written largely by themselves, and invited contributions from spiritualists, theosophists, Christian Scientists, Freemasons and others in their area. Its name was changed to *Unity* in 1898 and it became the organ of a movement which today is represented by churches in most of the larger American cities with some in Canada and Western Europe. There is also a Unity Centre in Missouri possessing a hundred million dollars worth of administrative, educational, library, prayer therapy, publishing and vocational plant and equipment, and publishing six periodicals which enter nearly two million homes a month, together with a seminary which ordains about fifty new Unity ministers each year.

Unity professes to teach rather than lay down dogmas, probably its only dogma being that a person should believe solely that which he is led to believe by contact with the Holy Spirit. Its teaching is highly Christ-centred, since it accepts that the Christ-spirit is incarnate in every man. Jesus was the perfect expression of the incarnation that all souls will ultimately achieve. This fulfilment in ultimate perfection and reunion in eternal spiritual life with God and Christ leads to Unity's emphasis on reincarnation and karma as the process that is gradually bringing about that perfection. Between lives the soul rests in a mode analogous to sleeping, absorbing its last life's experience into its character structure through a process similar to intermittent dreaming in sleep. Reincarnation may be avoided by those who concentrate their whole hearts upon God and seek to do his will always until his presence is vividly realised. When they leave the earth, such individuals will enter at once into full communion with God and need never return. Whether the soul arrives at this final destination soon or late, it does not lose its individuality but rather discovers its true identity with the eternal source of being.

Unlike theosophy, Unity regards karma as subservient to God. It is a tool he uses, not an immutable law to which he must bow.

Equally Christian in spirit and perhaps more heterodox, is the Association for Research and Enlightenment, Virginia Beach, USA. This was founded upon the work of Edgar Cayce, whose career and reincarnationist life readings are dealt with in greater detail in Chapter 6. Cayce himself was a typical Bible Belt fundamentalist Protestant who in trance produced ideas that he probably would have ascribed to the devil in his waking state, had they appeared alone unaccompanied by successful therapy of an extraordinary kind that has made him famous. His view of the destiny of the human soul was orthodox enough: 'the heritage of each soul is to know itself to be itself yet one with the Creative Force called God'. It was in his doctrine of Christ's reincarnation that he was heterodox.

The Elchasaites, an obscure Christian sect, believed in successive incarnations of Christ and, though he had almost certainly never heard of them, Cayce's trance revelations followed a
similar line of teaching. Christ was a divinity who had manifested himself several times on earth before he was able to provide a
human body of sufficiently advanced spirituality to sustain him
in his ultimate task of salvation. Some followers of Cayce spelled
out the process in more detail, adding Christ, as it were, to the
sequence of incarnations of Old Testament heroes listed in the
Cabala. Jesus was first created Adam as an encasement for the
soul of an entity, a part of the Creator, knowing separation in
death. He then became Enoch, so overcoming the result of the
law of disobedience as to merit the escaping of death. Thereafter
he was incarnated in turn as Melchisedek, Joseph, Joshua and
Jeshua. By obeying the dictates of the spiritual in each successive
life, he brought the physical body with its inherent desires more
into harmony with the spiritual until at last he had perfected the
physical instrument that was the vehicle of the Christ.

Shocking as this may appear at first sight to the orthodox (it is
in fact a variety of an early heresy, dynamic modalism), Cayce's
teaching does have a certain logic if reincarnation is a fact. For
Christianity teaches that Christ was God incarnate who
humbled himself to become man and, in the person of Jesus, son
of Mary, to experience birth, human life, death and the after-
death state ('descended into hell'), followed by resurrection,
which with all that it entails in the way of eternal life in the presence of God, the place he has gone to prepare for humanity, is his
gift to mankind. Since Christ's sharing and sanctifying of the
whole experience of men is an inherent part of the Christian
gospel, it can be argued that, if they are reincarnated, Christ
faced reincarnation too. The orthodox counter-argument that
the cross means that Christ must have done evil in a previous
existence for him to have suffered on the cross if reincarnation
was a fact for him is not a valid one, for to say that Christ bore our
sins is another way of saying that he bore our karmic entail. More
serious is the charge that in his first incarnation as Adam he committed the sin that started the whole train of evil-doing which led
to the crucifying of his last body—possibly a way of saying that

God is ultimately responsible for his whole creation and all the good and evil in it. The orthodox view is that Christ, uniquely sinless, *voluntarily* took upon himself the whole of evil on the cross and 'became sin for us'—he did not earn the cross by evil done by him.

Finally, Christian doctrines can be measured against each other. Fourteen headings may be shown, of which some, but not all, could be avoided by the Christian reincarnationist changing his denomination. In one or two instances orthodoxy would have to give way if it were to accommodate reincarnation and possibly karma.

1 The sacraments. Some fringe denominations do not practise the sacraments. Most accept baptism and the Eucharist. Some have more than these. Some churches believe baptism is essential to salvation, which means that only a tiny minority of mankind can be saved if one life is the human lot. If it is essential, reincarnationists can believe that sooner or later every man will experience it in one of his lives and, what is more, since it will become part of his eternal experience, its effects could carry on for all his existences yet to come.

2 Attendance at the Eucharist is necessary for salvation. If this is so, again, all men will come to it in one of their lives, and so with all the sacraments.

3 Membership of a certain church is essential for salvation. *Extra ecclesia nulla salus*. If this is true, just as it may take a man many lifetimes to reach the right religion, so it might take him a few more to reach the right denomination.

4 Soul-creation. A basic assumption of orthodox Christianity is that God creates a new soul for each human body born into the world, and that we owe our uniqueness as individuals to the combination of the two. Even if not specifically condemned, the pre-existence doctrine has incurred a tremendous weight of hostility throughout the Christian epoch. Soul-creation conflicts head-on with rebirth and destroys karma. The concepts cannot be reconciled and the Christian reincarnationist must recognise his heterodoxy—though he has some good company!

5 Predestination and its accompanying doctrine of the elect

cannot share the same creed with reincarnation and karma. But these articles of faith are by no means universally held by Christians and the New Testament mentions only predestination to salvation, which can be reconciled with rebirth. There *could* be an ultimate rejection after many lives which had been foreordained from the beginning, but it would be a very great waste of the Almighty's energy and as morally abhorrent as eternal hellfire after one life.

6   Eternal consignment to hell is still an official teaching of orthodoxy but is being increasingly rejected in the name of logic, common sense and a true understanding of God's love and justice.

7   Purgatory is a belief not inconsistent with both reincarnation and karma. In fact, purgatory and karma can be identical.

8   Belief in universal salvation is consonant with acceptance of rebirth.

9   Conditional immortality, where a soul is annihilated if it finally fails, is not; but as the failure of any soul is, as we have seen, a failure of God's love, which is impossible, it is also not consonant with at least some Christian understanding.

10   The resurrection of the body cannot logically live with reincarnation in the faith of a Christian, and the reincarnationist will ask 'Which body?' of all those we change every thirteen months. Few Christians, however, today believe that their physical bodies will arise and spiritualise the article in the Creed which says this. The Bible teaches, in fact, that flesh and blood cannot inherit the Kingdom of God—sense perception and carnal bodies cannot operate in the spiritual realm. What will be resurrected will be the unique existential entity that God has created us to be, each unique, immortal and distinguishable from every other. This may be associated with a 'spiritual body' which inhabits a series of different physical bodies—an idea not foreign to some reincarnationist beliefs.

11   Christian judgement theory varies among the denominations, some believing that a particular judgement is passed by God on an individual immediately after death, in which he is consigned at once to heaven, purgatory or hell, possibly followed by a final Day of Judgement at the end of time. Others

affirm that souls 'sleep' until the Great Assize. Both are incompatible with reincarnation, but there appears to be considerable doubt among even informed Christians as to what happens after death, and to many of them reincaration might come as a gospel—'good news'.

12 Reincarnation is not inconsistent with the work of the Godhead. God the Father, the Creator, can as well have created all souls at the beginning of time as at intervals dotted down the ages and be continuing his creative work in them as they move through their lives. God the Holy Spirit, communicating the knowledge of the Father and Creator to men, can do it rather more adequately in many lives than in one. God incarnate in Christ the Son can still provide a point that is focal to the history of the world; can still redeem and still atone, the only difference being that myriads of men and women who have certainly had no opportunity of knowing him and experiencing his salvation in the past will assuredly have it in the future.

13 The forgiveness of sins, mediated by the grace of God, is not put out of court by a belief in repeated lives, for it takes a level of spiritual development to understand and accept forgiveness which may need many lives to reach.

14 Original sin, as a tendency to evil innate in mankind, does not contradict the reincarnationist notion that souls have been created by God from the beginning and may even be emanations of himself sent into a good and evil world to learn to become morally perfect. The doctrine that Adam transmitted this tendency to the whole human race may be regarded as a myth attempting to explain what is an obvious fact of human experience. Only a very few extremely conservative fundamentalists believe that the taint was handed down in a physical sense by an actual individual.

Christian theology has sometimes tried to be static but it has never ceased to develop and reinterpret itself to suit the *Zeitgeist* of each succeeding age. It is true that Christ is said by his followers to have brought a complete and final revelation of God to which nothing can be added; but it is open to reinterpretation and added understanding in every generation—almost like a reincarnating entity itself, always basically the same but ever developing its potentiality in centuries of existence in different circumstances and cultures. It may be that the Christian Church will abandon some notions that have already been substantially rejected in all but credal articles. She will have officially to renounce eternal damnation and accept pre-existence of souls. Until that happens, no entirely orthodox Christian can be a reincarnationist, but a reincarnationist can come very close to being an orthodox Christian.

4

REINCARNATION EXPERIENCES

Types of reincarnation experience are manifold. Some of them—*déjà vu*, regressive hypnosis, Christos experiments and group reincarnation—are dealt with in succeeding chapters. Here are examples of various types of spontaneous and induced encounters with past lives. They may be grouped under spontaneous memories of children; spontaneous memories of adults; dreams and visions; revelations by sensitives and by spiritualistic techniques; experiences induced by drugs and by mental manipulation; possession cases.

Spontaneous memories of past lives by children are by far the largest group. So numerous are they that in Burma, for example, they have a group name, *winsa*. Of the some hundreds of cases that are known and have been investigated, the following are a selection.

Kumari Shanti Devi, born in October 1926 in Delhi, from the age of about four talked of her former life in Muttra, about a hundred miles away, saying that she had been a Choban by caste, that her husband, a cloth merchant, had been named Pt Kedar Nath Chaubey, and that her house had been yellow. Chaubey was found actually to exist in Muttra. His cousin interviewed the girl, who recognised him and convincingly answered questions concerning intimate details of her former life. In 1935 the husband with his second wife and former wife's ten-year-old son came to Delhi. Shanti, deeply moved, recognised him, answering more intimate questions convincingly. A few days later she, her parents and three investigators visited Muttra, where she identified her husband's elder brother and her father-in-law. She told the driver the correct route to her former house, mentioning that it had not been asphalted when she knew it, pointed

out various buildings erected since her death, and in her own
house identifed the *jai-zarur*, a local name for a privy not understood by Delhi-ans. Led away to a newer house now occupied by
Chaubey, she recognised her former brother, now aged twenty-
five, her uncle-in-law and other details, and later picked out her
former parents in a crowd of over fifty people. The first wife,
Lugdi, had died aged twenty-three in October 1925 after the
birth of a son. The intermission was therefore about three
months.[124]

Childhood memories of past lives usually disappear when the
present life fully occupies the horizon, but this process does not
always happen. Madame Laure Raynaud, 1868–1913, born at
Aumont near Amiens, when a child told a priest that his ideas of
heaven, hell and purgatory were wrong. She remembered from
childhood that she had lived before and told her friend Madame
Dutilleu of her previous home in a southern country. Married in
1904, she described to her husband her former house in a warm
blue-skied land. She herself had been brown with big black eyes.
She had suffered from a tubercular (?) cough which made her
pale, thin and exhausted and was sad at her impending death. In
character she had been haughty, proud, harsh and almost ma-
licious. She had spent more than fifty years in the beyond before
her birth at Aumont.

In 1913 when she was forty-five she went to Genoa, recognised the city as the scene of her former life, located the house she
had accurately described, and said she had been buried not in the
local cemetery but in a particular church some distance away.
Research showed that Jeanne S., a young widow, died in the
house on 21 October 1809, and was buried in the Church of
Nuestra Signora del Monte. The intermission was fifty-nine
years.[125]

A small American girl both amused and startled her family
with repeated references to an earlier life as a Canadian soldier.
She would tell herself fairy stories containing fragments of
knowledge no baby could have normally absorbed. Everything
she did was as if by habit, and if reproved she replied, 'I can't help
it—I've always done it this way.' She told her father, 'I've been
here lots of times, sometimes as a man, sometimes as a woman.

Once I went to Canada when I was a man. My name was Lishus Faber. I was a soldier and I took the gates.' Later, her older sister came across in a library a documentary history which included the capture of a little walled city by a small company of soldiers, among whom there was a young lieutenant who took the gate. His name was Aloysius Le Febre.[126]

John and Ellen Pollock of Hexham, England, in 1956 lost two daughters, Joanna and Jacqueline, aged 11 and 6, in a car accident. John first believed that they would return when his wife became pregnant some eight months later and insisted that she would have twins, although her doctor could hear only one heartbeat. He was proved right, Gillian and Jennifer being born. Jennifer had an unusual white scar slanting down her forehead above the right eye identical with one Jacqueline had had resulting from a fall when she (Jacqueline) was three, and also the same distinctive birthmark above her left hip. Although the fatal accident was never discussed, Gillian who had a striking memory 'hangover' described Jacqueline's injuries in detail, and was overheard by Ellen Pollock to say in play, 'The blood is coming out of your eyes where the car hit you.' Both girls correctly picked out the former sisters' toys in the attic, crying out, 'That's my Mary!' 'That's Susan', the same names as the dolls had been given before. One day John put on an old coat, in disuse since Ellen had worn it on the day of the accident, and Jennifer asked, 'Why are you wearing Mummy's coat, the one she used to wear at school?' Gillian had the same protective attitude to her younger sister as Joanna had had to Jacqueline.

The two were panicstricken when a car came at them in a lane, as if they were reliving the accident, although they had been told only that they had had two sisters who had died, nothing more. When the twins were taken to Hexham, whence the family had moved, they remembered where their school was and the playground where they 'used to go'.

Both parents were convinced that rebirth had occurred. There are weaknesses in the case from an evidential point of view in that Mr Pollock expected the two dead daughters to return, and twins had occurred in the same family before. To the argument made that her belief had led her to look for similarities, Mrs

Pollock replied that she didn't look for things that happened when she wasn't there.[127]

A Burmese (Karen) houseboy was born with malformation of his hands and feet. Across his right hand a fairly deep, straight indentation, deeper and sharper than normal hand-lines, divided it into two sections. There were similar marks lower on the hand and on his forearm, and the left hand was likewise marked though not so indented. Both feet and calves were similarly scarred. Three toes had been joined together at birth, but two were separated by home surgery by the boy's father. Sometimes his right arm would swell and pain was felt in all the afflicted parts, accompanied by depression and fear.

The boy told his mother that in a previous life he had inherited three houses containing silver and other treasures. A band of robbers broke in one night and bound him with wire in a crouching position, his head between his legs, while they ransacked the houses. For three days he remained in acute agony, unable to move. Blood dripping from deep cuts made by the wire in his hands congealed between three of his toes. He then died, seeing his body with a consciousness apart from it and located in a different and less substantial form. He then wandered round scenes of his former life without any sense of time, conscious of a sense of profound unhappiness, with an obsession to recover his lost treasure. After a long time he became aware of human beings, became attached to a certain young woman and was able to be reborn as her child.[128]

Djebel el Alla, a Druse boy of five, had been a rich man in Damascus, died, was reborn, died after six months and was again reborn to his parents, to whom he complained of his poverty. Taken to Damascus, he astonished relatives by his knowledge of the names of various places through which they passed on the way. In the city he led the way to a house which he declared had been his own. A woman was living there who he claimed had been his wife. He asked after the welfare of his children, relatives and acquaintances. The Druses of the place met together, and when Djebel had given a full account of his past life among them, including names of friends and details of property, all he said was found to be true. He revealed that he had hidden a named sum of money in the cellar, went to the place and counted it out before them. The intermission was about twenty years, because his wife and others were still living.[129]

Twin boys, Maung Gyi and Maung Ngé, were born in 1886 in Okshitgon, Burma, soon after which their parents moved to Kabyu. The twins used names between themselves which were found to be identical with those of a couple, one of whom was a girl, who had died in Okshitgon about the time the twins were born. They were taken to Okshitgon where they knew everything, roads, houses, people and the clothes they had worn. The younger twin, who had been the girl, remembered she had borrowed two rupees from a Mrs Thet which she had not repaid— Mrs Thet also remembered the debt. Physically, the younger twin looked like a girl. They described how, after death, they lived without bodies, wandering in the air or hiding in trees, until the time they were reborn.[130] The intermission seems to have been less than a year.

Shakuntala, born January 1934 at Allahabad, India, daughter of Sri Nundy Lal, moved with her family to Fatenpur in 1939. She began to sweep the floor because she had lived in the house before as the wife of a man who had died of a fever and an abscess on his back. She pointed out some alterations that had been made in the house. She had two sons, one named Kali Charan. She had given an image of Radha and Krishna to a brahmin woman before her death, mentioned a woman with six fingers on one hand who had recently died in the village, and recognised a third, over seventy years old, the wife of a brother of Sri Shewraj Bahadur, as her friend. The woman confirmed her story, naming her as Peshkarin, wife of Sri Ganesh Prosad. Peshkarin had improved the water of a well with amlokni fruits, a method unknown to her present family. She knew her husband's name but said it was not good manners to speak it. Three men remembered Peshkarin, who had survived her husband by fifteen years.

Shakuntala remembered nothing of the time between death and rebirth, but she recalled another life in a brahmin family at Thusi where, at that time, her present father lived. A servant who worked in both houses used to praise Nundy Lal, saying she would be pleased if Shakuntala were reborn into that family. This middle incarnation was an unhappy one because her family opposed her worshipping idols, which had been her chief occupation as Peshkarin. She died soon after, a married but barren woman, and was reborn as Nundy Lal's daughter. She said she could find the house in Jhusi but was not tested. The case has rare features, the coincidence that brought Shakuntala to her previous house, detailed remembrances of two previous incarnations and a wish about a next incarnation coming true.[131]

Gnanatilleka, born in February 1956 at Hedunawa, Ceylon, of Tamil-speaking parents, said that she had other parents. She was two years old. When four, she refused to enter a temple where there were some stone elephants, and refused to play with elephant toys because she had been killed by an elephant. On the evening of the temple visit she began talking Singhalese. She recalled her former life at Talawakelle, sixteen miles away, as a boy, the seventh child, with many sisters. She described the accident in which the elephant had caused her death from internal injuries. The details applied to Turin Tillakeratne, son of a post office employee, who had died aged twelve in November, 1954. Taken to Talawakelle, the girl recognised her previous mother, father, schoolteacher, sisters and elder brother, to whom she was cold because he had been unfriendly to Turin. She observed and remembered a number of telling details, a jewellery theft, Turin's belongings, her former father's different way of doing his hair, her mother's stoutness, and need to buy firewood because no coconut trees grew at Talawakelle. She had a scar on her knee and abdomen pains, corresponding to injuries received in the accident to Turin.

In a radio interview Gnanatilleka spoke both Singhalese and Tamil and described her former life. Features of this case are the change of sex (Turin seems to have been effeminate) and change of ethnological group, Singhalese to Tamil. The intermission was fifteen months.[132]

Several instances of spontaneous child memories allegedly include xenolalia, though they are too anecdotal to be very evidential. Melvyn Douglas, the film actor, tells of Robin Hull, a five-year-old boy who spoke words recognised by a professor of

Asiatic languages as from a dialect used in North Tibet. Robin, who had not yet attended school, said he had learned them 'before' at a school which, with his teachers, he described in detail. The professor was so impressed that he undertook the long journey to Tibet and found the school in the Kuen-Lun mountains, with lamas dressed as Robin had described them. The name of the professor is not given and the story sounds unlikely.[133]

'Jane Winthrop', pseudonym of an 'eminent woman scientist', became interested in reincarnation because of her involvement with a twelve-year-old boy who could speak fluent German and Persian while in spontaneous trance. Neither he nor his parents knew any other language than English, but scholars who studied him declared that his German was that spoken in the early sixteenth century and his Persian two centuries earlier. Again the scholars are anonymous, and anyone who has done research on 'speaking with tongues' knows how difficult it is to find hard evidence of the truth of such stories.[134]

A three-year-old girl sidled up to a Mr Roberts in Santa Barbara, California, while he was out walking, embraced his knee and called him father. She insisted to him and to her mother that she remembered having lived with Roberts and another mother in a small house near a brook with a planked bridge. One day her father disappeared, the family ran out of food and mother and daughter died, although the latter 'came back'.

Roberts revealed that eighteen years before he had eloped with an English girl to Australia. In the wilderness there he had cleared a farm and built a cabin and bridge as described by the girl. A daughter was born, and when she was two, Roberts was arrested without a chance of seeing his wife and child and taken back to England charged with committing a robbery the day he left the country. He proved his innocence, but too late for his wife and child whose skeletons were found by agents sent to investigate.[135]

The Lama Mé Thon-Tsampo, head of the Ky-Rong monastery, died. An eight-year-old boy with a childish face, nervous manner, and lack of understanding of the situation, was chosen to be the vehicle of the Lama's next incarnation. He was carried on a litter and placed on the knees of the Lama's embalmed body and both were covered with a veil. A cry was heard. The boy stepped forward, saying firmly, 'I am the Lama Mé Thon-Tsampo', and spoke with authority and power, his eyes sparkling, discussing doctrine, and prophesying. He also recognised articles owned by the Lama.[136]

This case of an immediate reincarnation taking over the body and psychic entity of an eight-year-old boy is interesting—what happened to the boy's personality, weak as it seems to have been?

Many of the spontaneous memories of adults are so subjective that, however convincing they may be to those who have them, they can mean nothing to the sceptic. They may come to those who experience them with the force of a religious conversion. The difficulty with conversions, however, is that so many believers are convinced by mutually exclusive religious experiences that only those who have the same viewpoint find themselves satisfied. Adult 'far memory' differs from that of children in that it grows stronger with time whereas childish memories fade, and the best adult cases are usually less evidential than the best children's.

H. K. Challoner,[137] for example, is convinced that he lived former lives in Atlantis, Egypt, Greece, Germany, Italy and England. There can be no records of the first three and there are none of the last. Mrs A. J. Stewart, a fine novelist, has had a growing assurance all her life that she was James IV who fell at the Battle of Flodden. She has expressed this in the title of her *Falcon: The Autobiography of His Grace James the 4, King of Scots*, well worth reading as an historical novel and deserving examination and evaluation by a competent historian of the period. Yet there is nothing in it that could not have been obtained by research combined with the skills that one would expect from a first-class novelist. But how does one get across a *real* reincarnation experience of which the same could not be said?

Joan Grant remembers more than thirty incarnations, about which she has written a number of books (see Bibliography). She was born in 1907, and her memories of past lives, most of them ordinary and humdrum, began when she was a child in England. In 1958 she met Dr Denys Kelsey. They recognised each other from several previous lifetimes together and married.

Dr Kelsey treated a number of his patients for paralysis and phobias discovered under hypnosis, in which they relived portions of past lives which revealed the causes of their current troubles. He and his wife believe that the 'supraphysical body' attaches itself to the ovum shortly after conception. It is not hereditary but is often drawn to its parents by some previously existing relationship in an earlier life. Sometimes a perfect stranger has so strong a desire for rebirth that he is born of parents with whom he has had no previous relationship.

Dorothy Wofford, a housewife from St Louis and a writer, found herself setting down lines of poetry which later proved to be words of a poetess, Anne Broadbent, who had lived in New England in 1612. Dorothy found on investigation that she shared certain traits with Anne, including a love of New England, and she, Dorothy, was moved by Elizabethan music. She does not consider herself a reincarnation of Anne, although she wonders, and the symptoms could equally be mediumship or possession. They could even be due to cryptomnesia.[138]

Another who found nothing mysterious or occult in his experiences, which to him were simply something he had always known, was A. C. Campbell, a retired insurance executive, who knew from a boy that he had lived in Sicily and Italy where he had been born early in the eighteenth century. He was irresistibly drawn towards cities and sites he had never seen in the twentieth century but which were nevertheless familiar.[139]

General George S. Patton, victor of the Battle of the Bulge, saw himself in the Greek phalanx meeting Cyrus the Persian, with Alexander the Great at the walls of Tyre, on Crecy's field in the Hundred Years' War, and as a general with Murat.[140] If these are more than the fantasies of a fighting man, they bring into question the purpose of reincarnation. Is it a series of lives developing one talent to the point of genius? Is its object the achievement of a complete and rounded personality? Or is it both, one talent being fully developed in a series of lives, then another in another sequence, until the whole person is fully evolved, the

process taking aeons of ages? Two commodities the reincarnationist has unlimited supplies of are time and the space of the universe.

Peter Ballbush (a pseudonym), born in 1902 at Zurich, developed violent stomach cramps in 1952. After five months, when
no cure was found, a psychically gifted friend suggested the
illness might be a karmic memory pattern and advised meditation exercises. After a week's concentration on the cause of his
ailment Peter had a vision involving smell and sound as well as
sight. He saw himself as Jan van Leyden, of whom he had never
heard, tied to a stake on a high platform in a medieval town
square, facing a church tribunal. A dignitary read a long accusation of which he understood only his then name. Next, a red-
cloaked executioner tore out his intestines and those of two other
victims with red-hot prongs. He lost consciousness. On regaining it he found himself in an iron cage hanging high over the
town. He could see two similar cages and people down in the
square. He wanted to rise but fell back, again losing consciousness. He awoke to his present life, in bed and drenched with
sweat. The cramps, which Ballbush then realised had been
brought on by the sight of a monkey cage at the zoo, disappeared
four weeks after the vision. Six weeks later he read the story of
Jan van Leyden, executed in 1536, illustrated by a picture of
three cages hanging from a church tower.[141]

Guiseppe Costa, a man of huge physique and martial
appearance, found as a child that memories were stirred in him
by a small picture of Constantinople and the Bosphorus. A fleeting vision of ships and fighting came to him. When he was ten, he
visited Venice which was familiar to him. The following night he
dreamed of himself as a thirty-year-old warrior commanding
some medieval ships. On the chief ship was a person honoured
by all, who talked cordially to him. There followed a voyage, dis-
embarking, fighting, an assault on Constantinople, and victory.
The dream was connected and chronological, and so impressed
Costa that he treated it as the memory of real events.

In adult life he became a soldier and was stationed at Vercelli
where, in Sant' Andrea Church, he felt he had been in olden
times and suffered great humiliation. Later he visited the Valley

d'Aosta and Castle Ussel which he knew and associated with sad events. The Castle of Verrès also 'vibrated with emotions and passion'. Visiting it again alone at night, he saw the apparition of a woman he knew he had loved. She addressed him as 'Ibleto' and told him to read the story of one of his earthly pasts, that of Ibleto di Challant, builder in 1380 of Verrès Castle.

Ibleto, born in 1330, was at the court of Count Amadeo VI of Savoy, loved Amadeo's sister but could not marry her. He accompanied the Count from Venice with 10,000 men, taking Gallipoli and Constantinople. Excommunicated by the pope in 1377 because he had taken Bishop Fieschi prisoner, he freed himself by an act of humiliation in Sant' Andrea Church and died in 1409 at Verrès. An extant painting of Ibleto was so like Costa that they could have been taken for each other. The intermission was 470 years.[142]

One of the fullest accounts of spontaneous memory of an alleged past life and one in which the memory seemed exactly like the memory of past events in a present life is that given by E. W. Ryall in his *Second Time Round*. Born in 1902, he early showed signs of the memories that were to develop later. He annoyed his grandmother by saying he did not have one (both grandmothers in his previous life had died before he was born). He used dialect words foreign to the speech of Essex where he was born, calling, for example, the Essex 'dyke' by the Somerset 'rhine' pronounced 'rairn'. His father pointed out Halley's Comet to him in 1910 and he remembered having seen it before (it appeared in 1682). When his memories developed fully, he claimed to have been John, born 24 June 1645, son of Martin Fletcher, a yeoman, and brother of Matthew. He named his grandfather and uncle and the members of the household— housekeeper, horseman and general factotum and dairymaid— and a couple of dozen other characters. John's particular friend was Jeremy Bragg who married Catherine Knight whose sister Mary became a minor mistress of Charles II. He mentioned Daniel Brewster, kin to William Brewster who in 1620 had sailed with the *Mayflower*. John had a love affair with Melanie Poulett of Hinton St George, Somerset (three Pouletts had been governors of Jersey), who could trace her ancestry to the Norman

Conquest, and in 1674 he married Cecily Fuller, daughter of Jeremy Fuller of Dunwear, and sister of Susannah, Parson Thomas Perratt officiating. Other parsons mentioned at a time of considerable religious turmoil were John Ruddock of South Petherton and Joseph Alleine, author of *An Alarme to the Unconverted*, who was ejected in 1662 from St Mary Magdalene, Taunton, and died in 1688. John Fletcher first met his bride defending her against Adrian Toombes, 'the strongest man in Somerset', and mentions a number of people who, one would think, could be traceable, such as Gregory Alford, Mayor of Axmouth, and his cousin Richard, Churchwarden of St Mary the Virgin, Weston Zoyland. Fletcher was killed in a skirmish just before the Battle of Sedgemoor, having been involved in Monmouth's rebellion almost accidentally.

How did Ryall's memories come? 'An impression or idea formed in my childish mind that I had somehow emerged into the light of day again after a long journey in a tunnel and that I did not know the people among whom I had arrived.' He seemed at various times to be transported without any effort of his to other scenes in which he met strange people who seemed not to notice his presence, although he could observe their movements and understand their speech. This stage passed. There followed 'the unfolding of more certain memories, as I know them still, in which I was in another life, another era, as an active participant, able to communicate with those around me, and to identify the people and places of those far-off days'. The process of recollection was easy and effortless except when he concentrated too long on his memories in order to clear up some detail. These had a bad physical effect on him. Ryall's memories of the seventeenth century bore the same relationship to his mind as those of his present life, and were not the product of any effort at profound recall except when he had to clear up a point that had become vague or doubtful.

The 217 years between Fletcher's death in 1685 and Ryall's birth in 1902 were a complete blank to him.

In an introductory essay to Ryall's book Dr Ian Stevenson points out how frequently a previous life ends, as Fletcher's did, in a violent death. His personal instinct is that Ryall was not a hoaxer, though he admits that there is no evidence for his opinion, which is based on a possibly mistaken intuition. Cryptomnesia was possible, but no source was identified, and Fletcher's part in the Sedgemoor preliminaries could be made to tally with contemporary accounts of the battle, which Ryall could have read. But there was much more to be accounted for, 'a mass of small details and allusions to objects, customs and events in seventeenth-century England which had no connection with the Battle of Sedgemoor and most of which are not mentioned in the descriptions I have studied of the Monmouth rebellion and the battle'. ESP could cull knowledge from printed materials or living knowledgeable persons but, as with most reincarnation subjects, Ryall showed no evidence of other ESP experiences beyond two, which are numerically common to many people. Nor was possession likely because Ryall showed no sign of the altered state of consciousness that might suggest an intrusion into his mind of that of a discarnate personality. He did not claim to *be* John Fletcher but that he *was* John Fletcher.

Ryall might be a descendant of John Fletcher and have inherited his memories, but if this were so, memories of such a detailed kind would be unique and as hard to believe as reincarnation.

Ryall's account has been criticised on several grounds. A study by Michael Green ARIBA FSA has shown that local church registers do not mention his remembered names. The site of the farmhouse in which he avers he lived was unreclaimed common land until after the Enclosure Acts. The Public Records Office does not support him. He shows an almost total incomprehension of the assumptions, manners, customs, morals, and cookery of the period. There are allegedly frequent anachronisms; and Ryall is accused of having subconsciously gained much of his 'atmosphere' from reading *Lorna Doone* and Conan Doyle's *Micah Clark*. Dr Stevenson has replied to many of these criticisms with some vigour, but the lack of evidence in the public records of the existence of Ryall's characters is telling. He has at least left enough data for a very detailed examination of his 'memories' and, if they should be conclusively proved false, the incubation of so detailed a life in his subconscious should make a fascinating study for psychologists.

It is a commonplace in some cultures that accept reincarnation that a woman shall dream of someone who announces to her that he is to be reborn as her child. Sometimes, when she is already pregnant, the dream-figure asks permission to enter the embryo. A bizarre example of the 'eternal triangle' is the case of a woman whose dead lover announced to her in a dream that he would enter the child begotten by her husband. Perhaps it is as well that mother and child died soon after the birth, but not before the woman had confided the story to a friend. Also bizarre and very confusing for genealogists is a case reported by Kekai Nandan Sahay whose cousin died of cholera at nineteen.[143] His wife was two months pregnant. In a vivid dream her husband appeared to her and spoke of his coming rebirth as her son. There would be a scar on his head for identification and he would not take her milk. When he was five years old, the son told his mother that he was her husband and that his grandparents were his parents. When grown up, the boy closely resembled his father. Interesting features here are the overlap of two months and the psychosomatic (?) scar. The mother may have spoken of her dream in the child's presence. There is some evidence that a child in the womb can hear what is said outside. Perhaps it may be affected, too, by the mother's dreams, thoughts and desires.

An example of influence upon an adult is the story of Philip Pryce Smith's mother. He was born in 1920 and died in 1925 and, to assuage her grief, she went on a cruise and learned in Burma that it was believed that children were reborn. Later she dreamed that Philip embraced her and said, 'I am coming back to you, Mummy.' In a second dream in March 1926, he promised to come back to her two months after Christmas. A son was born to Philip's mother on 23 February 1927, and given the same name.[144]

A reincarnation dream of a different kind but illustrative of a common type is that of a woman who dreamed from the age of five of living in an old rectory in Yorkshire, playing with a boy on a top gallery and falling from it on to a floor of black and white marble squares, followed by oblivion. The dream occurred whenever a change was about to take place in her life. In the course of time she was invited to visit an allegedly haunted house and found it was the house of her dreams. Two or three centuries before, a boy and girl had fallen from the gallery to their deaths. The woman could point out the very spot, and seeing two miniatures exclaimed, 'My father and mother!' The two depicted proved to be the parents of the children.[145]

A dramatic story comes from Hans Holzer of a reincarnationist dream. June Volpe, a 29-year-old Pennsylvanian housewife, went on her first major trip, to Silver Springs, Florida. She had a very vivid dream of herself as a nineteenth-century 'southern belle' visiting a house she owned. The next day, visiting a haunted house in a local derelict town, she recognised both as having been featured in her dream. She was told that a Mrs Elizabeth Simms had been murdered in the house, shot in the back in 1896 when she was 89. While Mrs Volpe was in the house she felt as if her body were being moved by some other entity within it. She escaped from the house, and looking back saw at a window a young girl in a long white dress with long brown hair. When she returned to Pennsylvania, her husband noticed a great change in her, almost as if she had become a different person, with sometimes a southern accent in her speech.

Regressed in two sessions of hypnosis to fifty years before her birth as June Volpe, she became Mary Elizabeth Tibbits, eighteen-year-old daughter of Frank and Catherine, with a brother, Melvin, aged 23, and a grandfather, Gordon, living in Atlanta, Georgia, during the time of President Jackson. She had a boy friend, Robert Simms, aged 22. Advanced ten years, she was now Mrs Simms with five children, living at Red Mill, Florida. She revealed that her killing was accidental, a rifle catching in the clothes of the supposed assassin. 'Mrs Simms' related how she had communicated with June coming to the Red Mill house. She was going to live in June's mind, 'with her, as her'. She talked of her sons and other aspects of her life.

June revealed another incarnation as Gloria Heimier, born 1750, daughter of Franz and Anna in Dusseldorf. She was Catholic, an only child, and died unmarried of a fever at 22. Later she spoke a peculiar German, a language she did not normally know. The historical details were checked by Holzer but not convincingly, and the peculiar German was probably German only in sound. The vivid dream in the southern belle scenario may have been precognitive, inspiring the possessed feeling in the house and a subjective vision outside it. These experiences were in their turn enough to produce the incubation of the hypnotic 'life'.[146]

A famous case of a waking vision is that of Madame Batista, wife of Captain Florindo Batista, who had a daughter named Blanche who died in 1902. The child had a Swiss nurse, Maria, who used to sing her a French lullaby. In August 1905, Blanche appeared in a waking vision to her mother and announced, 'Mummy, I am coming back.' In February 1906 the mother, who must therefore have been two months pregnant when the vision appeared, gave birth to a second Blanche who looked and developed just like the first. She sang the lullaby, forbidden in the house because of its painful associations, distinctly, with a French accent, to the end as if she had known it all her life. When her mother asked, 'Who taught you?' the child replied, 'I know it by myself.' It is possible that the mother may have sung it herself without realising it, though this does not explain the similarity of the two Blanches to each other, nor does it account for the French accent.[147]

Mr Neidhart, 1898–1966, born in Munich, as a boy of five recognised two scenes of an earlier life in France, one of his death by beheading by Louis XVI. His life was one of considerable misfortune. In spite of his boyhood experiences, he knew nothing about reincarnation, but one morning for no reason he began to see visions which revealed to him the life of a knight living about 1150 with names and other details. All his inner feelings identified with what he saw. He envisioned a castle which he found and identified as the present ruin of Weissemstein near Regan. He had been a knight named Künneberg with an enemy, Falkenstein, and remembered many scenes stretching over that whole lifetime. Further revelations came later to him of his life in France as a revolutionary called Arentin, which ended in execution. He knew people in that life who were known to him in his twentieth-century existence, and in the two previous incarnations the same individual had been his wife. He had further memories of two more lives, one a Stone Age existence and one in the South Seas, both ending in violent death and in both of which his second twentieth-century wife had played a part. The visions explained his misfortunes as a result of misdeeds in prior lives.[148]

A strange vision is that of Major Wellesley Tudor Pole, walking towards the ruins of the Temple of Amen Ra in Egypt. He saw what he took to be a pageant or a film rehearsal. His attention was particularly drawn to a slave-boy leading a camel, who turned round revealing to him the Major's own face. Shortly afterwards the vision of the procession vanished. The Major was convinced that this was a glimpse of a previous incarnation.[149]

An experience illustrating the 'mechanics' of reincarnation—if it is a method of survival—is that recorded by W. Martin who in 1911 at the age of sixteen was knocked unconscious by a hit on the head from a coping stone. In an out-of-the-body experience he watched people tending him, then willed himself to return home. But against his will he was carried to a bedroom where he recognised Mrs Wilson, a woman he knew, in childbirth. The doctor was holding her baby in his hands and an almost irresistible desire seized Martin to press his face through the back of the baby's head so that his face would occupy the same place as the baby's. The thought of his mother, however, carried him to her, and he accompanied his parents on their journey to him, yearning to comfort her as she sat beside his bed. He climbed into his body with an effort that made him sit up in bed fully conscious. He repeated conversations he had overheard, including those of his parents, and told them of Mrs Wilson and her baby. She had died that same day at 2.05 pm, after delivering a stillborn daughter.[150]

Visions and dreams associated with supplementary means of information are common. Half asleep after an operation, Mrs Catherine Warren-Browne, a Roman Catholic, said to her visiting priest, 'Here is good Master Coverdale come to comfort me.' She felt depressed during pregnancy for no reason and said, 'She, too, died of purpureal fever', which was true of Catherine

Parr, Henry VIII's last wife. Through a ouija board 'Tom Seymour, Lord Admiral' spoke to her, telling her that Catherine was buried at Sudeley, a fact found to be true. She had had a child called Mary, born on 17 August. Mrs Warren-Browne discovered that the girl was born on the 28th, but the communicator pointed out that the Julian calendar differed from the Gregorian by eleven days. Mrs Warren-Browne later recognised places she had known, for example, Pembroke Castle and the room in it in which Henry VII, her father-in-law, had been born. Regressed under hypnosis to Sudeley, belonging then to Admiral Seymour, she became Kate Parr under the care of a Dr Tahilcus. She mentioned Dr Herk the King's doctor, Anne her sister, Lucy Tibbett, her stepdaughter and others. She died suddenly and was buried in the castle chapel beneath the altar. All the historical facts were stated to be correct (I have not checked them myself) but all were easily ascertainable, and the story is explicable by cryptomnesia with, perhaps, elements of precognition inspired by a possibly incubated subconscious fantasy erected on forgotten reading.[151]

A classic case of a dream associated with spiritualistic elements is the story of Alexandrina, five-year-old daughter of Dr Carmelo and Adela Samona, who died in Palermo, Sicily, on 15 March 1910. On 18 March she promised her mother in a dream that she would return as her baby. On 21 March the dream was repeated. A friend interpreted these dreams as a prophecy that Alexandrina would be born to Adela, but an operation had made this impossible. Some days later, when Adela was grieving to her husband, three sharp knocks were heard. A number of family seances followed, at the first of which Alexandrina's spirit and that of Jeanne, an aunt who had died some years before, manifested themselves. Alexandrina said that it was she who had appeared in her mother's dreams and given the knocks, and that she and a twin sister would be reborn to Adela before Christmas.

On 22 November twins were born, one resembling Alexandrina and given her name, the other entirely different. Like her dead sister Alexandrina had hyperaemia of the left eye, seborrhea of the right ear and noticeable facial asymmetry. Other shared characteristics were left-handedness, a loathing of cheese, fastidiousness about having clean hands, calmness, neatness, contentedness in playing by herself, chattering to herself, and an endless folding, tidying and arranging such clothes or linen as were at hand. When they were ten, the twins were told of a proposed excursion to Monreale, where they had never been, but Alexandrina recalled that her mother had taken her to Monreale a few months before her death, accompanied by a lady 'with horns' (the unhappy woman had protuberances growing from her forehead). They had seen on the church roof there the statue of a man with his arms open, and 'little red priests', referring to the red cassocks of a seminary of ordinands at Monreale, a procession of which they had seen.[152]

Mediums or sensitives (not all sensitives are mediums) either 'see' the former incarnations of others or experience memories of their own, and are able to distinguish them from their controls or communicating spirits, if they believe in these. It is claimed that sometimes the same information about an individual's former lives is given by several sensitives unknown to each other, and that the revelations tally; telepathy could be an explanation.

A nurse responsible for a large institution felt its standards slipping and was so frustrated in all her efforts to improve conditions that she contemplated suicide by hanging. A psychic friend visited her and described to her a series of her past lives 'of which she became aware'. In the immediately past life the nurse had hanged herself but, realising her error, had asked if she might return to atone for it. Her request was granted. Her friend told her that she had expiated her mistake by her wholehearted service to others through her profession, and that she could justifiably retire. The revelation changed the nurse's outlook, enabled her to retire without guilt and gave her a security of outlook from which she never looked back.[153]

L. M., born in December 1939, reached the age of thirteen with undeveloped sexual organs and was taken to a doctor who fed him hormones. The boy became mentally deranged and aggressive, defying all attempts made to cure him by exorcism and other methods. A medium diagnosed twin spirits, male and female, existing within the boy. They were present because they had thought that twins were to be born, and the medium pronounced that the cure would be effected by taking out the female spirit. This process was successful, but the boy's body continued to have 'curious asymmetrics'. A medical explanation could be that the boy was an hermaphrodite and upset by the struggle by one side of his nature to assert itself over the other. The talking-out of the female side may have been a sufficiently strong symbol or suggestion for the struggle to be resolved in his mind.[154]

Two sensitives claiming to be reincarnated themselves have been studied in depth. Hélène Smith, pseudonym of Catherine Elise Muller (1862–1929), became a medium who developed total somnambulism in which she experienced three increasingly significant cycles of existence. A French incarnation is not important because French was Hélène's mother-tongue. But she claimed to have been Simandini, favourite wife of a Hindu prince, Sivrouka Nayaka, living in 1401, and to have spoken Sanskrit. She was investigated with great thoroughness by Thomas Flournoy (whom Hélène believed to be a reincarnation of her prince), Professor of Psychology at the University of Geneva. He discovered that Sanskrit was not spoken in Nayaka's country at that period but a Dravidian dialect, that women spoke Pracrit, not Sanskrit, and that Hélène's idiom was not Pracrit. Oriental scholars to whom Hélène's script was submitted thought that it was a medley of Sanskrit and invented words or that there were eight or ten Sanskrit syllables constituting a fragment of a sentence that had some meaning. Her poor pronunciation could have indicated a visual origin, and the details of her Hindu history were all contained too inclusively in a rare book printed in 1828, which she could have seen, De Marlès' six-volume history of India. As Chari comments, 'The Arabic, Sanskrit and alleged historical elements were woven by her trance personality into a mosaic of considerable plausibility . . . but the issues in parapsychology . . . are not about plausibility but about verifiability.'

Hélène's real contribution to the study of alleged reincarnation comes, however, not in a rebirth of her own, but in a spirit's who spoke through her. In 1894 Alexis Mirbel, the dead seventeen-year-old son of a widow attending Hélène's seances, spoke through her, subsequently emigrated spiritually to the planet Mars and in 1896 addressed his mother through Hélène in 'Martian'. The language was thoroughly analysed by Flournoy and later by Victor Henri, Professor of Sanskrit at the University of Paris, and discovered to be simply French with sounds and letters changed. Word order was identical, personal pronouns, articles and possessives were analogous to French and the vowels corresponded exactly with the same shades of pronunciation. Henri showed that French words were changed not arbitrarily but according to a logical, uniform system applied by the medium's subconscious mind.

The existence of such a false language, demonstrated beyond all reasonable doubt in one case of alleged xenolalia, must throw suspicion on the many cases of languages allegedly spoken by subjects reliving past incarnations and recorded usually by observers who did not know the language spoken. The one or two cases of genuine xenolalia are much rarer than a cursory examination of the literature suggests—although one really good case of responsive xenoglossy would be enough to cause an honest sceptic to question his position.[155]

Rosemary, the pseudonym of Ivy Carter Beaumont (d 1961), was a remarkable sensitive of the 1930s whose mediumship was documented in three books by a musician, Dr Frederic H. Wood, and an Egyptologist, Howard Hulme. Her case is rare in that there allegedly communicated through her Telika Venturi, Nona for short, a Babylonian princess who was wife to Pharaoh Amenhotep III (c 1406–1370 BC). She awakened within Rosemary memories of a former incarnation in Egypt when, as a temple-dancer named Vola, she had known Nona, and Rosemary is said to have recovered what no scholar knows and what therefore cannot be proved, the pronunciation of the Egyptian of those days. Her xenoglossy is astonishing and, whether genuine or not, warrants further study by experts, for Egyptologists disagree about it. Rosemary also remembered having been a martyr during the Neronic persecutions, a seventeenth-century inhabitant of New England and an upper-class French girl who fled to England during the French Revolution.

Where an 'other' spirit allegedly communicates through a sensitive who is simultaneously a vehicle for her own personality of a previous incarnation, how does one separate the two personalities? Differences between characters cannot count because there are differences in dissociated characters and both Nona and Vola could be these. If Nona were a dissociated part of Rosemary's personality, it would be simple to take the further step of creating Vola as her friend partly out of the Egyptian imaginings inspiring and inspired by Nona and partly out of a normally-educated person's general knowledge of Egypt. The very few facts that can be established as accurate could have been gleaned from normal sources. For the rest, the communications are dramatically impressive but are incapable of verification and therefore non-evidential. There are even possible anachronisms. And, sadly for reincarnationists, even if the Egyptian were proved to be genuine, it would not necessarily follow that Rosemary was a reincarnation of Vola, though her claim would be immensely strengthened.[156]

Possession cases differ from reincarnation cases in that whereas in the latter type the person remembers that he has lived before but is not now the individual he was then, in the former he *becomes* the individual he was, or is at least aware that another personality is struggling with his own for occupation of his body. A celebrated instance is that of the 'Watseka Wonder'. Mary Lurancy Vennum was born on 16 April 1864, at Watseka, USA, and was just over a year old when Mary Roff, whom she did not know, died. When she was thirteen, Lurancy became mentally ill, being possessed in turn by a sullen old hag and a young man who had run away from home, got into trouble and lost his life. In January 1878, Mr Roff heard of Lurancy's case and brought her into touch with a Dr E. Winchester Stevens, who hypnotised her. He penetrated to the 'sane and happy mind of Lurancy Vennum herself' who told him that an 'angel' named Mary Roff wanted to come to her instead of the two former evil spirits. Some days later, Lurancy went to live with the Roffs and became Mary Roff totally in life and memory, neither recognising any of her Vennum family nor knowing anything until then known by Lurancy. She remained like this for three months and ten days when Lurancy's personality returned and Mary's departed.[157]

Not so dramatic a case but still an impressive one is that of F. L. Thompson, who in 1905 began to paint in the style of a recently dead painter, R. Swain Gifford, so realistically that an observer would have taken the paintings to be Gifford's. Thompson sometimes had the vivid hallucination that he was Gifford himself. Whether this was a kind of partial possession or due to some other cause, it could not have been reincarnation, because Thompson and Gifford were contemporaries. Yet, if Gifford had lived a century before Thompson, the latter could have been convinced by his experiences that he was Gifford reincarnated, a fact that may put other reincarnation experiences into a different perspective.[158]

Drugs induce 'images, episodes and even entire thematic sequences that bear a striking similarity to the . . . death-rebirth mysteries of various cultures'. They also sometimes bring about reincarnationist experiences which may subjectively convince those who undergo them of the truth of the rebirth hypothesis, even if there is no documentary evidence. Waking from an anaesthetic, a Mr Richardson became Jacques Duval of the French court executed during the French Revolution. He talked 'stilted Parisian French'. This could have been a vivid hypnopompic dream and, in the absence of evidence, the xenoglossy may be just a story; for it is unlikely that any of the medical team would have recognised eighteenth-century French, stilted or otherwise—their patient might have recalled hesitant, awkward, schoolboy French.[159]

Finally, several techniques have been used to train in oneself or induce in others experiences that are strongly reincarnationist in flavour. Devotees of religions that include states of self-induced meditational trance are led to expect that they will remember past lives; if so, these may well be due to imagination working about otherwise forgotten or similar experiences in this existence.

A technique of induction of a form of reverie in which the subject is led to probe unconscious memories was practised in the 1930s by a study group under the leadership of the late A. R. Martin of Pennsylvania. In the usual procedure, the subject sat opposite Martin while two others of the group placed their fingers on his wrist pulses. Martin spoke to him softly, suggesting that the pulse would slow as he gradually relaxed and freed his mind of everyday pressures until his subconscious opened to far-off memories. During one series an American spoke fluent German, unknown to him in his conscious state, in a dialect of a district near Berlin. He said he was experiencing a life as a seventeenth century German soldier, and described customs and activities of that period. He followed this with an earlier life in which he had been a carpenter working on a scaffold that collapsed and injured him.[160]

In 1951, L. Ron Hubbard launched the dianetics movement, later named Scientology. Dianetic therapists called 'auditors', listen to the reveries of patients known as 'pre-clears', induced by relaxation. The Scientological techniques of integration are designed to free the individual from psychological bondage that derives from deep-lying impressions in the psyche, and patients sometimes vividly re-enact and intensely feel events that obviously have not taken place in the modern era. They have, for example, experiences of dying in ancient dress, or describe in vivid detail taking part in foreign customs. Some Scientologists have come to accept their experiences as valid past-life data.

Techniques of mental training such as the Silva mind control method seem to have as a side-effect with at least some of their subjects glimpses of apparent past lives, and the Christos experience is significant enough in this respect for Chapter 8 to be devoted to it.

The many varieties of reincarnation experience illustrated above might be quoted as tending to prove that the doctrine is true. But the argument is double-edged. It might equally show a tendency in the human mind to create for itself illusory reincarnation experience. This inclination might be controlled in the ordinary personality by common sense and the mental faculty that seems to guard the mind against irrelevant intrusions of *psi* material into normal living. But when the censor is removed, by sleep, drugs or abnormal conditions of some kind, or by deliberate acts as in techniques of mind 'training', the tendency may soar to the surface, proving only that it exists.

Much is not known—how much babies in the womb can absorb of the thoughts, convictions and conversations of their parents; how much the mind can affect the embryo physically, a dream becoming a self-fulfilling prophecy; or how far innate physical deformities (as of the Karen houseboy) can foster other-life fantasies to explain their existence. There may be special influences in certain cases. (Joan Grant's father, for example, is said to have been interested in Egyptology, which might explain her Egyptian incarnation, but does not account for her other far memories.)

There is also the fact that anything remembered from a past life that can be proved from documentary or other evidence can be obtained either normally or paranormally and is therefore always suspect. This condition will obtain until the limits of paranormal cognition can be established. The only incontrovertible proof would be a true memory of a life that could be confirmed by no other authority; and if no other authority was found to confirm it, how could the truth of it be proved?

5

DÉJÀ VU

Déjà vu is a name given to a group of similar phenomena experienced by possibly as many as six or seven out of every ten people. The phenomena include *déjà entendu, éprouvé, senti* and *raconté*, as well as *vu*. They range from a vague feeling of familiarity, 'I have been here before', when the subject knows or thinks he knows that he has not; through conversations which have been held before, though again the subject knows that the people present have never before talked of those topics in those circumstances; to similar talks in which he suddenly knows what is going to be said and by whom; to situations in which he knows what is going to be done (sometimes accompanied by a feeling of helplessness because he cannot prevent it); to an uncanny knowledge of a locality in which he knows he has never been, so detailed that the déjà viewer can guide a party round it, knows what is round the next corner, the arrangement of furniture in the room at the top of the stairs, or that a hidden bricked-up door once existed in a certain wall, or the name of the next street and what buildings stand or stood there. During a *déjà entendu* conversation the listener knows the very words his companions will use to such an extent that everything appears predestined. Sometimes meeting a new acquaintance brings with it a strong conviction of a previous encounter in another life with echoes of romance or hostility or simply a neutral but powerful and sometimes mutual recognition.

Many authors have recorded experiences of *déjà vu* of one kind or another. As early as the first century, extraordinary examples of recognition of people he had known in previous lives are recorded of Apollonius of Tyana. Nearer our own times De Quincey, Coleridge, Sir Walter Scott, Edgar Allen Poe, Nathaniel Hawthorne, Bulwer Lytton, all remarked on the phenomenon in their personal experience. John Buchan came close to declaring a belief in reincarnation when he wrote in *Memory Hold the Door*, 'I find myself in some scene which I cannot have visited before and which is yet perfectly familiar; I know that it was the stage of an action in which I once took part and am about to take part again.'

Many experiences of *déjà vu* can be demonstrated to have nothing to do with reincarnation. But when a tourist on a first visit to a foreign city has a paranormal knowledge of its past in such detail that accuracy can be established only after considerable research, there is a *prima facie* case for his accompanying conviction that he once lived there, and his claim needs to be examined seriously. For in the more intense examples of *déjà vu* not only is the scene familiar; the other senses come into play, so that the subjects hear, touch, smell and taste, and the sounds and odours of a city of old are as present with the déjà viewers as those of their own time. The experience frequently arouses memories of an alleged former life and often dramatic death, such as burning at the stake, which can be found to correspond with historical facts allegedly unknown to the subject. The memories are so vivid and convincing that he is certain that he was once that man who lived and died in that city during that century and nothing will shake his reincarnationist faith.

The literature of the paranormal has many accounts of *déjà vu* experiences susceptible of a reincarnationist interpretation. By no means all such experiences need or can be interpreted in such a way, and there are adequate alternative explanations advanced by those who are sceptical of rebirth.

Following is a selection of cases:

Case 1 A young lady, 'recognising' a house in Worcester, looked for a doorway which had, indeed, once existed but which had been walled and plastered up. Many such stories exist, some reasonably documented.[161]

Case 2 A French nurse seemed to know the turrets of the castle of St Germaine en Laye before visiting it. She said that there was a little sealed-up room at the top of a staircase, the existence of which was verified from city documents.[162]

Case 3 A woman from the Southern USA, visiting the ruins of Heidelberg Castle for the first time, drew a diagram of 'a peculiar room in an inaccessible portion of the building' before she had seen it. Secondly, she received the impression of a book and knew that the name of an old German professor would be found in it. A first search being made without success, a second followed on her insistence, and the book was found. She became convinced 'that I was in possession of the soul of a person who had known Heidelberg two or three centuries ago'.[163]

Case 4 Ruth Montgomery in her book *Here and Hereafter* claims she knew the way into the king's chamber in the Great Pyramid before she entered it on her first visit. She knew that she had been in that pyramid before. She had a feeling of belonging to Egypt and also to certain places in Palestine.[164]

Case 5 In 1906 a clergyman named Forbes claimed that on a first visit to Rome, the Baths of Caracella, the Appian Way, the Catacombs of St Calystus and the Colosseum all seemed to him 'perfectly familiar'. The Tivoli was 'as familiar to me . . . as my own parish', though his recognition of it suddenly failed, supporting a suggestion made by a scholar of reincarnation experiences and theory, Dr C. T. K. Chari, that perhaps *déjà vu* comes in sudden flashes. Forbes also claimed that on a first visit to Leatherhead he indicated the exact position of the Roman road near the town.[165]

Case 6 Friedrich Schwickert (1855–1930) visited Smyrna for the first time and was advised to ride to Ephesus. Very soon everything seemed so familiar to him that he dismissed his guide. Many years later a brahmin put Schwickert (how is not revealed) into a higher state of consciousness in which he saw his previous life pass before him like a film. He had been a cavalry leader who had fallen at the Battle of Ephesus.[166]

Case 7 Raynor Johnson asked his friend the Venerable Sumangalo if he had any recollection of former lives. Sumangalo replied that he at once recognised old enemies and was immediately ready to do battle with them, instancing one of Thailand's brainiest men whom he detested and who detested him for no good reason. Their enmity, both knew, dated from another life. Sumangalo and the first girl he had loved, both aged seventeen, knew that they had loved before but had never been able to do more than hold out their arms to each other. Always something happened. She died when she was twenty.[167]

Case 8 Another case recorded by Raynor Johnson and by Leslie Weatherhead, both of whom knew the protagonists, concerns a husband and wife. The wife felt 'psychically' that she should marry none of her early acquaintances until her true mate should turn up, which he did not do until she was in her middle thirties. Then he came from England to Australia to represent his firm, met her at a public function and with her was overwhelmed by a conviction that they had been man and wife in an earlier life. Some years before meeting her husband, the wife had had a vivid waking dream of being in bed after the birth of a child and bidding her husband farewell as he left her to ride on a forlorn hope on behalf of his king. When she met her husband-to-be, the lady knew that he had been the father of her child and the hero of her vision.[168]

Case 9 A lady had a recurring dream of a house which she immediately recognised when subsequently arranging to rent it. She herself was as immediately recognised by the letter as the 'ghost' who had for some time haunted the owner's bedroom.[169]

Case 10 When he was twenty, a youth named Najib Abu Faray moved some hundreds of miles from the district in which he had been living to the Djebel Druse which seemed to him 'more familiar than his own mountains'. He recognised a village and a house within it as his own and revealed a recess within the house, unknown to anyone else, in which he had hidden a bag of money. It was still there. This and other evidence identified him with a Mansour Atrash, who was killed in 1897, about the time that Faray was born. The boy mentioned a dispute about some vineyard boundaries that had occurred during his previous life. He was accepted as the reincarnated Atrash and as such given ten camel-loads of grain.[170]

Case 11 Hermann Grundei, a German businessman born in 1887, visited Italy seven times between 1924 and 1935 and had *déjà vu* experiences in the old parts of eight Italian cities though none in others. These recalled to him gradually memories of having been a tall, lean, severe-faced ascetic monk, entrusted as a learned man with diplomatic missions between courts and ecclesiastical authorities. He remembered his name, felt that he had lived in the fourteenth or fifteenth century and had died of consumption aged about forty-five.

In another *déjà vu* experience in Constantinople (Istanbul), Grundei pointed out a loggia in the Hagia Sophia where he had once sat as a fourth- or fifth-century bishop. He was then forty or fifty years old, had a short thick body and a round fleshy head, and wore clothes which, when he sketched them, agreed with bishops' garb of the time.

A third experience of Herr Grundei concerned his business premises in a Berlin building dated 1618. There he spent his Sundays in 1942 and 1943 on air-raid precaution duties, occupying his time in going over his books kept in an old safe in a dark passage. After some weeks he began to feel that he had lived under similar conditions before. He saw himself inspecting account books taken from an old safe in a dark corner on a feast day, finding himself ruined and shooting himself through the right temple. He remembered that he had been a merchant concerned with ships and perhaps timber, a tall, well-built man of about forty, living in a small German seaside town, who after discovering that he had been robbed by his book-keeper had killed himself in the period 1870 to 1885. After the war, Herr Grundei found a town in which a man of this description and suffering this fate had lived. The man's son, born in 1875, was still alive, and when Herr Grundei visited him in 1956 both felt like relatives meeting after long separation. They looked like brothers. Grundei recognised various features in the town, seemed to know certain family tokens and picked out 'his' two sons (but not two daughters) in a school photograph. He was especially impressed by photographs of 'his' wife and mother in his former incarnation.

As a boy Herr Grundei had a mannerism which his mother found upsetting of putting a finger to his right temple and saying, 'I'll shoot myself.'

A feature of the case is that the suicide took place on 23 November 1887, thirty-five days *after* Herr Grundei was born. If this is a case of reincarnation—and it is not the only instance in

which the physical vehicle of the later incarnation existed before
the death of the former—there has to be faced the problem of
what happened to the psyche presumably displaced by the reincarnating entity. Is there a game of celestial musical chairs, with
too many spirits competing for too few bodies? Grundei's
opinion was that it is not impossible that the soul of a man passing
over in an accident may displace a weaker soul from the body of a
baby. Professor H. Bender, a noted German parapsychologist,
and Professor Ian Stevenson both saw Herr Grundei and discussed the last case with him.[171]

Case 12 Mrs Maija Sonck-Hovi, a Finn born in 1896,
described as possessing a 'strong, matter-of-fact and down-
to-earth personality', had a *déjà vu* experience in the city of
Turku (Abo) and its cathedral, which she visited in about 1929.
This with other, mystical experiences recalled memories of a life
about 1500 or earlier, in which she had been a priest in charge of a
convent at Naantali and had there seduced a young nun (identified in her present life with a man, 'the love of her youth'). The
priest was later appointed head of the cathedral at Turku but,
before leaving Naantali, had to condemn the nun to be
unfrocked and burned alive. Ordered by the bishop to pay the
nun a final visit, the priest had led her to a cliff and pushed her
into the sea. Her mother (in the twentieth century Mrs Sonck-
Hovi's mother-in-law, a woman with a strong, apparently un-
justified, antipathy towards her) had denounced and cursed
the priest in Turku Cathedral and had been declared mad.

No documentary proof of this highly dramatic story has been
sought. Mrs Sonck-Hovi had a vague knowledge of other more
recent lives but feared to recall them completely.[172]

Case 13 A lady acquainted with the Rev Leslie Weatherhead,
in a letter to him dated October 1959, described some of the *déjà
vu* experiences of her son David. On a visit to a newly excavated
villa just outside Naples, the boy knelt down by the uncovered
bath, edged with tiles bearing the signs of the zodiac, calling out
that here were their bath and their tiles—his had a bull on it and
the fish was Marcus's. 'As he said the name "Marcus" he burst
into tears and called out: "Take me away, Mummy, take me
away—it was all so terrible, I can't bear it."'

He claimed on another occasion, when visiting some caves in Guernsey used at one time as prisons for French soldiers, to have watched a young man being walled up in a cave. The authorities denied that the cave existed, but when David persisted the walls were tapped, a bricked-up door was discovered and a skeleton stretched out upon the floor behind it. A search in the archives confirmed the name mentioned by the boy.

When he was about fourteen, David's mother took him to the British Museum where he saw a sarcophagus under which, he said, there should be three initials in white paint. Asked to draw these, he sketched three Egyptian birds, his name in hiero-glyphics at the time when he had been a kind of inspector whose work it was to mark the coffins if they were satisfactory.[173]

Case 14 A twenty-six-year-old married woman, described as quiet, careful and level-headed, while driving through Germany on holiday, came to a locality which struck her as fam-iliar. Turning into a side road in a wooded area, she cried out to her husband, 'Here is where I have lived before! I know exactly where everything is.' She knew that before the Second World War she had lived in the locality as Maria D., a peasant girl, with her parents and two brothers. She remembered how the village looked and which house she had lived in. This was confirmed when she entered the village whose every path, street and house she recognised in such detail that she could guide her husband round it. She pointed out the house where she had been born and recognised the owner, now grown old, of the unchanged village tavern. The innkeeper, questioned by the husband about the D. farm, said that the parents and one brother were dead, that Maria had been killed when young, kicked by a horse (an incident she was able to recall) and that the farm was run by the surviving brother.[174]

The account stops there. It is not related if the woman made contact with her former brother.

Case 15 When seven years old, Miss Deacon, on a train stopped near Yeovil, recognised the landscape as a place near which was a house in which she had lived. She remembered running down a hill in that field with two grown-ups holding her hands. All three fell and she hurt her leg badly. Her name, she said, had been Margaret, and she was able to describe the frocks worn by her and her companions.

Seventeen years later, she was motoring in Dorset and had occasion to stop at a cottage near Poole, about thirty-five miles from Yeovil. There she saw an old portrait on glass of a girl whom she recognised as herself, in the same frock that she had remembered. The woman who owned the picture told her that its subject was Margaret Kempthorne, the only child of a farmer for whom her mother had been dairymaid. When Margaret was five years old, she was running down a hill with the dairymaid and another woman, when one of them caught her foot in a rabbit-hole and fell, bringing down the others with her. The child broke her leg and died two months later. The woman did not know where the farm was, but the nearest market town was Yeovil. On the back of the picture was an inscription: 'Born Jan 25, 1830, died Oct 11, 1835.' Miss Deacon commented that on the day Margaret died, her father's mother was born, miles away, and her own birthday was 25 January 1900.[175]

Case 16 Myers, one of the founders of the Society for Psychical Research, reported the experience of the Rev W. S. Lach-Szyrma who was haunted in his youth by visions of a village with a stream, a little bridge and a church. When an undergraduate he visited for the first time Adderbury, which turned out to be the village of his dreams. It had been connected with his family since 1800 and his mother had spent part of her childhood there with an uncle. Lach-Szyrma also had persistent visions of a hill with a wood on its top and houses overlooking the blue sea, in one of which, on the north side, he felt that he had once lived. When he visited Clovelly in North Devon, his vision was realised in every detail. His maternal ancestors had long lived there, and there were seven family tombs in the church.[176]

Case 17 J. H. Hyslop, quoted by C. T. K. Chari,[177] tells of a Mrs D. who had a vivid recurrent vision in a crystal of a bright blue sky, a garden with a high-walled fence at the back of a house, and a peculiar chain-pump in the garden. One summer she returned to her childhood home in Ohio and there met an old lady whom she did not remember having met before, who invited her to tea. After tea, her hostess took Mrs D. into her

garden which she instantly recognised as the garden of her
vision, blue sky, high fence, strange pump and all. Conversation
revealed that when Mrs D. had been two or three years old she
used to visit the old lady, house and garden, but both women had
completely forgotten. There are many such cases.

While there are some instances of *déjà vu* that are impressive
and strongly supportive of reincarnation, Chari is right when he
says that they are too few to carry conviction, at least to those not
disposed to accept the belief. He affirms that the more scrupu-
lous reincarnationists acknowledge that *déjà vu* unaccompanied
by a recognition of verifiable details is suspect, probably merely
a false memory or recognition. On the other hand, a small
number of good cases are hard to explain by any thesis other than
that of rebirth.

Every psychical researcher becomes quickly aware of the
astonishing fallibility of human memory and the capacity of men
and women for exaggeration and self-deceit. Sometimes he finds
downright fraud on the part of those who, whether to demon-
strate the gullibility of their fellows or through a tendency to
exhibitionism or in order to satisfy some neurotic impulse within
themselves, practise cunning deceptions. He not infrequently
examines cases where the credentials of the protagonists seem
above suspicion and the evidence of the highest quality, only to
find as the investigation proceeds that the layers of exaggeration,
misrepresentation, subjective interpretation and stark untruth
peel off onion-like leaving practically nothing at the core. A
sceptic may therefore be forgiven for dismissing every case
history given above as nonsense.

There is no need for such an extreme position. For if it be
accepted that the cases are wholly or substantially true and correctly reported, there are several explanations other than that of
reincarnation. These may be divided into normal and abnormal.
None of them explains every instance of *déjà vu*, but a combination of several serve all but a very few. Among normal explanations are the following:

1 Cryptomnesia: the scene or circumstances may have been
genuinely experienced early in life and forgotten, as in *Case 17*
above.

2 False memory: the 'recognised' scene may so closely resemble another really seen before that the memory does not distinguish the two. Alternately, the 'recognised' scene may arouse an emotional response in the viewer identical with that inspired by a different scene. There may be rare coincidences where two scenes are almost identical.

3 There are several physiological explanations. One is a double functioning of the cerebral hemispheres. This imposes upon the subject a 'double exposure' whereby the same scene is viewed twice, the fraction of a second between the two viewings being extended by the brain to an apparently considerable period of time.

4 A second physiological explanation is that a blinking of the eyes at a critical moment of entrance to a room and an exaggeration by the mind of the time taken to adjust after the blink may give the viewer the feeling he has been there before. He *has* been there before—one-thousandth of a second before!

5 There are organic diseases of the temporal lobe of the brain in which disturbances of time-discrimination occur. There may be a very temporary mental aberration, an instantaneous 'flash' of such an illness, such as is paralleled by a stab of discomfort or pain felt physically by a body in good health in which something goes wrong just for a moment.

6 The orthodox psychological explanation is paramnesia, the opening of a false memory door. There are sundry ways in which paramnesia may be caused. All our lives we are exposed to peripheral experiences of which we are unaware, which are censored out from our consciousness as being irrelevant to our circumstances at the time. There may well be combinations of these experiences with each other and with dreams, reveries and emotions that are churned out in our subconscious and combine to give us a false sense of recognition. When paramnesia is linked with some of the paranormal explanations listed below, it goes far to explain most cases of *déjà vu*.

7 Another cause of paramnesia is the vivid images formed in childhood from the descriptions of adults, especially if they, too, are linked with paranormal factors.

8 A feeling of familiarity aroused by *part* of an experience may pervade the *whole* of it.

9 The philosopher Henri Bergson suggests that the state of *déjà vu* is due to a condition of inattention or distraction which moves the consciousness towards a dream state.

10 The Freudian school, as well as accepting the explanation of paramnesia, suggests that *déjà vu* may sometimes be due to a subconscious defence mechanism to avoid fear caused by a particular situation.

11 Certain abnormal psychological conditions may lead to *déjà vu* experiences, such as a brief personality split, a lowering of psychic tension or a diminution of synthetising activity. 'Transient pictures may arise from simple suggestions in predisposed subjects suffering from abnormal mental plasticity.'[178] The temporal disorientation sometimes following the use of marijuana and the suppressed memories recovered by LSD are hardly relevant to the ordinary déjà viewer, but they do show that normal characters under abnormal conditions are capable of having these experiences. It may be argued that since most people have only one or two *déjà vu* experiences in a lifetime and a few have them a great deal, they are the result of out-of-the-ordinary psychological dispositions—marijuana experiences without the marijuana, as it were. Reincarnationists will argue that the few are those who have seen the light of the reincarnationist gospel and are advanced in their spiritual evolution.

Explanations which demand an acceptance of some paranormal elements are as follows:

12 Precognition of several kinds including (i) that which some time before remains buried in the subconscious until the sight of the aforeseen landscape or sense of the aforeknown circumstances bring them to the forefront of consciousness; (ii) precognition slightly ahead of the happening; analagous perhaps to the subject who guesses a card or two ahead in a series; (iii) recognition of a place explored previously in a dream or an out-of-the-body experience. It is said by some authorities on precognitive dreams that they may be forgotten and not even remembered when they are fulfilled—though how this can be

proved when the subjects have forgotten their dreams is difficult to see.

It should be noted that precognition may not always impress the subject as a premonition or prediction of the future but may occur without a time-reference. It can arouse an overpowering feeling of familiarity just before its fulfilment, with a detailed recognition of strange places, persons and names.

Chari lists no fewer than nine varieties of precognitive *déjà vu* although I would not accept all of them as genuine examples of the phenomena.

13 Extrasensory perception (ESP) or clairvoyance: if ESP is enlarged to what is called general ESP (GESP), sometimes super-ESP, that is, extrasensory perception that is capable of obtaining information from any existing source, there is almost no limit to the explanation of *déjà vu* experiences by this means. As Chari writes, 'A walled-up doorway or a sealed-up room are not serious obstacles for a GESP hypothesis.' Many psychical researchers, however, find super-ESP too extravagant a hypothesis for acceptability, and too easy. 'All phenomena are explained by Super-ESP; this is a phenomenon; therefore this is explained by Super-ESP.'

14 There may be a 'psychometry' of localities which affects a natural sensitive or someone temporarily sensitive to its atmosphere, so that past events may appear as a mirage in time (which may be the explanation also of some ghostly appearances). This psychometry may also work only under certain conditions of, for example, temperature, light and humidity, and may need to match the 'vibrations' of a very limited number of people to be effective. A *déjà vu* experience of this kind is thus a matter of rare coincidence—though it could be potentially common.

15 Telepathy, especially between parents and children, may be a factor. Chari writes that 'the hypothesis of telepathic paramnesia, ie an illusory recognition mediated by an unconscious telepathic exchange, can take care of most of the alleged facts of Alexandrina Samona (page 130), which is not, however, a case of *déjà vu*.

16 Muller suggests that 'on rare occasions it could be that a

person experiences an altered state of consciousness connected with "unio mystico" of short duration, which can not only explain why one knows what is going to be said, but also the queer feeling which accompanies the experience."[179]

17 Retrogression, the experience of stepping back in time, of which several instances appear in the literature of the paranormal, may account for the seeing of a place as it was centuries ago.

18 Spiritualists, especially those who disbelieve in reincarnation, ascribe *déjà vu* experiences to the influence of spirit entities.

19 Some instances may indeed be memories of former lives. If reincarnation is a fact, the meeting with someone from, or the arising of a similar situation to one in, a former life may recall memories of that life.

Most researchers, including honest reincarnationists, would agree that rebirth should be accepted as the explanation of *déjà vu* experiences only after all other explanations have been tried and found wanting. Those who accept as facts precognition, GESP and telepathy can ascribe almost all cases of the phenomenon to a combination of these, and Chari, as honest and scholarly an investigator as Stevenson, argues that nearly every experience of *déjà vu* involving detailed and verifiable recognition of strange places, persons and names can be accounted for by paramnesia plus an occasional paranormal cognition. He maintains that an illusion of memory may have for its subconscious basis a paranormal cognition of past circumstances. He notes also the existence of what might be called negative *déjà vu* in which *familiar* people, places and objects become *strange*. The feeling of strangeness may affect a child in such a way that he treats his parents as strangers and claims unknown persons as blood-relations. This rare psychological state could be the reason for some of the claims of other parents made by certain of Stevenson's subjects, though it seems to me unlikely and negated by other evidence in almost every one of his published cases.

If the cases above are considered in the light of the various hypotheses, the pros and cons of a reincarnation explanation can be clearly seen. Cases *1* to *5* need only normal ESP to explain them. The Worcester house, in 'communicating' itself to its visitor via some form of ESP on her part, could have included the idea of the walled-up door. The visitor to Heidelberg could have picked up the first of her two impressions from some written account, book or mind of someone knowledgeable of the castle and her second from the book itself in which the professor's name was written. The French nurse's knowledge of the castle of St Germaine was confirmed from city documents, thus providing a source from which she could have obtained her knowledge paranormally—normally this could have been a case of cryptomnesia, a forgotten memory of some source read many years before. Ruth Montgomery might likewise have absorbed her knowledge of the Great Pyramid from some diagram; while Forbes's *déjà vu* could have come from a book of engravings seen in a school or college library and forgotten. Most Anglican clergy have been to the type of school and had the kind of education in which such books would be commonplace. Schwickert's ride to Ephesus has the added factor of the brahmin's intervention. Yet the 'higher state of consciousness' may simply have revealed to him an imaginary life incubated in his subconscious mind following his experience on the Ephesian road which may itself have been cryptomnesic in origin.

Sumangalo's feelings could have been purely subjective, prompted by a natural strong antipathy and affection, as may those of the Australian wife and her English husband. The sense of a former life may have been communicated from one to the other—lovers are often abnormally sensitive to each other—and the woman may very easily have projected her feelings for her husband back on to her very vivid dream. The lady who precognitively haunted the house she was going to rent provides no evidence for a former life although she might for the existence of an astral body. The familiarity of the Djebel Druse could be precognitive—Faray might have foreseen his travel there. Or, since his previous history is not known, it cannot be said for certain that he had never been there. The dispute about the vineyard boundaries could have been telepathised from old inhabitants, overheard as it was discussed when Faray was thought to be Atrash reborn, or simply deduced by him from leading questions. The knowledge of the hidden money—if the incident could be proved to have happened—would need GESP to explain it. If GESP is rejected, reincarnation must be accepted as a feasible alternative, for presumably no one but Atrash knew of the money, else they would have taken it. This one detail, taken with the other facts of the story, weighs the balance of argument slightly in favour of the reincarnation hypothesis.

The facts of the story—who can be sure that they were correctly reported?

Hermann Grundei's experiences are too subjective to be of much value to anyone else, convincing though they may have been to him. The third experience contains features that are interesting, but many are and others could be coincidental, the feelings of the suicide's son could have been subjective (Herr Grundei must have communicated to him his reasons for wanting to meet him before doing so) and the apparently paranormal and only partial recognitions of photographs and family tokens could easily have been unconsciously signalled to Grundei by the son. The overlap of thirty-five days is also a problem to the reincarnationist.

Mrs Sonck-Hovi's memories are too reminiscent of the processes of composition of a romantic historical novel and, since no evidence is forthcoming, are so subjective that they cannot be accepted as evidential to anyone but herself.

The evidence of David (*Case 13*) is almost too good to be true. He was obviously a sensitive which the majority of humankind are not. As such, he might have been aware of the localities in which he had spent other lives where most men would pass through the scenes of their former existences completely unawares. But it is strangely coincidental that in his short life—he died at an early age—he should hit on three localities as far apart geographically as his lives were in time, and that he should have been so closely connected with *those* tiles of the bath in *that* Neapolitan house, *that* cave in Guernsey and *that* sarcophagus in the British Museum. If a psychometry of locality exists this would seem a better explanation than rebirth, communicating to the viewing sensitive in the first person the feelings of a contemporary eye-witness as if they had been his own.

The anti-reincarnationist can explain the German woman's memories of her former life as Maria D. as being due either to the psychometry of the place or to GESP. If the facts are true and as detailed as the account suggests, many will feel that reincarnation is a better explanation of them, for psychometry of a whole village and its outskirts seems unlikely and super-ESP of this magnitude appears to some investigators a convenient, lazy and meaningless way of 'explaining' great areas of the otherwise inexplicable. Sensitives may by means of GESP flashes have access to detailed knowledge of the past; if this is so, there must be some record of the past imprinted somewhere, and the notion of the *akashic* records does not stretch the credulity as much as it does at first hearing. Retrogression is scarcely an explanation in this instance. Those who claim to have experienced retrogression observe scenes from the past without themselves being involved except as observers, and the German woman's account is one of memory of a former life, not of observation of it.

The Rev Lach-Szyrma did not seem to have considered reincarnation a possible explanation of his experience, in spite of his feeling that he had once lived in a house in Clovelly. Nor did the lady who dreamed of the house she 'haunted' believe she had once lived in it. If the same type of memory fails to arouse conviction of a belief in some people while inspiring it in others, this is evidence only for the fact that people differ. In the cleric's experience, precognition or some form of psychic communication from his mother, both possibilities that would be accepted by many psychical researchers, are sufficient explanations of his experience.

The support of *déjà vu* for the doctrine of reincarnation depends on the individual's threshold of credulity. For those who accept all the paranormal interpretations given above, there is no reason to postulate reincarnation as the explanation of any experience. For those who find super-ESP too much to believe, reincarnation looms larger as a possibility; and cases such as those of Miss Deacon and the German woman are, in our present state of psychic knowledge, difficult to explain without it.

6

EDGAR CAYCE

Every generation seems to cast up one or two highly gifted psychics. Whether their gifts are explicable by natural laws yet undiscovered or are derived from some spiritual dimension discernible only by the eye of faith, they produce extraordinary phenomena that challenge normal ways of thought and being. Edgar Cayce (pronounced Casey) was such a man. Born on 18 March 1877 in Kentucky, of uneducated farming parents, he left school after reaching ninth grade (aged about fifteen) and worked successively as a clerk in a bookstore, an insurance salesman and, after losing his voice through laryngitis when he was twenty-one, a photographer. By faith he was an orthodox Protestant Christian of the fundamentalist Bible Belt type, with ambitions to be a preacher. He never lost his simple faith, was a Sunday-school teacher much beloved by his pupils all his life and fulfilled an intention made as a boy to read the Bible completely through once for every year of his life.

Cayce's loss of voice proved a blessing not only to him but to many hundreds of sufferers from a vast variety of complaints in the years to come. A travelling hypnotist induced him to talk normally while hypnotised though he could not prolong the cure into wakefulness. A second hypnotist named Layne suggested to Cayce in trance that he should diagnose his own condition and its cure. Cayce did this and spoke normally in his waking condition for the first time for over a year. There were occasional relapses, but these were treated successfully under further hypnosis.

Layne's own condition (a stomach ailment) was then diagnosed and a cure suggested by Cayce in trance, and these events were the start of a career of healing that lasted until the psychic's death in 1945. It was found that a simple process was all that was needed. Cayce lay down. In a few moments he put himself into a hypnotic sleep. A helper said, 'You have before you the body of so-and-so of such an address [this could be hundreds of miles away, even in a different continent]. Examine the body, diagnose its condition, suggest a cure and answer any questions I ask you.' Cayce would then give an accurate diagnosis of the condition of people of whom he knew nothing and would usually never meet, using medical terms of which he was completely ignorant in his waking state, and would suggest methods of cure which, if followed faithfully by his patients, worked in miraculous fashion in literally thousands of cases. This is not the place to discuss them; there is a considerable literature about Cayce's healing work and a thriving living memorial to him in Virginia Beach where the Association for Research and Enlightenment, which arose out of his work, has his cases on record and where his cures are studied by medical practitioners and others from all over the world.

Besides medical cases the healer gave what came to be known as 'life readings' which purported to reveal former lives of the inquirers, usually for therapeutic purposes. These began from a meeting in 1923 with a Dayton, Ohio, printer named Arthur Lammas who was interested in occult subjects and believed that a man who in trance could solve medical problems might also reveal other hidden truths. The hypnotised Cayce, questioned by Lammers about astrology and his (Lammers') horoscope, said, among many other things, 'He was once a monk.' The statement suggested to Lammers that Cayce could confirm that reincarnation was a fact.

To Cayce's Bible-informed mind reincarnation was a novel and fantastic idea, but he agreed to the use of a new formula: 'You will have before you [name] born [date] in/at [place of birth]. You will give the relation of this entity and the universe and the universal forces, giving the condition which are as personalities, latent and exhibited, in the present life; also the former appearances on the earth plane, giving time, place and the name; and that in each life which built or retarded the entity's development.'[180]

Cayce gave 2,500 life readings between 1923 and 1945, which are filed at Virginia Beach. Their purpose was to reveal the influence that former lives had on the present existence, and to show the attitudes, inclinations, personality characteristics and experiences carried over from the past and affecting the present. Psychological traits were often accounted for by former life experiences, and Cayce's object in giving them was as therapeutic as his physical readings. Perhaps more so, for the healing and development of the eternal spirit must be more important and urgent than the cure of temporary bodily ills.

Some life readings concerned his own family and circle, others—by far the greater number—people of whom he knew nothing. From his cases arose a 'theology' of reincarnation which he held alongside and reconciled with his staunch Christian faith. This theology was not only implicit in his revelations of alleged past lives but often explicit in reply to direct questioning while he was in trance. By studying a selection of his cases and a summary of his teaching, the reader can estimate the value of Cayce's contribution to twentieth-century reincarnationist thought. There is probably no other one man who has provided so much material.

Reincarnation, like charity, can begin at home, and Cayce, in life readings given for himself, revealed a number of previous lives. He had been a member of five groups and religions. In ancient Egypt he had been married to his wife of the present existence, Gertrude, then a priestess, and had been a high priest named Rata, possessing great occult powers but self-willed and sensuous. In one incarnation he had been a Persian physician, in another a Persian or Arab tribal desert leader and mystic with the name of Uhjltd. Once wounded in desert warfare, he had suffered hideously for three days and nights without food, water and shelter. He was once Lucius, kinsman of St Luke and associate of St Paul. Many centuries later, born of Cornish stock in 1742, he was John Bainbridge, a gambler, fond of women and wine, and a soldier in the British army in America prior to the War of Independence. Flying from Fort Dearborn, the present site of Chicago, when it fell to the Indians, he helped a group to attempt escape on a raft. The escape failed because the Indians kept pace with the raft and the survivors died of exposure and starvation. Bainbridge lost his life helping a young woman to safety. Charmingly, Cayce once met a child who 'remembered' him from having been on the raft with him in their previous life together. In the twentieth century Cayce's life was given him as an opportunity to serve mankind selflessly and redeem the pride, materialism and sensuality of his past.

Many of Cayce's circle in this life had been relatives, friends and associates in the past—friendly or unfriendly. Gladys Davis, his secretary, had been daughter of Rata in the Egyptian incarnation. She died then aged four. She and Cayce had been members of a close-knit family in a Persian life, and a phobia she had in her present existence about cutting instruments was the result of her having died in a Persian incarnation from a stab wound in the breast. As a Frenchwoman living in the reign of Louis XIV, she had grieved so deeply over the death of her three-year-old son that, inconsolable, she had entered a convent where she soon died. From this experience arose her longing for a son in this life and her choice of her own mother, whose only child prior to Gladys had died nine months before Gladys was born.

Mae Gimbert StClair, at one time researcher and receptionist at the Association for Research and Enlightenment, had lived unhappily in poverty and ill-health, with two failed marriages behind her. Life readings for her revealed that she had had lives in Atlantis, Egypt and Palestine in the days of the early Church and had had associations with members of her present family and others from her present life. For example, a New York woman who intended to remain at the ARE headquarters for two weeks left the day after she arrived because of her intense antagonism to Mae. She turned out to be the woman for whom Mae's husband had left her in the Palestine incarnation.

In another incarnation Mae had been a lady-in-waiting who had become the mistress of Louis XIV and later retired to a convent. Cayce said that Mae's first husband was a reincarnation of Louis XIV. Finally she had been married to a tavern-keeper at Fort Dearborn and was the young woman saved by John Bainbridge who died by drowning in the attempt. One of her brothers today had been her husband then, another had served in the tavern and a third had also been her brother in that distant existence. Her present father had been sheriff at Fort Dearborn, her mother had been her confidante and landlady, her second husband had been married to her present sister, and various other relations were incarnated then as other relatives and acquaintances.

Beverly Simmons, born on 24 August 1910, proved to be a reincarnation of Leila Beverly Cayce, Edgar's sister, who had died before he was born, aged just under three. Beverly also nearly died just before her third birthday and bore a marked likeness to the Cayce family. In giving her life reading, Cayce claimed to draw his information from the *akashic* records, referring to a 'keeper of the records'. Beverly had had five incarnations, including three in Atlantis, prehistoric Egypt and the Holy Land. In two of these she had been Cayce's sister. As Nimmuo in the Palestinian incarnation she had married a Roman political adviser who reincarnated as Riley Simmons, Beverly's present husband. He had also been Ex-der-Enemus, official insurer for Egyptian workmen killed or injured in government construction work, a job not unlike his modern work in the mutual insurance field.

On meeting Eula Allen (author of *Before the Beginning* and *The River of Time*), Cayce felt that the two of them had known each other before, and Eula had revealed to her former lives in Atlantis, Rome, Syria, Peru and the American West before the Civil War. She was later 'recognised' in California by another woman who had been her contemporary in the American West and greeted as 'Etta', a dancing-girl from the Barbary Coast, whose existence was afterwards confirmed from a poster of the period.

Yet another group of reincarnations in the Cayce family concerned Hugh Lynn, his son. In a prehistoric Egyptian incarnation, Hugh Lynn's brother had stolen his wife, whom Hugh Lynn had again known as a woman in an English life at the time of the Norse invasions. He had married her then and strangled her for infidelity. One of Hugh Lynn's school friends, given a reading, was found to be the brother who had stolen the wife, and the wife turned up later in the shape of a girl to whom Hugh Lynn became engaged. The former 'brother' and 'wife' met without being told of their Egyptian romance and fell in love, the result being the breaking-off of the engagement.

The theme of reincarnation in groups was continued when Hugh Lynn was told in a reading to go to Washington-Lee University at Lexington, because there he would meet many boys with whom he had been associated in past lives and would be able to make practical tests of reincarnation. Another life had been lived during the Crusades, and in an Austrian village after the Second World War he had a vision which filled him with a 'strange awareness' of a Crusader army marching through the place. He knew he had once lived there, and located ruins of structures he had known.

Cayce had lost another son who later reincarnated in another boy to whom he gave a life reading. Before the relationship was revealed, Gertrude, Cayce's wife, was 'so magnetically drawn to the boy that she had difficulty in concealing her true feelings'.[181]

A sceptic might argue that in readings so closely connected within the family there might be subjectivity, wishful thinking, self-delusion or, at worst, conspiracy and downright fraud. Supporters of the Cayce claims, on the other hand, can point to hundreds of instances of strangers whose ills in this life were diagnosed correctly by reference to causes of them in past existences and allege that although most of these lives lack historical confirmation, many others have remarkable documentary evidence to support them. In addition, Cayce often listed events and dates in the current life which he had no means of knowing normally, together with dominant character traits. His accuracy in these reports was never challenged by a single subject.[182]

Following is a selection of cases from the considerable literature published on Edgar Cayce. I have not had the opportunity of consulting the records at first hand, as would have been ideal, and have had therefore to rely on secondary sources, to the authors of which due acknowledgement is made.

Julia Chandler, drama critic, dramatist, feature writer and radio producer (d 1966), had a childhood vision which she never forgot of herself as a Greek dancer aged about sixteen. The vision recurred intermittently until she was about eighteen.

After a lapse of fifteen years it returned with startling clarity, and a few days later Flower Newhouse, a Californian mystic and lecturer, told her that she had been a temple dancer in Greece five hundred years before Christ. Later, Edgar Cayce tuned in to the same period.[183]

This case could be explained by cryptomnesia and telepathy. Miss Chandler as a very small child could have been stirred emotionally by, say, a picture of a Greek dancer, have identified herself subconsciously with the girl and telepathically communicated her impression to the two sensitives, perhaps conveying also to Cayce the 'same period' which she had obtained from Flower Newhouse.

C. J. Ducasse, himself a considerable writer on life after death, was given a life reading by Cayce in which he was told that he had been a Jean de Larquen, who had come to America from France as an intelligence officer associated with Lafayette. No one of that name has been traced in either France or America, and it is possible that the French-sounding or appearing name Ducasse suggested a French origin.[184]

There is, however, historical confirmation of a reading given to a blind musician who combined a passion for railroads with an enthusiastic interest in the American Civil War. Cayce said that he had been a Southern States soldier in that war named Barnett Seay, and that records of the man could still be found in the State of Virginia. The Virginian Department of Old Records confirmed that a Barnett A. Seay, aged twenty-one and living in Henrico County, Virginia, had been a railroad man by profession and had enlisted as a colour-bearer in Lee's army in 1862. His date of discharge was also recorded.[185]

A sceptic could argue that Cayce, living in Virginia, might without realising it have seen Seay's records and reproduced the information by cryptomnesia when a suitable subject applied for a life reading. It would be argued against him that Cayce usually worked simply from names and addresses, and that to pick a suitable subject would be a coincidence too extreme to be credible.

A telegraph operator in New York City, intrigued by the telegrams she was required to send to Virginia Beach, asked for a life reading for herself. Told that she had been a competent artist in several lifetimes and could be one again, she changed her career and not only became a highly successful commercial artist but transformed her personality.

The following cases are all to be found at greater length in Noel Langley's *Edgar Cayce on Reincarnation*.[186]

David Greenwood, born on 26 August 1913 and fourteen years old when he was given his reading on 29 August 1927, was told of five previous lives. The earliest was pre-10,000 BC when he had been heir to a throne in Atlantis. Next, he had been an Egyptian named Isois, living about 10,000 BC, when the land had been conquered and he had been useful to the conquerors as an intermediary between priests and people. He lived his third life as Abiel, a court physician in Persia, possibly at the time of Alexander the Great's invasion and conquest. In his fourth existence he became Colval, a tradesman who obtained and abused a position of power in his city on the isthmus of Thessalonika. Finally he had previously lived in the reigns of Louis XIII and XIV as Neil, a kind of master of the robes, personally responsible for the king's wardrobe and an arbiter of fashion. He had served faithfully in this capacity.

His life reading warned David of digestive troubles (Neil had been a gourmet) and a quick temper, and advised him to make a career with people whose trade pertained to materials and clothing. Although he had no apparent interest in clothing, David became salesman to a clothing company in 1940, after some time in a dead-end job, and became hugely successful. But he suffered from food allergies and had to live on the most Spartan of diets.

Three lives were ascribed to Grover Jansen, aged nineteen in 1939. He had been Ex-en, an Egyptian, living during a period of reconstruction following the inundation of the Atlantean lands. He had instructed and edified various groups, assisting their efforts for better conservation. His next incarnation was as Agrilda, who served under three Roman emperors in England, Ireland, France, Spain, Portugal, Africa, Greece and Palestine, estimating what could best be produced in those lands for the benefits of the Roman Empire. Then he became Elder Mosse who worked during the American War of Independence as an agriculturist whose work was to estimate the amount of produce to be obtained from a given terrain.

Conservation was to be Jansen's life work. He took the advice given and lived a happy, useful and fulfilled life in the National Park Service of the American Department of the Interior and then as a United States game management agent.

Nurse Stella Kirby, sent to look after a man in the last stages of imbecility and loathsomely unclean, could not continue and resigned her post. A life reading revealed that she and her patient had met twice in previous lives, once in Egypt, when he had been her son, and once in the Middle East, when she had been one of a number of young women used to satisfy his abnormal sexual lusts. Cayce pointed out that both the man and Stella had met their karma, and advised her to work hers out—it would otherwise continue to another life—by returning to and caring for her patient. Stella did so. She won the dog-like devotion of the imbecile, who realised within the limits of his understanding that he was once more loved. He died in two years and Stella went on to live her own, balanced life.

Flora Lingstrand, born in 1879, inherited from her neurotic mother a terror of death in childbirth. As a result she left her husband, had her ovaries removed and became addicted to narcotics because of the drugs administered to her. She became utterly self-absorbed. Her life reading showed that she had to go very far back to find her soul yet uncorrupted. In prehistoric Egypt she had 'stood immaculate and tall' in one of the temples of initiation, and had followed this by a good life in Greece. Her forfeiting of domestic happiness began when she had been clerk at the court of one of the French Charles's prior to 1515 when she (he) had squandered the life then given in excesses of debauchery. In a later life, previous to her present, she had been Sara Golden, who as one of the lost colony of Roanoke in 1590 had been forced to witness her five children 'taken and scourged in the fire'. She had cursed God, rejecting all hope of forgiveness from the God she had reviled, and from this experience had grown her dread of bearing children.

Patricia Farrier, a forty-five-year-old spinster, suffered from claustrophobia and fear of crowds. Cayce revealed to her that she had ended a previous life as a thirteen-year-old girl by being smothered in a farmhouse cellar, when an earth tremor caused the floor to collapse.

John Schofield, aged twenty-three, in a dead-end job and oppressed by a possessive family, was told that he had been involved in fresco-designing in previous lives in Egypt, Greece and Rome. He was advised to get away from his family and train for the same kind of work. He obeyed and was rewarded by a successful career.

Children killed prematurely, as in war, tended to reincarnate too soon and into uncongenial families. Theresa Schwalendal, who lived on the borders of Lorraine and Germany, was scared of city life, because she had died after experiencing Nazi hooliganism. She re-entered the material world less than nine months after dying, with the fear of cities as part of her nature. Another four-year-old died violently in France during the Second World War, and eager to re-enter life was born again of American parents only nine months later. But the intermission was too short for the memories of bombardments and fires to be erased.[187]

A case which could be evidential of reincarnation is that of a woman to whom Cayce revealed that she had lived ten thousand years ago in what is now New Mexico. She had made certain hieroglyphics. Neither Cayce nor she had ever been to New Mexico (both might have known of the hieroglyphics cryptomnesically or even telepathically, since their existence was known), and when the woman later saw the hieroglyphics, she felt inwardly that she had lived in the locality and had made the marks. As she had already been told this, the feeling could have been subjective.[188]

For a simple Bible Christian, Edgar Cayce developed, or had thrust upon him by his experiences, a complicated theology of reincarnation. He reacted to the first revelation of what he had replied in trance to Lammers' questioning with understandable alarm; the ideas he had promulgated, in so far as he could understand them then, seemed utterly at variance with his own faith, and he even thought them possibly devil-inspired. Yet, as his experience and knowledge grew in time, he reconciled them with his beliefs which developed to include much that Christians of his brand of orthodoxy, and others, found strange.

He accepted the existence of the *akashic* records, *akasha* being a Sanskrit word which refers to the fundamental etheric substance of the universe, described by modern believers as 'electrospiritual' in composition. On this substance there remains indelibly impressed every sound, action, movement and thought that has happened since the beginning of time. Sensitives are able to have access to portions of this information relevant to the needs of their subjects. To a Christian, the *akashic* records may be acceptable as a version of that terrible account book kept by the recording angel which is to be opened at the Day of Judgement. Indeed, Cerminara suggests that the Day of Judgement may be the time when the karmic debt falls due,[189] although this is at variance with the view that reincarnation is a process that does not end until all karma is resolved.

It should be noted that if the *akashic* records include a complete record of human behaviour and thought, they will contain all the erroneous conceptions as well as the true. Revelations by sensitives, including Cayce, are therefore not infallible, and every pronouncement must be judged individually on its own merits. There is no requirement that an admirer of Cayce should accept everything he said as truth, and he certainly produced some questionable conceptions.

A second source of Cayce's information was the subconscious minds of the individuals with whom he was put into direct touch when he went into trance.[190]

His theology may be summarised as follows. God, desiring self-expression and companionship, projected from himself a cosmos of souls. He created all the souls that exist in the beginning—none have been made since—and each contains within itself an infinitesimal spark of the divine. Cayce therefore accepted the principle of pre-existence, even possibly of coexistence with God. Each soul was a new individual issuing from the dependent upon God, but aware of an existence apart from him. Each possessed two states of consciousness, that of the spirit, which carried a knowledge of its identity with God, and that of the new individual, which bore the knowledge of everything it experienced.

The soul's destiny was a cycle of experience of unlimited scope and duration which would eventually enable it to perfect its individuality and bring to it the knowledge of all creation. This process did not necessarily include identification with and participation in all forms of substance. When a soul attained a state in which its will's desire was no longer different from the thought of God, then its two consciousnesses would merge and it would return to God its source, to be joined with him as the companion it was destined to be. It would retain its consciousness of separate individuality, aware that it had acted as a part of God of its own free will. Loss of individuality could not occur because God's awareness of everything that happens includes the consciousness of each individual. The return of the soul is the return of the image to God who imagined it, and the consciousness could not be destroyed without annihilating part of God himself. When a soul returns to God it is aware of itself not only as a part of God but as a part of every other soul and of everything else. Its ultimate destiny is to become not only a companion but a co-creator with God. Its heritage is to know itself to be itself yet one with the Creative Force called God. 'We become one with the ocean of life, but it is not so much that we are lost in the ocean as that the ocean has entered into us.'[19] What is lost is the ego, the desire to do other than the will of God, a desire that is voluntarily surrendered.

The soul is not a permanent personality. Each personality of a soul is a separate experience in no way related to other experiences except by common inclusion in a larger enterprise. The consciousness of the separate personalities is absorbed at the end of each life into the subconscious which becomes the record of all the lives of the soul. At death the conscious mind of the body is discarded, and all that remains from the sojourn upon earth is the total recall of its worldly experiences, stored in its memory bank. The subconscious mind survives because it neither consists of nor depends on matter, and it becomes the conscious mind of the soul. The superconscious mind assumes the functions relinquished by the subconscious, and the soul is articulate as it never can be upon earth.

When it comes to entry into the next life, the soul may be allowed to choose its parents. Infant deaths may be deliberate, a realisation on the entity's part that it has made a mistake. Children killed prematurely in war, for example, sometimes reincarnate too soon into uncongenial families (a view supported by Joan Grant and Denys Kelsey, who have found this in the hypnotic regression of some of their subjects). Development of the soul is probably faster in advanced cultures.

Only a comparative few have come into the experience of the solar system, though many have gone through or are going through similar processes in other systems. Arcturus is the next step for those leaving the solar system, and represents a choice for the soul's next venture.

During the earth cycle the soul experiences a series of incarnations interspersed with periods of involvement in other dimensions of consciousness in the solar system. The first incarnations entail a descent into earthiness, and the separation of the conscious from the unconscious mind. The nadir is reached when an entity believes only in what it can see, feel and prove in terms of the conscious mind. Then it begins to fight its way back and up, using the only tools left to it, suffering, patience and mental power, until every thought and action of the physical body is in accord with the original plan for the soul. When the body no longer hinders the soul's free expression, when the conscious merges with the subconscious and the atomic structure of the body can be so controlled that the soul is as free in as out of it, the earth cycle ends and the soul can progress to new ventures.

A personality is shaped by three or four incarnations but is only an aspect of an individuality. Our conscious minds are records of our current lives. Conscious thoughts pass to the imaginative or introspective mind (Cayce gives various glands and parts of the body as the seats of these different minds) where they are compared with all that has gone before that is in any way related to them. Properly conditioned and judged, they then pass to the subconscious or soul mind, where they are kept on record. If constructive, they quicken the spirit and lower the barrier between the soul and the pure essence of life. If destructive and repeated, they build up the barrier and dim the radiance of the life essence that shines through the subconscious to the imaginative and thence by refraction, intuition and yearning, into the subconscious.

During the intermission between incarnations, which may vary in length from a hundred to a thousand years, souls who have made some progress are able to choose their own entrances and their own tasks, but those who have made too many mistakes or become too subject to earthly appetites are sent back by law at a time and in circumstances best suited to help them. Where there is a choice, a soul may assume any of several personalities, each of which would express a portion of itself. As it approaches completion of its time in the solar system, the personality becomes more complex, expressing greater proportions of its individuality. Diminishing adverse karma results in more freedom for the expression of individuality, and when the personality is the complete expression of the soul's individuality, the sum total of all of his thought, experienced and felt throughout the ages of its existence in the cycle, then the cycle is completed and the soul moves on.

Choice of incarnation, when choice is allowed, is usually made at conception, a pattern being woven by the mingling of the soul patterns of the parents and attracting the to-be-born-again soul for the working-out of whose karma the opportunity is presented. Many factors can be taken into account, such as the contemporary situation and former association in past lives with the parents and other entities reincarnated at the same time with whom karmic relationships have to be resolved. Cayce taught that not only were groups reincarnated together in cycles but that between lives they agreed to take up earthly existence together at a particular time. He warned his circle that animosity between people would link them in life after life, and that the only way to dissolve a bond forged by hostility was to begin to be reconciled now.

Cayce had no doubts about the divinity of Christ, but his Christology was markedly unorthodox. Before his incarnation as a divinity (orthodox Christians would say *the* Divinity, God himself), manifesting himself through Jesus ben Joseph, Christ had lived as Enoch, Melchizedek, Joseph, Joshua and Jeshua— the scribe of Enoch who rewrote the Bible [sic]. He had to manifest himself several times on earth before he was able to prepare a human body of sufficiently advanced spirituality to sustain his divinity in its ultimate task of salvation. [192] Through his activities in his several incarnations he overcame the world and by 'bearing the cross' in every experience he reached the final cross with all power and knowledge, and willingly accepted crucifixion. As a by-product of the incarnation of Christ was the sentiment expressed by Cayce that the most permanent benediction that a soul can bring with it to its lives on earth was the memory of a blessing bestowed on it by Jesus himself.

Cayce, quoting the usual proof texts (see pages 94–6), believed that Jesus taught reincarnation. He added the argument that since no man dies perfect and Jesus had taught that unless a man was perfect he could not enter the kingdom of heaven, there must therefore be further lives in which perfection was eventually attained. Some of the life readings asserted that the Church embraced reincarnation for its first three hundred years until its recognition by the Emperor Constantine caused its ranks to be opened to every sycophant at his court. Upon this, Church leaders dropped the doctrine of reincarnation. It was difficult to explain, difficult to believe. It complicated living and made virtue even more necessary, demanding too much of the 'new' Christians, for a man had to be brave to face the fact that one life of suffering was only a single step to heaven. On the other hand it inspired carelessness by removing the fear of hell from those who examined the implications of a belief in rebirth only superficially.

The gnostics kept the line of belief unbroken between the old Christianity and the new, but the Church fought, beat and suppressed them. Cayce maintained that the Church leaders had been wise to drop the idea of reincarnation, as the reaction of some of his subjects to their life readings showed.

If a present life were inferior to a past, it showed that the soul was on the downgrade. A life reading was a balance sheet, and if an asset once possessed were missing, there was cause for alarm.

Some souls possessed greater virtue in earlier lives, but it was the virtue of innocence. The soul's path ran downwards until it made a turn upwards of its own free will. So there was no reason for pride in a good life lived thousands of years ago, and the goodness lost had to be attained again, this time not through innocence and ignorance but by the use of the will in overcoming evil and temptation.

Cayce's thought and philosophy were influenced by his trance utterances, which were perhaps a greater revelation to him than they were even to many of his hearers. Lammers' first questions to him were about astrology, to which he had replied that the solar system provided a cycle of experiences for the evolving soul. Man alternated experiences on earth with experiences in other dimensions of consciousness. Earth was the 'third dimension', a sort of laboratory for the whole system, because only here was free will completely dominant. On the other planes some measure of control was kept over the soul to see that it learned its proper lessons. Astrology, though containing some truth, fell short of complete accuracy because it did not take rebirth into account.

Cayce also had a developed doctrine of karma, close to that of the theosophists, as 'the cosmic principle of rewards and punishments for acts done in a previous life or lives'. Debts incurred in the flesh must be met in the flesh—an eye for an eye and a tooth for a tooth; this *lex talionis* was a natural law, ascribable neither to God nor man but to the nature of things (although, for a deist, God created the nature of things and natural laws are of his making). Despite its expression in physical effects, karma was primarily a psychological law, enabling the subject of the karmic effect to make progress by a right reaction to the handicaps or advantages conferred on him. The reversal or reaction on the objective physical plane was not as exact as it was on the psychological.

Karma could be of several kinds, and could be deferred for many lives until conditions were right for its fulfilment. A common form is 'boomerang' karma, where an entity becomes the victim of ills he has in the past imposed upon others. A college professor, born totally blind, had in a barbarous Persian tribe existing in about 1000 BC carried out its practice of blinding its enemies with red-hot irons. A caricaturist at the French court of Louis XVI, who lampooned homosexuals, now struggled against the same tendencies in himself. A girl with both legs crippled and feet stunted by infantile paralysis had in an Atlantean incarnation made people 'weak in limb and unable to do anything else but follow'.[193] *Many Mansions* gives seven examples of people who suffered from severe physical afflictions because in previous incarnations they had scoffed at those who had been disfigured or who were weak because of their ideals (mostly Christians in Rome).[194]

Organismic karma affects the body—gluttony in two previous incarnations resulted in a weak digestion in the present. Symbolic karma repaid debts in former lives with physical handicaps or benefits that were metaphors in flesh, as it were, of former deeds. Five lives back a subject had seized control ruthlessly of the country of Peru, shedding much blood, resulting in anaemia in the present existence. Beauty now was sometimes the reward of selflessness and service in previous times. Vocational karma, as exemplified in the case of John Schofield (page 163) could qualify a man in his present life for work for which he had been fitted in previous existences.

There could be karmic credits and debts within families and circles of acquaintances for, as Cayce taught, the same groups of people tended to reincarnate together in cycles and sequences. One frequent sequence was Atlantis, ancient Egypt, Rome, the Crusades and the early American colonial period. Another was Rome, France during the reigns of Louis XIV, XV or XVI, and the American Civil War. Former incarnations were found also in China, India, Cambodia, Peru, Norseland, Africa, Central America, Sicily, Spain, Japan and other countries. And at least sixty-five contemporary Americans are said to have lived in the days of Jesus Christ and the Acts. Many individuals were told by Cayce that they had been among the holy women who had followed Christ on earth.

Cayce also believed in a leapfrog system, whereby groups of souls living during one era, *A*, tended to be reborn together in a succeeding time, *X*, while those living in era *B*, were reincarnated in period *Y*, like shifts in a factory.[195] Those bound by ties of family, friendship, hostility or common interests were likely to be related or connected in succeeding lives.

Not only individuals and close circles engendered karma, but there was karma attached to tribes, races and nations. It can be imagined, for example, that Hitlerite Germany might as a nation have brought upon themselves by their persecution of the Jews a karma that would need to be neutralised by their being subjected to persecution as a nation in their turn.

Karma was not necessarily fulfilled immediately. Centuries might pass before a suitable opportunity or an appropriate culture epoch presented itself, the lives between being used for the healing of other character defects and the attainment of qualities and strengths necessary to meet the coming karma. For example, Atlanteans were being reincarnated today in large numbers, for only now was civilisation beginning to reach the technological levels that they had attained in the years before the continent sank beneath the Atlantic, and only now, therefore, could they work out their karma fully.

Karma could express itself in changes in sex, race, colour, culture and health. Sex could change from life to life as necessary, although it was usual for there to be a succession of lives in the same sex. An overloading of and perhaps indulgence in male or female sexuality in one life could lead to lesbianism or homosexuality in a following. Racialism, religious intolerance or contempt of a class or culture could result in lives where the subject belonged to the race, religion, class or culture despised. Ill-health, too, could be karmic. 'All illness is sin', Cayce taught, not necessarily sin committed in this life, but sin expressing itself in illness because it had not been expiated by the soul.

Karma could have an effect opposite to racialism in having an attractive effect. Lafcadio Hearn, for example, an American, found his spiritual home in Japan, marrying a Japanese girl, assuming a Japanese name, becoming a teacher in a Japanese school, possessed of an intuitive grasp of the Japanese point of view and an ability to interpret East to West and West to East. He could have derived all this from a previous Japanese incarnation.

T. E. Lawrence's empathy with the Arabs has been ascribed to a similar cause.

There were, according to Cayce, two escapes from karma. Free will was for him always stronger than preordained destiny. No soul was ever so encumbered with old debts that it had to resign itself to pay and pay for ever. The law of grace was a perpetually available alternative to the soul; in other words, atonement was a reality to Cayce, who still accepted the doctrine that a soul could turn from its old ways to Christ and obtain salvation from the immutable law of cause and effect through his mercy and love. 'To achieve the Christ consciousness [which is love] is to dissolve all Karma', he said.

Cayce was subjected to the same arguments against reincarnation as all those who find a place for it in their scheme of faith. It is not ethical, he was told, to hold a personality responsible for deeds done by another. He replied that there was an 'eternal identity' that remembered all its past lives (like an actor knowing all Shakespeare) and a temporary personality which is like one role of the actor who, while acting Hamlet, does not think of the part of Shylock, although he knows it and it is present within him.

When challenged—Why did we not remember past lives?—Cayce replied that we do not remember that we are remembering. We don't remember the agony of learning our tables in this life, but the results of that agony are with us. Empathy with people is a memory of meeting them in past lives. When asked if an entity could leave some record of its existence which it might recognise in a later life, Cayce replied, 'By living the *record*. If a man loved deeply and developed spiritually, he developed the faculty of remembering what he had done, where, when and how.' He added, 'God's Book of Remembrance may be read only by those in the shadows of his love.'

Lammers' reply to the same question was that if we remembered we should learn nothing. We would carry over with us all our prejudices, weaknesses, strengths, likes and dislikes in active rather than suppressed form, which would affect the action of our free will. 'What we have been builds our character and intellect and makes us charming or hateful: then, with free will as an active agent, we go forth with this equipment in a world that is like a succession of laboratory tests.'[196]

Could some souls be lost? Cayce replied, no; what could be lost was the individuality of the soul that separates itself. Reincarnation gave continuous opportunities for soul-improvement. When pressed to answer what happened to a soul if it failed to improve itself, he replied, 'Can the soul of man continue to defy its Maker?'

Cayce's life readings and the philosophy behind them may be challenged by sceptics on a number of grounds, although every challenge can be met by his disciples with counter-arguments. Lammers, who had studied the occult and eastern religions, may have suggested or even telepathised to the entranced prophet the astrological and reincarnationist ideas which could have prompted a whole incubation of similar ideas founded upon casual reading or contact. The impact of the media in the 1920s was far weaker than it is today, but even then an American would have had access to journals containing articles on every conceivable subject, including the occult. Sceptical minds may balk, too, at the 'legendary' stuff of Atlantis, the mention of ancient Egypt with its high priests and temples (were there no fellahin in those far-off days?) and the many contemporaries of Christ that Cayce discovered among his subjects. At best, all this is incapable of proof; at worst, much of it belongs to an occult dreamland of esoteric powers, knowledge and prophecy associated with the land of the pharaohs, the Mystic East, the grand masters of Tibet, great pyramidism and 'B' films with titles such as *The Curse of the Mummy* on the lunatic fringe of ideas. Some details may be queried—are the names Neil and Angel, for example, likely to have been borne by seventeenth-century Frenchmen? How is it that no written records support the existence of some allegedly quite prominent men? Why so few, if any, reincarnations from primitive tribes, which throughout the world must have far outnumbered the great civilisations of the past? Why so few, if any, from other great civilisations, such as those of Sumeria, Assyria, Babylon and ancient China?

The fellahin argument is answered by the contention that by far the greater number of life readings deal with very ordinary past lives and that celebrities represent a tiny minority. Cayce's view was that most souls make their greatest spiritual advance while living obscure uneventful lives. The fact that Atlantis, Egypt, Tibet and the rest have caught the fancy of the occultists should not detract from the long and honourable tradition of the existence and destruction of Atlantis, going back to Plato, nor from accepting that other civilisations and cultures may have developed psychological treatments, techniques and processes unknown to the modern West. As for reincarnation from primitive peoples, since Cayce dealt only with meaningful past lives, it was natural that he should concentrate on lives in growth-making civilisations.

It is easy, say the sceptics, to invent previous incarnations so obscure that no documentary evidence for them could be expected to exist. But, reply the believers, readings agree with historical details where records can be found. Indeed, Cayce told some of his subjects that confirmation would be found in local records. To this the sceptics answer that here fraud, conscious or unconscious, might have been perpetrated. It *could* have happened that Cayce, among many lives whose truth could not be verified, deliberately read up some obscure American records and slipped them in occasionally with a suitable subject. Or there could have been subconscious fraud in that his emphasis on certain periods of history resulted from a fondness for them, engendered perhaps, by his reading and subconscious incubation of themes inspired by it. Subjects of life readings were usually not in a position to judge their accuracy and in some cases might find them congenial—there is romance in discovering that you were a Civil War soldier or a dancing girl in a Wild West saloon.

Those who knew Cayce personally would reply that his character was the answer to charges of conscious fraud. A faithful Christian and Sunday-school teacher all his life, he would have regarded deliberate deception as an unpardonable sin. His gifts brought him fame, and a secret lust for fame might have led him to fraud (but see below). If he wanted money or ease, he does not seem to have succeeded, for his life was never very financially secure and there were times of failure and disappointment, to say nothing of exhaustion during his last years when the demand for wartime readings sapped his resources beyond endurance.

Nor is it possible to separate his physical readings from his life readings. The technique for both was the same; and it may be argued that if his diagnoses and cures of physical ailments were largely accurate, his accounts of previous incarnations were equally so. Equally it can be argued that paranormally accurate knowledge in one respect does not imply accuracy in others. Indeed, some of Cayce's prophecies have been unfulfilled and some concepts strain the limits of credibility.

But fraud, conscious or subconscious, is ruled out by other considerations. Mingled with his reincarnationist readings were remarkably accurate clairvoyant details in which he saw his subject often hundreds, sometimes thousands, of miles away and was able to give an exact running commentary on his surroundings and actions. He is also said to have frequently spoken foreign languages in trance, Homeric Greek to a Greek scholar, fluent Italian to a friend sitting in for an Italian (did the friend speak the language?), idiomatic German to a German, and French, Spanish and some unidentified tongues besides. These abilities might count for little; but the character analyses of perfect strangers, given on no other data than their names and addresses, were accurate in every case—in none did the subjects deny their accuracy. Predictions of vocational abilities and other characteristics proved accurate in the case of newborn children and of adults, though it could be argued that these were self-fulfilling prophecies. Yet they transformed the lives of many adults psychologically, vocationally and physically. Psychological traits were accounted for by past-life experiences, though again it may be argued that, given an 'explanation' of a characteristic, its owner may fit the one to the other. A potent argument is the self-consistency of the readings over a period of twenty-two years. In instances where readings were given to the same people sometimes years apart, they agree with each other not only in basic principles but in minute detail.

But it is Cayce's character that is the most potent argument for the sincerity of his beliefs and the genuineness of his phenomena, whatever their explanation and however some of their details may be questioned. The loyalty he inspired in those around him and the affection and reverence with which those who knew him speak of him today confirm that he was a good man and an altruist of the highest order. Nevertheless, an inquirer into the truth or falsehood of reincarnationist theory must use the same critical standards in assessing Edgar Cayce's work and beliefs that he brings to his judgement of all other men and phenomena.

7

HYPNOTIC REGRESSION

Among students of psychical phenomena there has been a recent surge of interest in hypnotic regression into past lives. A number of television and radio programmes in Great Britain have publicised the Bloxham tapes and the work of Joe Keeton, and in the United States subjects have been regressed in front of television cameras. To the casual viewer and listener the impression is given that such work is new, although many people are aware that Morey Bernstein, an amateur American hypnotist, caused something of a furore in the early 1950s when he published his book on *The Search for Bridey Murphy*. Rather fewer know that as early as 1956–7 Emile Franckel conducted live past-life experiments in a Los Angeles television programme entitled *Adventures in Hypnotism*. Yet work in this field has been going on for nearly a century.

Although the word *hypnosis* is comparatively modern, its practice is as old as that of magic. It entered the purview of western, scientific man with the work of the Austrian physician Mesmer (1733–1815) and has been used therapeutically and in less reputable ways since.

There is a great deal of misunderstanding as to what hypnosis is and does. Although self-hypnosis is possible, there are normally two parties to the process, the hypnotist and the subject. Hypnotists are not people with special powers of eye or touch or who possess some occult ability denied to ordinary people; they have taken the trouble to master techniques which can be learned by anyone, and if some are more successful than others, it is because they are capable of establishing empathy with a large number of their subjects and are genuinely interested in helping them. The unsympathetic and unimaginative are not likely to make good hypnotists. There are, no doubt, Rasputins and

Svengalis who overwhelm even at first unwilling subjects with the power of their personality, but it could be argued here that their reputations create a suggestibility which operates before ever hypnotist and victim meet. Normally an operator must learn his patient's pattern of thought and response and use them to achieve the therapeutic results he needs. The popular picture of the hypnotist as a man of immense will-power who beats down the feeble efforts at resistance of an unwilling subject by some kind of occult 'fluence' so as to get him into his power—even for his own good—is wildly wrong.

For his part, the subject must trust the hypnotist completely and understand that co-operation with him will release within himself the healing powers that will cure him of a neurosis or a habit, such as smoking. Hypnotist and subject are a team.

Hypnosis induces in the subject a psychological state which may vary in depth from what seems to him to be no more than gentle relaxation—many patients are unaware that anything has happened and, if not informed beforehand, may be disappointed—to deep somnambulism of which they remember nothing when they awake. Various phenomena can be manifested in the hypnotic states varying from subject to subject and according to the depths of the trance. Every subject behaves differently; in hypnotic regression into past lives, many subjects will be completely consistent when taken back into the same 'life', sometimes after considerable intervals; others will be wildly inconsistent in dates and other details. The phenomena that have to be taken into account in cases of regression are suggestibility and hypermnesia. Through suggestibility the subject opens himself often enthusiastically to ideas received consciously or even subconsciously from the hypnotist, giving the hypnotist what he thinks he wants. It may be enough that the subject knows that the hypnotist is investigating the possibility of regression into past lives for him to manufacture such a life for him when he goes into trance; and, if any regressions are memories of genuine past lives, the hypnotist has to be prepared by research to separate the true from the false. Hypermnesia is the ability to tap memory to an abnormal extent, so that a subject can, for example, remember every detail of his fifth birthday from the time he woke up to the time he went to bed. It can be suggested to him that he *remember* or that he *relive* the day. The ability to relive, so that a thirty-year-old man writes in the hand he used when he was five and recaptures his intellectual and emotional outlook at that age with complete forgetfulness of his subsequent development, encouraged some hypnotists to regress their subjects to birth and even womb experiences. From there it was a short step to probing into preconception experiences (if any), and thus the discovery was made that access could be had to apparent previous existences.

The amount of material is enormous. As early as 1887 Fernando Colavida, a Spaniard, attempted 'age regression',[197] although I know no details of his experiments or the extent of his regressions. Dr Mortis Stark is said to have been the first therapist to explore the possibility of regressing subjects to a life before the present (in 1906) but he was most likely anticipated by Colonel Albert de Rochas. The Frenchman published in 1911 an account of the work he carried out in the first decade of the twentieth century and almost certainly began earlier. He regressed a large number of subjects, many into multiple past lives. In 1906 a normal explanation was found, though by paranormal means, for an apparently veridical case. What are described by Professor C. D. Broad as the best examples of reincarnationist regression are ascribed to a Swede, John Björkhem MD (1910–63), and described in his book *De Hypnotiska Hallucinationerna*. He conducted hundreds of experiments, and in many of his cases it was established that the previous lives had in fact been lived. By the early 1950s Alexander Cannon claimed to have regressed over thirteen hundred subjects and Arnall Bloxham some four hundred. At about the same time the case of Bridey Murphy brought the phenomenon of regression to public attention on a wide scale, largely because of the debate it inspired in certain American newspapers which took sides in upholding and attacking the genuineness of the Bridey Murphy life. In the 1960s and 1970s other books dealing specifically with regression into past lives came from the press—Dr J. Rodney's *Explorations of a Hypnotist* (1959), Hans Holzer's *Born Again* (1975), Jess Stearn's *The Second Life of Susan Ganier* (1970),

Peter Underwood's and Leonard Wilder's *Lives to Remember* (1975) and Peter Moss's and Joe Keeton's *Encounters with the Past* (with recordings of actual regressions) (1979). From many other books issued in the last thirty years further individual cases of the phenomenon can be culled.

A. de Rochas begins with Josephine, a girl of eighteen, who became a man with a man's voice, Jean-Claude Bourdon, born in 1812 at Champvent in the commune of Polliat. Jean-Claude, atheist, drunkard and callous libertine, served for four years with the Seventh Artillery at Besançon, but could not remember the names of his officers. Having left the army, he kept Jeannette, his fiancée as his mistress, having learned that he did not need to marry her. He grew old alone, estranged from his nearest family. When he died, he followed his own funeral, saw how the *curé*'s prayers, actions and holy water protected him from the assaults of evil spirits, and suffered much from feeling his physical body decompose. His 'astral' body then took a more compact form but remained in darkness because of his sins, which he realised. He decided to reincarnate as a woman because women suffer more than men, and he could expiate the wrongs he had done to women. Having chosen his mother-to-be, he 'surrounded' her until her child was born and then entered its body little by little. Until the girl was nearly seven years old, he stayed around the body like a mist and knew many things about his previous existence that he had forgotten since. The *curé* of Polliat said that no Bourdon was known in the commune but that the name was widespread in the neighbouring countryside.

Other personalities emerged in Josephine in other hypnotic sessions. She became a spiteful old woman who loved doing evil to people. Born in 1702 as Philomène Charpigny, granddaughter of Pierre Machon, she lived at Ozan, married a man named Carteron at Chevroux, and had two children, both of whom died. Describing her life Philomène spoke in calm, dry tones, confessing to not being loved and knowing how to revenge herself. In feeble tones she depicted her post-mortem state as one of thick darkness in which she was surrounded by tormenting evil spirits of hideous aspect. Her great suffering was emphasised by the convulsions of Josephine's face and the writing of her body in her chair. Families of Charpigny and Carteron existed at Ozan, but there was no trace of a Philomène.

Prior to her life as Philomène, Josephine was a child named Alice, who died in infancy, before that a bandit, before the bandit several other incarnations including one as a dweller in the woods killing wolves (her face became ferocious) and the earliest of all as a large monkey like a man. Josephine said that animals, like men, had good and bad natures and that, on becoming a man, one kept the instincts one had possessed as a beast.

De Rochas believed that by using longitudinal passes in hypnosis he took his subject into the past, whereas transversal passes took them into the future. The future lives were as vivid as the past, but when they could be checked after the passing of the years they were shown to be fantasy.

Nearly all de Rochas' subjects were women of varying ages, types and marital status. Certain features repeat themselves in his regressions. The alleged previous incarnations are more or less equally mixed sexually, for example one woman remembering six female and five male lives. In the historical episodes, which are full of names and atmospheric details, there are numerous anachronisms, but many unexpected accuracies. Some of these could be coincidence and others were due to cryptomnesia, as de Rochas traced them to novels his subjects had read and forgotten. In yet other instances, his suggestion to subjects that they should forget everything they had read that had inspired their fantasies did not prevent the same lives reappearing.

Several subjects repeated the idea that they had 'surrounded' the mother-to-be of their next incarnation and the child when it was born, entering it only little by little over a period of years. After death, too, several subjects entered a 'grey' or 'black' domain, according to their previous earthly lives. One wonders if the hypnotist, having heard these conceptions from early subjects, subconsciously passed them on to later ones.

De Rochas, whose work deserves study, suggested several hypotheses to explain past lives. They might be dreams, but he questioned whether human imagination could create an impression of a life as if really lived ten centuries ago. One life might be possible but not several, and the consistency of accounts at different times was uncharacteristic of dreams (although some dreams, especially recurring nightmares, are consistent). Nothing in spiritualistic or psychic knowledge allows attribution to the imagination under hypnosis of detailed accounts of existences wholly re-seen and relived. Another possible explanation was the subconscious imprint of talk by parents from which the past-life personality was constructed in the hypnotic condition. This again could be an adequate explanation of one life, but scarcely of several; it was unlikely that all information would have come from parents or family talk. A third hypothesis—certainly true in some cases—was that historical facts learned and absorbed might be incubated to form a past life. Fourthly, the subject might indeed have lived in the past, in spite of anachronisms and chronological inaccuracies, for his memory might be of facts rather than dates, and researchers must investigate with every possible care accepting only those details as true that were sufficiently supported by evidence. 'It is not memories of past lives that one awakens,' de Rochas concluded. 'What one evokes are the successive changes of personality.'

A classic case of unconscious incubation based on fiction is to be found in the 1906 Proceedings of the Society for Psychical Research.[198] An unnamed clergyman's daughter, of good general education, under hypnosis experienced a past life in Richard II's reign. She knew Blanche Poynings, friend of Maud, Countess of Salisbury, married to the Earl of Salisbury and formerly to Sir Alan de Buxhall, gave the names of her children by the Earl and of her stepson, her maiden name, and those of the Earl's brothers. She mentioned that the Earl was a Lollard, his family name was Montacute, he was Lord of the Isle of Man, and that they used to ride to his manor of Bisham from London. Blanche's maiden name was de Mowbray, after Poynings' death she married Sir John Worth, and she, with the Dame de Molyneux, was expelled from court by Arnold, one of the Lords Appellant. Joan, Richard II's mother, the 'Fair Maid of Kent', was also mentioned, and many others. The costume of the time and details of food eaten were described and given. Almost every fact was found to be true, and the hypnotised girl had no memory of ever having read them.

A communication through a planchette board revealed, however, that she had once read but completely forgotten even the existence of a book, *Countess Maud* by Emily Holt, in which every person and fact, except for some trifling details, were mentioned. 'Though Miss C. got her facts from the novel, she made up [presumably on the basis of miscellaneous theosophic reading] a quite new setting. She selected as her interviewer in this imaginary world a subordinate character, not the heroine of the book, the Countess Maud.'

Alexander Cannon conducted 1,382 reincarnation sittings which convinced him of the truth of the doctrine. He maintained that complexes and phobias were brought over from previous lives, the intermissions varying from a hundred to two, three or more thousand years. A man terrified of lifts had some centuries earlier been a Chinese general who had fallen to his death from a great height. A woman with a terrible dread of water had drowned as a Roman galley-slave in chains weighted with stones. Another slave of a Roman official who was always threatening him with cruel treatment reincarnated in his present life as a man dogged with a sense of impending disaster.

Cannon's subjects experienced conditions during their intermissions different from those of de Rochas. A woman regressed to the time before her birth said she was in the beautifully coloured 'garden of waiting' where all astral forms ready for reincarnation spent two years. 'White brothers' ushered waiting souls into male bodies, 'blue sisters' into female bodies, when the time for reincarnation came. Prior to entry into the garden of waiting, the soul had lived on the planet Venus, or some other planet, where instruction in the art of living was given. No choice of body was allowed to those reincarnating—one's physical body was determined by how one had lived one's previous life on earth or in the intervening period on other planets.

Cannon claimed that the statements made by some of his subjects confirmed what was known of, for example, Roman history, filled in gaps and corrected some accepted ideas. Most of his subjects were either murdered, committed suicide or died

of some serious accident or disease, a fact that suggests that, if
reincarnation is to be believed, those who ended their previous
lives violently are the most likely to remember them.

As was noted above, hypnotic regression into past lives first
came to wide public attention with Morey Bernstein's *The
Search for Bridey Murphy* which not only produced a fierce
debate in a number of prominent American newspapers but also
inspired a film. Bernstein was an amateur hypnotist who, in a
series of sessions from November 1952 to October 1953
regressed 'Ruth Mills Simmons', a pseudonym for Virginia
Burns Tighe, into two previous lives of which the first was that of
a child who had died in babyhood. By far the more detailed was
that of Bridey (Bridget) Murphy. Mrs Tighe, twenty-nine years
old at the time, was a native of Madison, Wisconsin, and had
lived at Chicago from when she was three until her marriage. She
had never visited Ireland nor had much to do with Irish people,
in spite of some allegation to the contrary, which she strongly
denied.

The case not only attracted great public attention at the time
but exhibits many typical features of regressions; facts confirmed, facts unconfirmed, facts proved incorrect, memories of
insignificant details and ignorance of important events of the
time, and highly convincing character-change. Here, then, is
Bridey (Bridget) Murphy's life.

She was born on 20 December 1798, daughter of Duncan
Murphy, a barrister and cropper, and his wife Kathleen, and
granddaughter of Bridget. They were a Protestant family living
at The Meadows, Cork, and she had a brother, Duncan Blaine,
born 1796, who later married Aimée, daughter of Mrs Strayne,
who kept a day school attended by Bridey when she was fifteen.
Duncan was also a cropper of flax, hay, tobacco and corn, and
there was an incident when he cut himself with a scythe, though
Bridey surprisingly could not remember the name of the tool.
When ten years old she went on a trip to Antrim. She had two
friends, Mary Katherine and Kevin Moore. In 1818 (?) she
married Sean (which she pronounced Se-an) Brian Joseph Mac-
Carthy, a Catholic, son of a barrister, nephew of a Mr Plazz (the

correct popular spelling of Blaize), who married an 'Orange', and grandson of Mrs Delilinan MacCarthy. The newlyweds travelled by carriage to Belfast through Carlingford, Mourne and Balings (Bailings) Crossing, the latter two places too small to be found on any map but found to exist, the Glens of Antrim and Doby (possibly Dopy, a village on the old coach road, not to be found on modern maps, or Dovea) in a livery hired from the stables belonging to Mrs Strayne's husband. Brian wrote about law cases in the *Belfast News Letter* and would have signed his name. Bridey was unable to give her Belfast address, but worshipped at St Theresa's Church in a street off Dooley Road, whose priest was Father John Joseph Gorman. The church would have kept some records of Bridget Murphy MacCarthy because all family details had to be put on the church board and she and her husband would have had to give a tithing to the church.

Bridey shopped at Caden (Cadenns) House (women's clothes), Farr's (food), John Carrigan (greengrocer), using as money pounds, sixpences, tuppences and copper halfpennies, knew of a big rope company and a tobacco house, and described Belfast as being lit by 'poles with lights on them'. She remembered three men at Queen's University, William McGlone, Fitz-Hugh and FitzMaurice. She died on a Sunday in 1864 aged sixty-six by falling downstairs and breaking her hip. At her funeral a man played the uilleann pipes.

Mrs Tighe's Irish accent developed as the first conversation proceeded and was marked in subsequent trances. When asked for Irish words, she produced colleen, brate (properly *quait*, a small wishing or toasting cup), wake, ditch (for bury—this was questioned by some experts but others maintained that the word was applied to the mass burials following the great famine of 1845–7), banshee, tup (meaning fellow or chap, but a word with no nineteenth-century connection with Ireland), slip (correctly, to describe a child's pinafore or frock), linen, for handkerchief made of linen, another now obsolete use of a word, and 'flats' for platters. She mentioned as rivers of Ireland *Lough* Carlingford and *Lough* Foyle, and at that time 'lough' was indeed used for 'river' although today it means only 'lake'. Bridget knew the story of Cuchulain, had read *The Sorrows of Deirdre* and *The Tales of Emir* but had not heard of Conchibar. She remembered troubles in the south when people there felt enmity towards England, but other memories were personal—the anger of her father when she pulled straws from the thatch on the barn and the emigration of friends of her parents named Whitty to Pennsylvania. Her favourite food was 'platters' (flats of potato cake).

Bridey was a good dancer, having learned at Mrs Strayne's, and mentioned 'The Sorcerer's Jig', 'The Fairies' Dance' and 'The Morning Jig'. The existence of the first of these was verified in detail by a lady as having been danced by her parents, and she sent complete instructions for its performance; and there was a curious episode when Mrs Tighe, aroused from trance and yet not fully conscious, danced 'The Morning Jig', ending with a stylised yawn as conclusion of the dance. Bridey played the 'leer' (lyre) but not well, and the songs she knew included 'The Londonderry Air', 'Sean', 'Father's girl's a dancing doll' and 'The Minstrel's March'. She mentioned a book, *The Green Bay*, borrowed from the 'lender' (library), and played 'fancy' with cards. She described correctly the Blarney-stone kissing procedure used in Bridey's day but not now.

Verification of the facts of so obscure a life is not easy. Registers of births, marriages and deaths were not kept in Cork before 1864. It would have been common practice to keep such records in a family Bible, but none is known for this Murphy family. There is therefore no known record that such a family lived in Cork in 1798, that their daughter married a MacCarthy, or that she died in 1864 in Belfast. An 1801 map of Cork shows a handsome suburban part of the city called Mardike Meadows. Small quantities of tobacco *were* grown around Cork. The Catholic Relief Act 1793 enabled Catholics to enter the legal profession. Nothing is known of a St Theresa's Church in the Belfast of Bridey's day, nor of a Father John Joseph Gorman. Carrigan and Farr, however, are both listed in the Belfast city directory for 1865–6, though neither earlier nor later directories mention them, and they were the only foodstuffs traders at the time. It is also established that the rope company and tobacco house existed in the city. Though Queen's was a Protestant university, neither students nor instructors were barred on the grounds of religion, and it was confirmed that a FitzMaurice was a member of the university and a McGloin (not McGlone) a fellow. The uilleann pipes were customarily used at funerals because of their softer tones.

The Song of Deirdre and the Death of the Sons of Usnach was published in a paper cover in both English and Gaelic (Erse) in 1808. 'The Londonderry Air' was popular at the time. Great play was made by Bridey Murphy's opponents of the fact that she referred to a metal bed, supposed to be an anachronism—such beds were said to have been unknown in Ireland before 1850, until it was shown that they were advertised as early as 1802.

The Bridey Murphy case was investigated by William J. Barker, a feature writer for the Denver *Post*'s Sunday Magazine, *Empire*. Convinced of the genuineness of the case by hearing six tape recordings, though Mrs Tighe refused to be hypnotised in his presence, Barker featured 'The Strange Search for Bridey Murphy' in the *Empire* magazine in 1954, and again in 1956, following a three-week visit to Ireland to check the story on the spot. Rival newspapers and a collection of essays by psychologists tried to debunk the reports but, to an objective researcher, their arguments appear too *ad hominem* and some are based on demonstrable inaccuracies.

Bridey's account of her intermission is interesting in its contrast with other intermission stories. She remained in her home until Father John died and could talk to him after his death but not to Brian, who when he died did not join Bridey. She then left and returned to Cork where she saw her brother but could not communicate with him. In her discarnate state she met many people she did not know and some she did, including her little brother who had died young. In the spirit life there was no sleep, day, night, heat, cold, wars, senses (except sight and hearing), disease, old age, grief, pain, love, hate, family attachments nor marriages, just 'satisfaction'. Relatives don't necessarily stay together, although her father saw her mother. There were no laws or regulations nor any guidance. One went where and did what one willed, and she travelled from Belfast to Cork simply by willing herself to be at her destination. There were no insane people in the astral world. No differences existed between men and women though one knew the difference intuitively. Bridey could foretell the future for people on earth. When the time came for her to be reincarnated, she was told by 'some woman'.

The Bridey Murphy case caused great controversy, but those who upheld the genuineness of her experience, whatever its explanation, got the better of the argument. The opinion of a person of 'national prominence' was that 'the spontaneity and character of her responses—and her association of thoughts—indicate that this is a person who is actually relating her own experiences and not merely repeating a tale'.[199] The usual comment was made that, if this were fraud, then Mrs Tighe was an actress of genius. Fraud, however, was impossible because so much of the information found on research to be correct was available to no one on the American side of the Atlantic. The explanation that she had read some story, incubated it and produced it under hypnosis was belied by the quality of the brogue, the drabness of the life and the after-death episode which, it is argued, would not have been part of the incubation.

Contemporary with Bridey Murphy but unknown to the general public was the work of a psychiatrist, Dr Blanche Baker of San Francisco. She began in 1950 to use a light hypnotic and free association technique which regressed her patients to what appeared to be previous incarnations. She did not suggest to them that they should return to past lives, but most of them began to see themselves in strange dramatic scenes of violence, death or curious interpersonal relationships. These visual experiences were accompanied by vivid sensations of smell, taste, touch and, sometimes, physical pain and acute emotional anguish. The material was often very drab and commonplace, but when it derived from historical epochs it was found on checking to be historically accurate in atmosphere, events, costumes, customs and dates. One example was a patient of Scots–English–American ancestry, born in Utah, of meagre education, who had a total of forty-seven lives, twenty-three as a man, twenty-four as a woman. It is claimed that literally hundreds of details from these lives were verified in historical reference books, such as the help given the patient in one female life by a woman doctor named Dr Marie Boivin who was later found to have practised medicine in Paris in 1820. Whatever the truth of these claims—and psychical researchers are taught by experience to be sceptical of such generalised statements—the experiences allegedly relived resulted in great therapeutic bene-fits, both physical difficulties and neuroses disappearing. It is denied that the apparent previous lives can be paraphrased childhood memories or due to coincidence or independent acts of telepathy and clairvoyance. But could it be that the human subconscious mind, aware as the conscious mind is not, of the nature of its neurosis or disability, creates a scenario to explain, dramatise or justify it which, when brought to the surface in trance or to the attention of the conscious mind, has a therapeu-tic effect? Physical antibodies exist—may they not have their mental counterparts?

Emile Franchel, the first hypnotist to conduct past-life experiments before television cameras, believed that reincarna-tionist memories were due to leading questions by the hypnotist or genetic memory. But there were some cases which could not be explained thus. For example, Beverly Richardson of North-ridge, California, in an unrehearsed television broadcast, went back to an existence in Corning, a small Ohio town where in 1898 she was Mrs Jean MacDonald, forty years old. Neither she nor her parents had ever been to Corning. Yet two elderly people, old-time residents of Corning, remembered the town as she described it, and others confirmed her accounts of people and places they recalled. Under hypnosis she identified six pictures of Corning scenes correctly and was aware of and puzzled by changes made since her 'life' there.

Nor is it easy to explain the case of a twenty-nine-year-old housewife, Mrs Norbert Williams of Indianapolis, which was reported in 1958 in a number of United States newspapers. In seven hypnotic sessions she regressed to the life of a Confederate soldier, Jean Donaldson, supplying detailed information of various Civil War battles, in one of which he lost an eye and in another, two years later, his life. The man did exist. He was born 4 March 1841 on a farm near Shreveport, Louisiana, and in 1862 joined the Confederate army. His best friend was killed at the Battle of Shiloh. Documentary evidence showed that the Donaldson family did live at a farm south-west of Shreveport before the Civil War, that Jean was a member of it and that the facts given about him were correct, that a James Duncan, named as a neighbour by Mrs Williams while regressed, owned property south of Shreveport, that Jean was a member of a militia unit in Louisiana in 1862 and that Walter Street, named in the regression, had existed in early Shreveport. Mrs Williams felt her face alter to that of a youth and could see herself loading a cannon 'just as plain as if I'd been there'. A very thorough further investigation was planned but not carried out due to an illness contracted by Mrs Williams.[200]

There is an embarrassment of riches in the number of individual cases. Ruth Maguire, of English–Irish–Danish ancestry, had never left the United States except for a short time in Canada. It was claimed that she sometimes behaved far beyond her usual capabilities and showed professional ability in such activities as playing a concerto by Max Steiner as if she knew it, painting landscapes, dancing a Hindu folk dance and making Danish pastry, the suggestion being that she had learned these talents in former lives. In addition to the two lives described below, she had memories of a fourteenth-century French garden and a longing for things Greek.

Regressed to 1613 under hypnosis she became Magdalene Darling, aged twelve, an English Puritan exile in Leyden, waiting with her family to go to the New World. Her father was John Darling, from Horton in the North Riding of Yorkshire, her mother Johanna, *née* Bliss, from 'Durham near Newcastle'. Magdalene died in Leyden. More vivid memories surfaced when Ruth became a Sussex girl, Martha, sister to Ann and daughter of a lawyer, George Andrews. Martha lost her mother, Mabel, *née* Bream, in 1800, when she was two. The Andrews had a housekeeper, Mrs Benton, and worshipped at St Hildegard's Church where Holly Benton was the minister. Towns mentioned in the regression were Stokeley and Buckminster, of which the former does not exist, but there is a Buckminster on the Leicestershire–Lincolnshire border near which there is a

Stoneby, and there is a Stokesley in Yorkshire. Martha married an army officer in a vividly remembered wedding at a stone church in England: Ronald Whiting, of His Majesty's Troops Dragoons of the 67th Regiment. Its commanding officer was named Edgeworth and the Colonel's wife Dora. There followed memories of a marketplace in Calcutta, of the Indian Mutiny, of being raped by a sepoy at Lucknow in 1857, of Martha's resulting pregnancy and consequent suicide by falling from the ship that was taking her back to England. Ruth also described her experience after death in which she learned about herself preparatory to another life on earth.[201]

Vividness is no guarantee of the truth of a regression. Barbara Larson, a graduate of Indiana University, a teacher until her marriage and mother of three children was hypnotised at the age of forty and became Sam Sneed, a cocky young gambler and cardsharp. Nineteen years old in 1872, he swaggered his way across the American continent, hopping trains just one jump ahead of the sheriffs of the towns in which he played. His whole career from gambler, salesman, entrepreneur, to straight solid citizen was portrayed until in 1888 he began selling advertising for the Sacramento *Bee*. He also wrote editorials for the paper and was eventually shot in May 1896 by a Frank Jordan, whom he had accused of corruption. He was buried in Sacramento cemetery 'just across the bridge'. These are the bare bones of an intensely vivid regression which sounds like a film script (and could, indeed, have been inspired by a film—it seems to me to echo some cinema experience of my own long ago, down to the very names). As an observer wrote, 'To watch the transformation of swaggering, boastful Sam Sneed into a charming, attractive Californian matron was an astonishing experience. For two hours I had been so caught up with the life of this Personality Kid that I felt I knew him better than most of my friends, because this seemed to be the inner man speaking.'[202]

Investigation did not reveal that Sam Sneed had ever lived. As Mrs Larson had lived for a few months in an outlying suburb of Sacramento she may have been subconsciously influenced to use it as the scene of Sam's activities, whereas the events described may have occurred elsewhere. Confusion of present and 'far' memory does appear in other examples where reincarnationists believe that regression into genuine past lives had been achieved and can be demonstrated. Rehypnotised and challenged about the proved errors, Mrs Larson insisted her story was true. No one who had met Sam Sneed would have expected anything else.

Dr J. Rodney in his *Explorations of a Hypnotist* reported similar experiences of failure to confirm facts in some of the cases he took time to investigate. This was in spite of, or perhaps because of, a wealth of vivid details, names, relationships and historical events. He noted also that whole fantasies could be built up on suggestions given by the hypnotist. But one of his cases was remarkable. A Mrs Anne Baker returned to a life where she became Marielle Pacasse, twenty-three years old, working at a fruit shop with Jules, her husband, aged thirty-seven, at the time of the French Revolution. King Louis and Marie-Antoinette had been executed and the rulers of France were Marat, Danton and Robespierre. Mrs Baker replied in allegedly archaic French (Dr Rodney does not state his authority for asserting this) to questions put to her in English. She said that she hated the English. When Mrs Baker awoke, she stated that she had never learned French.

In a second session Mrs Baker was taken back to 1794. Marielle Pacasse emerged again, now twenty-five years old. Tallien has arrested Robespierre. Jules is now a soldier, there is a great general, Napoleon Bonaparte, she lives in rue de St Pierre, looks after the fruit shop alone, drinks beer, has never heard of tea and regards the very expensive coffee as a drink for royalists. In his investigations Dr Rodney found not only that the French was archaic but that, at the time of the Revolution, a street called rue St-Pierre-aux-Boefs had existed on the Isle de la Cité close to Notre-Dame, and that 'Marielle', now obsolete, had been in use as a forename in eighteenth-century France. So here was a woman who in her waking life had no knowledge of French life, language or topography, talking French, using an obsolete name and correctly locating a vanished street near Notre-Dame.[203]

Another remarkable case is recorded by R. Montgomery in *Here and Hereafter*[204]. Dr James L. Rowland, 'a prominent Midwestern physician', regressed an athletic teenaged girl who suddenly became terrified of water while competing in a diving contest. She was hypnotised and said that she had seen a moving shadow in the water. Then regressed to a previous life in Louisiana, she had been a child who, just before jumping into the water, had seen a moving shadow beneath the surface. This proved to be an alligator, by whose jaws she met a hideous death.

A detailed study of Joanne MacIver's previous life as Susan Ganier was made by Jess Stearn and published in 1969. Joanne, eldest of five children, lived at Orillia, some eighty miles north of Toronto; regressed under hypnosis during her teens by her father, she produced several other lives. In one she had been Suzette, living in 1792, drowned while trying unsuccessfully to rescue her granddaughter Annette from a river; in another, Michael, a French boy, whom his mother caused to be executed; in a third, as an African girl living at a time when many of her people were dying of fever and eaten by ants; a fourth as 'Marguerite' and a fifth, in 1701, as a fugitive slave.

In comparison with Susan Ganier's life, the others were mere fragments. Susan's story, as revealed under hypnosis, was that she was born about 1835 in St Vincent Township, Grey County, Ontario, some ninety miles from Sydenham Township, later Owen Sound, near which the MacIvers were to live a century later. There Susan settled in a village called Massie after her marriage in July 1849 to Thomas Marrow, a tenant farmer. They were married by an itinerant preacher called McEachern. Thomas was killed in an accident in 1863 and Susan, after a completely uneventful existence as a farmer's wife and widow in the undeveloped Canada of the nineteenth century, died in 1903. Her life was such that it was almost impossible to check, especially as no provincial birth or death records were kept prior to 1879.

Yet some confirmation was found. Ganier's farm was shown on a map issued by the Ontario Department of Lands and Forests. There was a central Ontario town called Massie, still known by residents in the area by that name, although it does not appear on most maps. Vail's Point, mentioned by Susan, did exist. Susan had a close friend, Mrs Speedie, a postmistress, who died in 1909 and whose tombstone can still be seen in

Annan, a nearby village. Arthur Eagles, an octogenarian when the book was being researched, remembered Susan Marrow and the Ganier family. He confirmed facts about Susan Ganier's neighbours, knew that Susan and Thomas Marrow were man and wife and, from what his parents had told him, that Thomas had died when he was about three years old, and was well acquainted with Susan from his fourteenth to twenty-first years. He used to drive her to Owen Sound. The Toronto Department of Public Records and Archives produced the names of Mrs Speedie, Robert MacGregor, the blacksmith in Massie, Joshua Milligan, storekeeper, and William Brown of the flour-mill, confirming memories of Susan Ganier.

'Susan' was strikingly correct in some details of the life of that time. Sugar did come in packages at ten cents a box; saddles did sell at from seven and a half to twelve dollars; oranges, even when small and hard, were a prize indeed; and a 'democrat' was a kind of wagon, peculiar to that time and locality. Owen Sound, the county seat, had been Sydenham, changing its name shortly after the 1810s.

Joanne's subjective memories included recognition of the places where and near where Susan Ganier allegedly lived (the Ganier farm is now in an army tank range), including the churchyard, a barn and her old home. She identified a well where none was known to exist. At one period she actually felt herself to be Susan Ganier and felt as if she were moving in two worlds simultaneously, with confusion of memories of past and present lives. When regressed, her voice changed from its normal huskiness to a lighter, musical treble, and the reality of her characterisation of Susan under hypnosis and the depth of her emotion—her joy, for example, after marrying Tommy—inspired the usual comment, 'She would have had to be a Bernhardt to fake it.' Stearn comments that such details as dates are not particularly important when she can recreate scenes so completely delineating her relationships. One could read a dozen books, he adds, and not get the pictures she gives us of the Canadian wilderness.

Joanne believed that she would meet Tommy in another earth life because their love was eternal and would recognise him by his eyes. In heaven (by which presumably she meant the place of intermission), one knows everything but forgets it when one returns to earth. The returning entity sees its future father and mother—Joanne saw the MacIvers and entered the body of the baby which Mrs MacIver was carrying just before she was born. When she was born, she forgot everything.

Arnall Bloxham, a hypnotherapist, has regressed some four hundred subjects into past lives. A large number of these former existences were extremely dull, but a few, featured in the book *More Lives than One* and in broadcasts, are intensely dramatic and at least in some details apparently veridical. It is interesting to note that a high percentage of previous lives end in violence or sudden death, a feature observed by other researchers—Dr Stevenson says that 40–80 per cent of the Asian cases he has studied end violently.

Bloxham's best-known subjects are probably Jane Evans and Graham Huxtable. Mrs Evans is a Welsh housewife and worker in a business office who has experienced six lives under hypnosis:

Livonia, a tutor's wife, living in the third century AD in the Roman British city of Eboracum (York).

Rebecca, a Jewess massacred at York, 1190.

Alison, the teenage servant of a French merchant prince, Jacques Coeur. She died in 1451.

Anna, servant to Catherine of Aragon, 1485–1536.

Ann Tasker, a London serving-girl in the reign of Queen Anne, 1665–1714.

Sister Grace, *née* Ellis, a nun in Maryland, USA, who died about 1920, two decades before Jane Evans's birth.

In the first life, Mrs Evans was Livonia, living in AD 286, wife of Titus, tutor in Latin, Greek and poetry to Constantine, later emperor of Rome, son of a prominent Roman named Constantius and his wife Helena, at Eboracum (York). Livonia and Titus were converted to Christianity by a woodcarver named Albanus (St Alban?) and met violent deaths in the reign of Diocletian. Livonia's names and historical references, checked by Professor Brian Hartley of Leeds University, an expert on Roman Britain, were mostly correct where they could be checked, and his verdict was that they were 'fairly convincing'. He was unhappy about some details, such as the statement that Roman ladies rode on horseback. He agreed that it was possible for Constantius to have been governor of Britain AD 283–290, for these are missing years of which historians know nothing. He stated also that Livonia 'knew some quite remarkable historical facts'.

What is significant is that there is no known source of Mrs Evans' statement that Constantine was in Britain in 286. If the statement is true and no known authority exists to prove it true, it would be almost watertight proof of reincarnation. But the moment authority is found to prove its truth, opponents of the doctrine of reincarnation can argue that Mrs Evans picked up the information by clairvoyance on super-ESP!

Jane Evans was regressed to the life of Rebecca in front of television cameras, showing a personality entirely different from her normal one. She was massacred with many of her fellow-Jews in the crypt of the church of St Mary's, Castlegate, where no crypt was known—but one was subsequently discovered by a workman when the church was being turned into a museum. Professor Barrie Dobson, Reader in History at the University of York and author of a book on the 1190 massacre, commented that Jane's story was true to what was known of the events and the time themselves; that much of the detail was impressively accurate; and that disputed facts could well be true, while a few could have been known only to professional historians. Other commentators have pointed out apparent anachronisms which could suggest an occasional confusion between present memory and 'far' memory, but in the main the story is impressive and the terror shown by the subject when the murderers enter the crypt is, as usual, such as one would expect only from a superb professional actress.

It is argued by opponents of the reincarnation theory that the knowledge about Jacques Coeur shown by Mrs Evans is much more accessible to British readers than has been suggested, and that all the facts given by Alison are readily available. She described the merchant's mansion at Bourges in the Loire Valley with its courtyard, style of architecture and even the paintings and people who had filled its galleries and rooms in 1450. She also showed a knowledge of French history and the personal history of her master, yet was ignorant of the fact that he was married and had five children (if her knowledge *had* depended on books she would certainly have known this). She referred to Charles VII by his contemporary nickname of 'Heron Legs'— his thin shanks looked ridiculous in yellow tights; and talked of his mistress, Agnes Sorel, the Duchess Yolande, his mother, with much contemporary gossip such as that the Dauphin Louis (later XI) had killed his wife, Margaret of Scotland. Alison also mentioned a golden 'apple' containing jewels, which was listed as a *grenade* (that is, pomegranate), of 'gold' in an obscure catalogue of items confiscated by the Treasury from Coeur.

As Anna, lady-in-waiting to Catherine of Aragon about to leave for England, Mrs Evans again gave correct historical details but revealed nothing remarkable, nor could much have been expected from Ann Tasker, a serving-maid in Queen Anne's reign. She referred to the death of the Queen's 'only child' which critics fasten upon as an obvious inaccuracy, yet it is true in the sense that he was her only child at the time, the rest having predeceased her.

The most modern life proved to be the most difficult to check, and Sister Grace, member of an enclosed order, formerly of Des Moines, Iowa, born in the nineteenth century, has not been identified. No registration of births in Iowa was required until the 1920s, and although censuses existed they were not wholly accurate. Sister Grace showed an awareness of current events like the First World War which was not linked with Jane's school knowledge.

All Mrs Evans' incarnations were female, whereas Ann Ockenden, the subject of a detailed study written by Mrs Dulcie Bloxham, *Who Was Ann Ockenden?*, had both male and female lives.

As convincing as any of Mrs Evans' lives was the one regression of Graham Huxtable, 'a charming and soft-spoken Swansea man', with no interest in the sea, who became a 'swearing, illiterate gunner's mate, with a hacking cough and earthy chuckle', fighting in the sea war between England and France at the turn of the eighteenth century. His voice became deeper with a strong South-of-England country accent, and he used archaic naval slang and referred to out-of-date shipboard practices confirmed as accurate by historians at the National Maritime Museum, Greenwich. A historian, Oliver Warner, asked to research the information on the tape by the late Earl Mountbatten, a former First Lord of the Admiralty, found convincing 'the reality of the conditions described [and] the man's general attitude' and was impressed 'as much by his overall ignorance as by any facts of history he appears to be familiar with'. The gunner's mate served on the *Aggie* (short for *Agamemnon*?) under a Captain Pearce, but neither ship nor man has been identified. The tape ends with the screams of agony given by the sailor when his leg is shot off in an unidentified action against the French; whether the episode is a genuine reliving of a past existence or some quirk of the subconscious dramatisation, there can be no doubt of its grim actuality to the experiencing subject.

Huxtable's regression illustrates one difficulty of the research. Since the gunner's mate is illiterate he cannot read his ship's proper name nor communicate a hundred details that any sailor would know today. It is almost impossible to realise the inadequacy of information possessed by and communicated between the illiterate masses of past centuries, and demands that historical facts should be confirmed by such characters as Ann Tasker or the gunner's mate are almost bound to be disappointed. The horizons of such people were limited by the neighbourhoods in which they lived or the ships on which they served, and the doings of the great were far removed from them.

A number of detailed studies of regression have been made about single subjects. Leonard Wilder[205] hypnotised Peggy Bailey, born in 1921, and regressed her to the life of one Sally Fraser, aged seventeen in 1733, living on a farm in Devon and speaking with an authentic Devonshire accent, which she found impossible to reproduce when awake. Her birthday was 4 June 1716, she had a brother Tom, at nineteen she married Sam Barnes, five years her senior, had two children, Terry and Mary, and died aged sixty-seven in 1783. When at a subsequent session Peggy was taken back to 1756, she instantly became Sally Barnes with her Devon burr, and after a seventeen-year gap between sessions, taken back to 1733 she was again Sally Fraser aged nineteen, though there were some slight inconsistencies in her accounts.

It is sometimes claimed that subjects do not lie or deceive under hypnosis, though they are often sly and reluctant to give information which may nail their regressions to checkable facts. Wilder instructed Peggy under hypnosis that unless Sally Fraser was authentic she would be completely inhibited from fabricating any part of her life. Sally still appeared. Later, when Wilder had researched the topography of the locality where Sally had allegedly lived, the girl showed no signs of picking up the information from him, thus answering the argument sometimes made that subject learn from the hypnotist by telepathy. But her knowledge of important local events about which she should have known was minimal.

Taken forward from Sally's death in 1783, Peggy produced Liza, born twenty years later in about 1803 and dying in 1850. She was a London cockney girl, taken from the Foundlings, Millbank, to work as a kitchen-maid in Piccadilly for Lord Frobisher and later, aged twenty, promoted to personal maid to Lady Frobisher. She mentioned as members of the household Mr Jenkins the butler, Mrs Bates the cook and Sid the bootboy. She married Harry Bloggs when she was twenty-seven or thirty (a discrepancy in dating here). Harry had been a soldier and then worked in the vegetable trade in Covent Garden. They lived at 33 Cutts Walk. In her late forties, Liza was treated by a Dr Levy for angina pectoris, and the treatment she described was correct for the period.

Records showed that the Foundling Hospital did not exist at Millbank but elsewhere. There was no trace of Cutts Walk, and in 1837, when Liza said that Victoria was on the throne, the monarch was William IV. Critics have pointed out that since hypnotic subjects taken back to a particular year are supposed to have no knowledge of the future—that is, events happening *after* the year to which they are regressed—Liza could not possibly have known in 1837 that Victoria would be queen and this, in their opinion, invalidates the Liza regression. It is also another argument against telepathy, as Wilder knew that William was reigning in 1837. Harry's uniform as described by Liza of a little round hat, blue trousers and red jacket could have been one of the Guards regiments. No Dr Levy or Levi could be traced, but there was a Dr Lever working in Lambeth at the time. Acknowledging that many details of Liza's story were false, Wilder and Peter Underwood, his co-author, nevertheless found the personification extremely convincing.

A third life appeared in the person of Alice who was six years old in 1903, lived in a big house near St James's Park, was lame from birth, never went out, was attended by a doctor, Sir Harold Somers, and died in 1920 aged twenty-one [sic] within a year of Peggy Bailey's birth. At another session the date of death was changed to between 1916 and 1919. Alice described her experience of dying, of meeting her mother and of her joy in discovering that she could walk. In the next session, she said that in 1912 she was eighteen, her mother had died when she was born and that her father, formerly a colonel in India and now working at a Strand bank, was Sir George Browning. On one occasion when Wilder was trying to make contact with Liza by regressing Peggy to 1816, Alice appeared, living at 15 Portman Square (Peggy had that day visited an osteopath at *16* Portman Square), daughter of a man called Sinclair, who worked in the City. Alice's doctor was a Dr James, and she died between the ages of fourteen and sixteen. On yet another occasion Alice appeared in 1883 aged eleven, this time the daughter of Sir Robert Lansdowne, living in Berkeley Square. Outside all Alice's homes there was always to be found a statue of a little black boy.

The falsity of this regression seems self-evident and, apart from the fact that there was a Coutts Bank in the Strand from 1904 to 1973, none of the persons named could be traced. Yet the Alice characterisation appeared as genuine as others that have been exhibited by hypnotic subjects. When subjects are told under hypnosis to act out a fantasy they are not convincing, and the problem is presented as to how and why a self-produced fantasy can be acted so convincingly while a suggested fantasy cannot. Underwood suggests that the alleged regressions are 'pretend people' and may well be right in some instances. This, however, neither solves the problem nor explains the many details of historical confirmation that are often to be found. A possible solution of the Alice regression is that Alice was confined not only because she was lame but because she was insane, a fact that could account for her different fathers, domiciles and doctors, but this still leaves the problem that she popped up at different periods of history where she had no business to be and when Peggy Bailey should have been someone else. This inconsistency is unusual; hypnotic regressions are generally remarkable for the uniformity of the information they impart.

In the news at the time of writing is the work of Joe Keeton who has conducted over 8,000 regressions in twenty-five years' work, spending as many as eighty hours on individual subjects. Statistically at least he must be the most experienced worker in the field of hypnotic regression and one whose opinions are to be taken seriously. His account of his findings with a number of selected subjects, *Encounters with the Past*, written with Peter Moss's collaboration, is admirably objective.

An unnamed twenty-three-year-old woman became the eighteen-year-old Joan Waterhouse of Hadfield, on trial for witchcraft at Chelmsford Assizes in 1556, prosecuted by one Gerard. She actually experienced in a physical and mental sense all the emotions felt by the original Joan, and the details she gave of the trial were historically correct.[206]

During sixty hours of regression Anne Dowling, a middle-aged housewife, consistently became Sarah Williams, an orphan living in the Everton slums during the first half of the nineteenth century. The atmosphere of the regression, the knowledge shown of a large number of obscure and verifiable facts such as Jenny Lind's visit to Liverpool in 1850, the experience of her father's death when the neighbours descended like harpies and removed every stick of furniture and other possessions from the five-year-old orphan, and that of her own squalid murder, make the regression immensely veridical, whatever its explanation may be.

Michael O'Mara, a Philadelphia businessman, regressed to a

drunken Irishman, Stephen Garrett, living at the end of the nineteenth century. He was asked questions about the politicians of the time which he could not answer, but when brought back to the waking state said that although the names of all the politicians were screaming in his mind, nothing would induce Stephen to utter them because it seemed that they meant nothing to him. This dual consciousness is common in the hypnotic state.

Edna Greenan, another middle-aged housewife, for over eighty hours of sessions became Nell Gwyn, actress and mistress of Charles II. Keeton and Moss divide the material she provided into historically correct, definitely incorrect, near misses, half-truths and lucky guesses, small talk or imagination, and new historical material which, if corroborative evidence could be found for it, would be of great value. It can be argued that everyone knows of the existence of Nell Gwyn, one of the folk-heroines of British history, and that a great deal of material about her is available. But not only did Mrs Green consciously deny having read any, she showed ignorance under hypnosis of any book or other source of information about Nell; and the information she produced with its familiarities, nicknames and small talk was the stuff of which Nell's conversation would have been made. Even if a subject learns facts with the intention of producing them under hypnosis, his experience is that he cannot utter them. 'All the learned facts sit imprisoned, silent and helpless at the back of the mind, while the unknown rules free.'[207]

Frances Isaacson, a sixty-year-old craft teacher, regressed to two American-born personalities, achieved a third, Anna Karlsson, who could not understand English, but understood Swedish; she had come of Swedish stock and could have absorbed the language as a baby. More striking is the case of the Jewish-American wife 'T.E.' hypnotised by her doctor husband, reported at length and evaluated by Dr Ian Stevenson in his book *Xenoglossy*. 'T.E.', speaking in a deep male voice in either broken English or Swedish, became Jensen Jacoby, a Swedish peasant who had lived some centuries earlier and met a violent death. The subject seems to have had no opportunity during her life of learning Swedish nor to have mixed with

Swedish-speaking persons, and the case appears to be one of genuinely responsive xenoglossy—that is, paranormal conversation in a foreign language with questions understood and replies given, and not simply language remembered subconsciously and repeated parrotwise. The transcript of the tapes covers 165 printed pages.

In a scientific study of hypnotic regression carried out for a BA thesis at Southampton University, Miss Dianne Barker came to the conclusion that 'there are cases that are more indicative of reincarnation than others, and it could be suggested that either an element of ESP, a particular traumatic past life or individual differences with respect of memory or imagining are plausible alternatives to these isolated cases'. Miss Barker herself was hypnotically regressed to two previous lives, in which the personalities of a thirty-year-old woman, Madelaine [sic] Kattelly, and a sixteen-year-old girl, Helen Adder, emerged. These both recounted considerable detail of their lives, much of which was substantiated, but showed the usual feature of being apparently unaware of important events and the names of ruling monarchs. Instructed by her hypnotist to remember in detail her subjective experience during these regressions so that she might gain insight into the cognitive processes occurring during the reliving of past lives, Miss Barker noted that her experiences appeared to be genuine in that she was completely divorced from her normal waking self and all memories connected with it, and that the new personalities seemed to appear spontaneously and vividly. She could not account for her inability to produce factual information, a fact that led her hypnotist to postulate that imaginative role-playing involvement was the explanation of her case. Miss Barker then played these personalities, when her experience was the same as in the hypnotic.

She next herself induced fifteen personality changes in four subjects first under hypnosis, then by suggestion of imaginative role-playing in a waking condition. Both regression and role-playing without regression were suggested under hypnosis. Her subjects developed different personalities under the two treatments but apparently equally strong ones in both. This runs counter to the experience of Wilder and Underwood above, where *suggested* fantasies were found to be unconvincing and unsuggested regressions lifelike. One subject, Jenny, became a four-year-old boy, Gary, of an unknown time or place, who was kicked and made to cry. When she came out of hypnosis, she felt horribly isolated. Another, Roger, was the only one of the four to show any voice change, becoming Joss, a contemporary caravan-dweller, speaking in a rough, slangy voice, and, later, George, whose voice was soft, with a strong Devon accent. The features of an unhappy past life, such as Gary's, and change of accent are to be noticed in many cases of alleged regression; in fact, Joss, being contemporary, was not a regression at all.

Miss Barker noted that 'there is a noticeable increase in elaboration of answers and a more positive orientation towards involvement in a specific role, as interaction between experimenter and subject progresses'. She also makes the point that previous lives can be evoked in different ways, either by suggesting to the subject that he *relives* an incident or that he *recalls* it.

She suggests five possible explanations; cryptomnesia, psychodynamics, clairvoyance, dissociation, and role-playing. Psychodynamics (the study of personality in terms of past and present experiences with regard to motivation) suggests that the phenomena of personality changes could be based on unconscious memories, revealing a relationship between the subject's personality and the nature of his personality change. Miss Barker quotes Zolik (see below) as believing that the crucial elements of the Bridey Murphy life were based on unconscious memories, which when studied revealed such a relationship. She criticises Zolik's work on the grounds that he referred in detail to only two of his own subjects and that his instructions were such as would elicit a fantasy creation, thereby negating any chance of the production of a genuine past life. Cayce, whose insights in his life readings had markedly clairvoyant elements, is instanced as an example of clairvoyance.

Dissociation, or the existence of multiple personalities, is mentioned in passing, possibly because it is usually recognised as a pathological state. Miss Barker believes that phenomena in this study can most adequately be explained by the role-playing theory of hypnosis, or in terms of the fundamental principles of social psychology. She points out that hypnosis is a social interaction between two persons and that, according to what is called the 'non-state theory', hypnotic subjects, by their nature, are highly motivated, have a positive attitude towards hypnosis and are able to become very involved in suggestion-related imaginings administered by the hypnotist. According to the alternative 'state theory', memories of previous lives are elicited by the very nature of the hypnotic trance, which possibly brings about an altered state of consciousness.

E. S. Zolik, referred to by Dianne Barker, asserted that there were three factors in regression:[208] the subject was eager to give the hypnotist what the subject felt the hypnotist wanted; he drew on his subconscious memory for many of the details, inventing others to fill the gaps; the previous existence coincided with previous events or were based on subconscious memories. He quoted the experience of two subjects in support of his thesis.

The first became Brian O'Malley, a British soldier born in 1850, living in County Cork, an officer in Her Majesty's Irish Guards. He had several Irish and French mistresses (one at a time!) and was killed in 1892 at the age of forty-two in a fall from his horse while jumping hurdles. At one point he mumbled, 'He killed . . . horse . . . horse', squirming in his seat and tossing his head from side to side.

Hypnotised but not regressed, the subject revealed that there had been a Timothy O'Malley, who had been an enemy of his grandfather, had run him out of Ireland, inspiring detestation in him, and had been killed in an accident with a horse. The grandfather disliked the subject who had overheard him tell his parents that the subject had bad blood in him. On one occasion the subject had borrowed his grandfather's mare and infuriated him. The dynamic basis of the fantasy was the identification of the subject with O'Malley, the ambivalence of the grandfather and the latter's relationship with O'Malley. It is easy to see how the hostility between subject and grandfather could be paralleled in the fantasy by the real hostility between O'Malley and the grandfather, how the 'bad blood' could be interpreted in the mistresses concept and how the horse incident and O'Malley's death could be dramatised as his own death while riding.

The second subject became Dick Wonchalk, living in 1850 and dying in 1876 after living a solitary life following the annihilation of his entire family by Indians when he was a child. The plot was based on that of a film. The fantasy revealed the psychological conflict in the subject resulting from a feeling of isolation since his childhood, concern about loneliness and being accepted by people, and self-blame.

Every theory that attempts to account for regression into past lives satisfactorily explains some details. Cryptomnesia has been shown to be the cause of 'Miss C.'s' life in Richard II's reign, but cannot account for some of the Bridey Murphy data nor many of the details revealed by Bloxham's and Keeton's subjects. Psychodynamics would seem to be an inadquate explanation of apparently well-integrated personalities who under hypnosis produce from half a dozen to thirty or forty lives. If one interprets and extends clairvoyance so as to include powers attributed to super-ESP so that the hypnotised subject can telepathically locate distant persons with relevant pieces of information, seize them from their subconscious minds, collate them with other material gleaned from documents in existence anywhere and use all this information imaginatively, so as to produce a personality living in a past century, such a theory satisfactorily explains not only every regression but nearly all psychic phenomena.

Dissociation and the existence of multiple personalities, though pathological when exaggerated beyond a reasonable level, may exist incipiently in all 'normal' people and be revealed only by hypnosis or the inducement of some similar altered state of consciousness. There are certainly cases in medical history where subpersonalities have emerged by accident when hypnosis has been used to treat quite other conditions. All human beings have undeveloped potentialities of character, and they may compensate for what they feel subconsciously is a loss by allowing these potentialities to develop a life or lives in some part of their being that does not interfere with their normal, conscious living. The Walter Mitty pattern often comes to the surface in daydreaming, but the apparently unimaginative, the single-minded or the disciplined personality may drive such fantasies deep into his subconscious. There they may compensate by developing a rich life of their own, normally never to be revealed except by flashes in dreams.

Such lives may well be linked with role-playing, especially if revealed under hypnosis, brought to the knowledge of the conscious mind by posthypnotic suggestion and repeated in the conscious state. But, again, role-playing does not account for every aspect of all regressions, for instance, for the obscure historical details revealed in many of them. The same objection can be made to the suggestion that subjects give hypnotists what they feel they want, picking up hints from leading questions or suggestions from their operators. It is true that the skilful, objectively researching hypnotist does his best not to give such clues. But unless his every word is recorded and, indeed, his every expression, it is impossible to judge how much he influences his subject. It is not only by leading questions and overt hints that he may bring pressure to bear. Hypnotic patients can be enormously suggestible and may seize upon the slightest expression or word of the operator upon which to build a whole fantasy.

There may be telepathic communication of a kind, not of facts but of beliefs and attitudes. *Facts* known to the hypnotist and any observers present often do not pass to the subject's mind. But the personal faith and outlook of the hypnotist may penetrate telepathically to the subject's subconsciousness and influence his fantasies and behaviour.

Although some subjects want to please their operators by producing the vivid regressions they know will delight him, suggestions can be rejected. The belief that patients cannot deceive is belied by instances when hypnotists have suggested to them that obvious fantasies were not true, yet they have insisted on their truth. If there is such unconscious deception in some cases, this makes all regressions suspect and only to be trusted if they can be checked by external authority.

Why, since in our conscious role-playing in daydreams we tend to see ourselves as successful, famous and happy, do subjects 'please' their hypnotists by producing for the most part drab, often wretched lives, often ending in violent and squalid deaths? The appalling suffering and misery shown in some instances, as in the case of the blowing-off of the gunner's mate's leg or the burning at the stake of the witch Joan Waterhouse, are the kind of role-playing we should shrink from, not embrace—unless it were unalterably true or we were convinced that it was true.

Whatever the subject's convictions, there are other explanations of drab or tragic lives. Daydreaming is usually happy; night-dreaming often the reverse. Nightmares can be cathartic, purging the personality of fears, anxieties and unhappy memories, though they may also symbolically reveal to the dreamer failures and inadequacies of personality. If past lives are manufactured by the subconscious mind, they may very well act therapeutically in the same way, as a safety valve and revealer of reasons for neuroses and unbalance. Subjects often find that their present lives are healed by the realisation that shortcomings are due to occurrences or tendencies in alleged past existences. Sometimes there is healing in the reverse process, when they can rationalise adverse conditions in the present life as being due to karma working itself out because of failures in past existences.

This does not necessarily prove that former lives are true. The mythopoeic faculty that exists apparently so remarkably in the subconscious mind, enabling sensitives and others to act, sing, imitate, write and perform in every way far beyond their normal capabilities, may create drab and even tragic and desperately painful lives, for two reasons. First, there may be an unconscious realisation that as reincarnationists are often accused of claiming to have been only the famous, beautiful and clever, they must deliberately avoid these, choosing the humble and the downtrodden. Secondly, recognising its neuroses and inadequacies, the subconscious mind may create lives which will account for these and which, when brought to the surface by hypnosis or any other means, will act remedially upon their personalities—the 'mental antibodies' suggested above.

The theory that there exists a cosmic, universal memory or consciousness that can be tapped—the *akashic* records—is attractive but unproven and probably unprovable, and poses the problem of selection. This could be solved by the hypothesis that the personality intuitively chooses a life or lives which will act therapeutically upon its present existence. Immediate genetic memory seems to be disqualified by the fact that there is often clearly no relationship between the present entity and a previous life—Mrs Evans, for example, could not have descended from Sister Grace, the Maryland nun. Ancestral memory may be far wider than is generally thought and many people are more closely related than they realise (it is calculated by a leading genealogist that everyone belonging to any family that has lived in England for a hundred years must be at least sixteenth cousin to everyone else in all similarly qualified families). But ancestral memory cannot account for lives from immediate past generations. Some of the older lives in conditions of slum dwelling, impoverishment, torture and death because of religious persecution or accusation of witchcraft, could be due to folk memories of risks and terrors which at some periods of history were imprinted upon whole generations. A Jewish friend of mine, too young to know consciously of the Nazi concentration camps at the time when they existed, tells me that she had realistic nightmares of being confined in one, and wonders if there might not have been some sort of common Jewish subconscious folk fear that communicated itself to her.

Certain features are to be found in subjects of quite different backgrounds and cultures. There is the common experience of 'surrounding' the mother-to-be and either of entering her womb or insinuation of the reincarnating entity little by little into the body of the child from birth until about the seventh year. There is the frequent rebirth in localities comparatively close to those in which the present life is being lived. Reincarnation from other continents or land-masses is comparatively rare, as is that from other races or cultures, unless these are ancient. Thus, English previous lives are to be found normally in England, French in France, American in America or in the European country of origin. These features are not confined to alleged reincarnations revealed in hypnotic trance, and consideration of them and others will be given when the whole field has been surveyed.

8

THE CHRISTOS
PHENOMENON

In 1971 G. M. Glaskin, an Australian author of over twenty books and plays, read an article headed 'A Method to Remember Past Lives' in *The Christos Experiment—Introductory Principles*, published by Open Mind Publications of Western Australia. As a result he conducted experiments on himself and a number of his friends, and his and their experiences inspired him to write three books (see Bibliography) in which he recorded and discussed the results.

A Christos experience which, with subsequent discussion, lasts about three hours, is induced by a simple technique. How this was originally discovered or evolved is not known. Mrs Jacqueline Parkhurst, of the Open Mind magazine, learned it from her first husband who was taught it by a Mr Bill Swygard of Miami, Florida. It has been surmised, though without evidence at present, by one of Glaskin's friends, Dr Khalil Messiha, a Cairo general practitioner and parapsychologist, that the technique described below of massaging the centre of the forehead could have been used in the ceremonial anointing practised in the Old and Middle Kingdoms of Egypt. Thence the procedure could have been adapted by the cult of Aesculapius.[209] The word 'Christos' (Christ) means 'The Anointed One', and the use of the word here has no specifically Christian significance. The centre of the forehead is, according to occultists, the position of the 'third eye' which is the organ of psychic vision.

The procedure is as follows. The subject lies on his back on the floor, eyes closed, without shoes and with his head supported by a cushion. The experimenter uses the edge of his clenched hand to massage the lower centre of the subject's forehead vigorously with a circular motion for about five minutes, until the head is really buzzing. At the same time a helper massages the subject's feet and ankles. The subject is then told to imagine himself growing two inches taller through the soles of his feet, then to shrink back, and the process is repeated several times. The stretching and shrinking is next applied to the head. The exercises are repeated with the stretching extended to twelve inches and then to twenty-four. The subject is next asked to imagine himself expanding in every direction like a giant balloon, following which he is told to visualise his own front door and describe it in detail. Many subjects remember details they have never consciously noticed with clairvoyant vividness.

The next step is for the subject to visualise himself on the roof of his house and to describe everything he can see, then to ascend five hundred feet into the air and again describe the scene below him, alternately by night and day. The descriptions given by the best subjects are allegedly extremely vivid and, where they can be checked, accurate. The subject is finally asked to fly through the air and descend when he is ready, and when he lands the Christos experience proper can be said to begin. The main vision may be preceded by insignificant fleeting images.

Then the subject, asked to look down and describe himself, will have changed. His feet may be bare, his legs black or brown, his height, age and personality different, his clothes strange. The landscape may be unfamiliar or remind him of one far away that he has known or journeyed through. He may find himself apparently in another life in another age. And yet he will remain conscious of the experimenter's voice and answer his questions and know that he is lying on the floor of a room in a twentieth-century house. It is claimed that the Christos procedure 'makes it possible to dream while one is fully awake, and ... possibly even reveals past lives and/or future events'.[210] As sometimes happens in dreams, the subject is aware of himself both as observer and as participant.

Glaskin discovered later that 'haptic' people needed a different technique as they sometimes found the visual exercises inhibiting and distressing. A haptic person (Greek *haptikos*, 'able to lay hold of') is one who is primarily concerned with his own body sensations and subjective emotional involvement in his experiences. Lauenfeld and Brittain in their book *Creative and Mental Growth*, from which Glaskin quotes, classified 23 per cent of their 1,128 subjects as haptic, 47 per cent as visual and 30 per cent as borderline. 'Visual' people register experience by starting objectively as spectators of their environment or surroundings. If they are rendered sightless by, for example, being placed in a completely darkened room, they are lost.

Glaskin's first Christos experience was that he saw himself as the elected leader of a community living in a district in the upper reaches of the Nile, visiting a mausoleum containing sarcophagi in which were laid the bodies of former leaders. He was coffee-coloured, nearly seven feet tall, dressed in a loose knee-length garment, and wearing specific rings and ornaments as insignia of his rank. From the mausoleum he walked to the nearby city and to a primitive building which was his palace; a room there contained a stone desk on which stood a hieroglyphic-carved stone tablet on which he had been working for several of the twenty-eight or so years he had lived. During this experience he was conscious of being *inside* the Egyptian body and of being simultaneously aware of both his environments, for example, the chill of the mausoleum and the warmth of the radiator on his body. When he returned to the twentieth century he could remember every detail of his experience and answer questions about it, for unlike rapidly evanescent dreams, the Christos experience remains in the memory. Research later showed Glaskin that many of the details of his experience could be reconciled with a period and place in Egypt about 4000 BC. During a visit to Egypt he identified the locality and stood on the very spot he had seen in his vision. In a Cairo museum he saw *stelae* like the one on which he had been working, and a scribe portrayed in precisely the type of robe in which he had visualised himself. Other details that corresponded to the neolithic age in which he felt he had lived were sandals, the style of the hieroglyphics, the type of tools, enamels and sarcophagi, all depicted clearly and all related to one small area of the world. Glaskin describes the experience of standing on the actual spot remembered from his vision as 'shattering'.[211]

A second Christos experience took the author back to a rugged coastline on which he found himself as a Cro-Magnon or even more primitive man, wearing a fur and with huge bare feet, coarse ragged toenails and thick muscular hairy legs. In spite of feeling very cold he remained conscious of the warmth of his body and his presence in the modern sitting-room, but these disappeared as he concentrated on his new surroundings. He knew he was back in that savage state where children were left to fend for themselves against hostile men and beasts immediately they were old enough. Finding a tunnel several miles long, lit by some form of artificial light (an anachronistic detail which indicates that dream-elements may enter what seems to be a reincarnation experience), he passed through it to a village, advanced by the standards of those days, inhabited by agriculturists who cooked in stone pots and used language to which Glaskin in his prehistoric state had not yet attained.

The two regressions had significance for the author's present life which will be discussed later, together with that of the other Christos experiences which follow.

In his books Glaskin numbers over twenty acquaintances who attempted such experiences, many of which were remarkable but not all successful, and other, unpublished records are touched on below. Notable among Glaskin's subjects are the following.

Joy 'dreamed' that she was a very frivolous twenty-four-year-old unmarried girl named Minne, from a rich family. She loved animals, played on the harp and lived on the heights of Rome a little before Christ. She was conscious of having beautiful hands, the fingernails painted with birds and jars. Her toenails were also painted. She had a tiny body, long neck, reddish-brown hair (she is blonde in real life) bound into many plaits with a blue metal ribbon through it, and alabaster skin. She wore a simple white sleeveless garment without underclothes. She found herself feeling disturbed, walking among buildings of classical type among people who seemed not to see her and who looked sad. She then saw a man whom she knew to be her father, also sad. She realised she was dead; she had died that morning from a pain in her head and, going to her home and into her room, saw her body. Everything seemed beautiful to her and she realised that death was not to be feared—it was like walking into another room. Like Glaskin she was conscious simultaneously of her two environments, of being in Rome and lying on the floor.

A second trip took Joy to the time of Christ. She found herself a man of about thirty-five named Yahbi, conscious of possessing a man's genitals, clothed in a loose white corded garment. She had long hair and big feet hardened by walking barefoot, wore Arab headgear and carried a metal staff with a strap at the top which went round her wrist. Yahbi described the landscape and his home in detail and himself as a contented person, who wanted only a simple life, friendly with birds, animals and children, to whom he told stories. He was on his way to visit a man named Krala and met Jesus of Nazareth. Except for his eyes, which made Yahbi feel inadequate, Jesus looked like everyone else; but Yahbi, sensing a challenge about to come from him, retreated within his friend's house.

Roy, a Norwegian living with his wife in Western Australia, also had two trips. In the first he went back to his native country to a life and experience he felt to have happened thousands of years ago. He was conscious of long hair, a beard covering almost all of his face, huge hands and crude boots. He lived a lonely life in a village beside a lake where he worked with boats. The experience was extremely vivid but did not prevent Roy from being conscious simultaneously of the warmth of the room and the cold of prehistoric Norway.

His second trip took him back to the same place and time as before, but on this occasion there were no people nor habitations. After walking through forest glades in moonlight to a beautiful place of huge trees and a waterfall, he became increasingly desolate and lonely, wanted to return, and woke.

Other experiences suggestive of reincarnation were those of David B., Richard B. and Julie W., to which may be tentatively added that of Ruby B.

David B., a law student, saw himself as a Queensland farmer at the turn of the century living a happy life in a cottage outside a village to which he had gone to escape from family and relations.

He would have liked a companion but wanted neither wife nor children.

Richard B., bisexual by nature regressed to the life of a Roman soldier stationed somewhere in Britain. He visited a bath-house where in two pools men and women were openly playing with each other, men with men, men with women and women with women, and where in cubicles couples or groups played sexual games. He found what he wanted in the person of a youth who fellated him (the Richard in the sitting-room showed no sign of sexual excitement).

Julie W. became a twelve-year-old girl, quite different physically from her modern self, living in an old farmhouse in Kansas a century ago. She described her surroundings in detail. Her mother had died in childbirth and she was conscious of tension between her father and his mistress, who was living with them. The father wanted the woman to leave, she to stay.

Ruby B.'s experience can be described as suggestive of reincarnation only if the doctrine of the transmigration of souls is accepted. For she saw nothing but empty ocean and herself flying over it as a bird, identified when she returned as an albatross.

Nicholas and Jacqueline Parkhurst experienced many revelations of past lives. In one of these Mrs Parkhurst, whose parents lived in Lewes, England, was conscious of herself as a young Englishman, about twenty-six years old, in a deckchair in Lewes in about 1914. The chair was in the garden of an Edwardian house in a street named Langford or Angford. She knew that the young man died of wounds in France in 1915 in a battle with a name like that of the Somme. After much research Edwardian houses of the type she had described were found in Landport Road.

One of the Parkhursts' subjects has experienced being thrown to the lions as a Christian, another being burned at the stake by Roman soldiers after seeing her husband and children suffer violent deaths at their hands; and a third was stabbed in the throat after leaving a tavern in Verona about AD 1500—the subject made choking noises and a large mark appeared on his throat.

Further work has been done using the Christos technique by Alastair McIntosh, founder of the Aberdeen Parapsychological Society, who has written a commentary on the technique in *Worlds Within* and a so-far unpublished monograph. He used fifteen subjects, seven male and eight female, of whom two, both male, failed to get any results. With one subject, Ann, he made seventeen runs, in one of which she became 'John', a cleaner-out of a ship's hold and occupier of a bed [*sic*] under one used by 'Pete' on a ship bound for West Africa in 1768 to pick up a cargo. In another she was walking along a stone rampart looking across a hot, apparently foreign country, brown-skinned, leather-sandalled and with a ring on her hand. She also travelled to India, to a marketplace full of people, many of whom she knew, including a friend named Savinya Barata. Derick, a nineteen-year-old student, became a soya-bean farmer of fifty-eight. Mary became a warehouseman at what was probably a military camp, talking to another man, Richard, in days when quill pens were used.

To these experiences may be added that of Kathryn McNaughton, who was sighted up to the age of eight but who at nineteen years old was almost totally blind. During her Christos experience she saw as though she were not blind some scenes from her childhood and others she had never seen before, full of colour. Perhaps these came from another life.

The Christos phenomenon, however, includes other than allegedly reincarnation experiences, although all of them may be due to different types of ASC (altered states of consciousness) which the technique effects in different types of human being. Thus, some experiences are this-life memories. One student's only trip, under the guidance of Mr McIntosh, took her back to a time when she was six years old. She found herself wandering in a completely deserted village, a reflection of an actual childhood experience. Peter C. became a three-year-old playing on a beach with his sister of five. Told to go into the water and dragged towards it, he was afraid and ran away. The incident had happened, though he had forgotten it. Here the Christos experience had the same effect as hypnotic regression to childhood, though no such suggestion was made to either subject.

A possible birth trauma may be represented in another experience of Mary, mentioned above, in which she had a dramatic vision. She saw herself as a man named Lawrence, set in a stained-glass window looking into a church. She had arrived there after a battle in which she had been killed, floating back into the window, and had then gone through the battle again, in which she was again killed, by a spear. Mary's dream, if not a birth trauma, might be symbolic reincarnation—a painful death followed by a period of peace with a beautiful feeling of having a new physical being.

In other experiences there is an element of precognition. A girl who was unable to 'land' and could visualise only a beach which she had once visited had a terrible feeling of melancholy which proved to be a foretaste of what she felt when separating from her husband a year later. R. G. Chaney[212] envisioned a village which he did not see until two months later, on a visit to Scotland. It was identical in almost every detail and the 'experience of seeing dream manifested into reality [was] quite shattering'.

One of Glaskin's subjects, Stephen M., had a precognitive vision in which he was himself, though named John, six years older than his then age. He was at a funeral attended by his brother, two sisters, real father and stepfather in Karrakatta, a suburb of Perth, Australia. They were all older than at the time of his dream, and he knew that the funeral 'had happened but not yet'. Later he realised that the funeral would be his mother's and was brought back with obvious relief; he had found his experience distressing. Happily, the prophecy was unfulfilled. Stephen refrained from buying a suit on a visit to London like one he had seen himself wearing at the dream funeral, and although he was recalled home because of his mother's dangerous illness, she survived. Her son was convinced that his not buying the suit had averted her death. Perhaps this is an example of Jung's principle of synchronicity—the avoidance of one factor neutralised the other.

Precognition is relevant to the reincarnation debate, as will be seen below, and so is the clairvoyance which can appear in Christos visions. McIntosh's subject Ann, for example, in her fourth run saw her friend Paula sitting an exam (it would have been even more convincing evidence of clairvoyance had she been able to read the question-paper and Paula's answers); and in her fifth correctly described a girl at that very moment visiting Paula's room whom she had never seen before.

The visions of several of Glaskin's subjects were like normal dreams in their kaleidoscopic shifting of scene, period and personality, but the details remained vividly in the memory afterwards. All Christos dreams seem to be lucid dreams (in which the dreamer knows that he is dreaming and feels fully conscious in the dream itself), mostly with typical dream-type environments. Some subjects tend to see strange unidentifiable animals, unlikely ever to have existed in any past life. One who was given to real dreams of monsters had a kind of nightmare in which he became a human monster with green skin. John M. had an impossible vision in which he descended in brilliant daylight on to a palm-girt temperate island where he found a house prepared, he felt, for him. He had come to the island to escape from a place across the sea where people lived meaningless and miserable lives. He found a strange mixture of fauna on his island who played together happily, there were no unpleasant insects and only the things *he* liked. No past life, this, nor even a future one, but merely a romantic dreamwish, symbolic perhaps of some present discontent.

Symbolism, even in what appear to be definite reincarnation visions, is present everywhere and can often be easily interpreted. The Parkhursts seem originally to have believed that Christos experiments rarely if ever succeeded unless subjects were already convinced or had an open mind about reincarnation, and genuinely wanted to try to glimpse a past life. But in a letter to McIntosh in March 1974 they 'now place far more emphasis on the symbolic "meaning" of experiences than the possibility of their relating to a supposed past incarnation'. In the *Sunday Times* of 9 and 16 June 1974, out of a series of twenty-eight dreams they classified only five as being of the reincarnation type, nine of the others being related to the subjects' problems and the remaining fourteen to Jung's archetypes or symbols.

Glaskin himself recognises the symbolic meanings of his experiences and those of some of his subjects. Previous to his Egyptian and prehistoric trips he had been suffering 'writer's block', a drying-up of ideas and an inability to express himself. His Egyptian experience, in which he had felt an impatience with the limitations of the primitive hieroglyphics of that day, and the prehistoric state, which taught him the value of language, were enough to remove the block and enable him to write fluently again. Roy's experience might be a warning to him and his wife, living in Western Australia, to avoid Norway in spite of the yearning they both felt to return to Europe. The message of David B.'s dream was plain to him; he did not want to be a city lawyer but might like to take up farming. Richard B.'s vision showed him the futility of a life of casual affairs.

Symbolism need not exclude reincarnation. For what, in a series of lives, has gone to the making of any individual must be relevant to the present life. If some factor in the current existence is demonstrated and/or cured by an alleged revelation from a past life, this argues more for than against the possibility of rebirth. Traumatic events in past lives could have a detrimental effect on one's present existence, and if these are realised and faced karmic clearance can be obtained in the same way as this-life neuroses can be cured by their causes being brought from the unconscious to the conscious. Similarly, if character defects appear in past lives and are still with the subject, he may see them objectively and mend his ways. Joy, who died of a 'pain in the head', in her present life suffers from migraines, and her characteristics include frivolity and kittenish traits. Whether the experience of her Roman incarnation helped her in health and personality is not known, but phobias have been released and physical ailments and neuroses allegedly cured in other cases.

Whether the symbolism speaks of a past life or a present attitude is impossible to surmise in some cases. Stephen, a Communist, dreamed that he had been exploited by a certain farmer. It could be argued that he was a Communist in this life because he had suffered exploitation in a past existence; or the dream could be represented as some kind of justification for his political views.

Not all Christos subjects succeed. Apart from the haptic type there are those who resist the visions and push them away. There may be emotional blockages; Jane could not complete the stretching exercises until she confessed to loneliness, an admission which removed the block. Reincarnationists suggest that there may be a blockage because of a violent end to a previous life, or some handicap such as blindness, which the subconscious did not want to experience again.

Although Glaskin's experience in Egypt when he stood on the very site of his first Christos vision struck him with the force almost of a religious conversion, he acknowledged earlier that there was no scientific proof of reincarnation in it, although he had never known so detailed a dream in sleep nor one whose particulars proved so related to an actual time and place in history. After the Egyptian visit he added that 'Despite all this incredible evidence and confirmation of detail, the logical and pragmatic part of my mind can still find no adequate proof'.[213] Yet he instinctively feels that the 'eternal self . . . has to progress from primitive incarnations to that ultimate greatness . . . our sole purpose for living'.[214]

Alastair McIntosh, whose approach is parapsychological where Glaskin's is personal, is also cautious about the possibility of reincarnation. His work is subtitled 'A Study of Some Induced Altered States of Consciousness', and he distinguishes between lucid dreams, out-of-the-body experiences (OOBEs) in which the subject finds himself separated from his physical body, mediumistic states of consciousness, and mystical and peak experiences. In lucid dreams contents of the personal unconscious are made accessible to consciousness, within a dreamlike environment. The dreamer may experience a confusion of identity in which it is possible that a 'subpersonality' may be released, a dual identity comprising simultaneously a sense of 'I am now' and 'I was then'. Such an experience could in reality be only a psychological phenomenon.

The experience of Mimi, one of McIntosh's subjects, supports the idea of different identities within the personality. During her Christos experience she referred to her lucid dream/ OOBE entity as the physical body, and she underwent moments of separation from it as she associated with some less tangible image of herself. The ASC then involved the concept of two bodily systems which, with her true physical body, seemingly forgotten as her experience deepened, fits a tripartite scheme of material physical body, psychical body and formless, transcendent and spiritual body. OOBEs are sometimes called 'travelling on the astral plane', and Muldoon, one of the foremost authorities on the phenomenon, is quoted by McIntosh as writing, 'It seems that on the astral the mind *creates* its own environment . . . Hence the common term, the "Plane of Illusion".' An apparently reincarnationist Christos experience may be simply an illusion created by the mind.

ASCs are not clear-cut in their divisions and may easily merge into each other. If, says McIntosh, the subject of an OOBE should employ his imagination to create a fantasy world, technically speaking he falls back into the lucid dream state even though he may still be displaying the behavioural characteristics of an OOBE percipient. Conversely, the best lucid dream subjects could be brought into OOBE or similar states simply by their being asked to come back from their dream, re-enter the room and try to see their physical body lying on the bed (or floor).[215] Where there are such confusion and so many types of experience none of them may be anything but a dream illusion; the case for any of them being reincarnationist is weakened rather than strengthened by the phenomena.

A further argument against the reincarnationist explanation of some Christos experiences is that Glaskin found that three blind subjects had no more imagery in their dreams than they had in life; surely they would have done had they lived sighted lives before. He found a counter-argument in the hypothesis that mind and memory, even of the finest quality, could not function through the medium of an inferior brain. They would have to function not only without sight but without even the knowledge of it.

The arguments against reincarnationist memories being a factor in any Christos experience are recognised honestly by Glaskin. Beginning with the most common-sensical, there is the possibility of a concoction of fantasy from the immeasurable material stored in the subconscious in the only life we know certainly, our present. The case of Lady Blanche (page 182) shows how from the seed of a single book can spring the tree of a whole life incubated in the subliminal mind. Allied with this is the desire of the subject to be successful, if only to please the operator; and the latter might unwittingly, suggest rebirth experiences. The Parkhursts' original view that subjects needed to believe in or at least have an open mind about reincarnation could in itself set in motion the creation of a former life from material lying in the dreamer's mental depths.

Equally acceptable to common sense is the view that Christos experiences are symbolic of changes in the person or of his emotional and mental state at the time, and that these changes and states may be represented by the projection of secondary repressed personalities or complexes into the field of consciousness. Harmless dreams about ostensible former incarnations dramatise the subject's this-life needs.

For those who accept precognition, sufficient explanation is that the visions foretell future experiences. Thus, all the elements of Glaskin's Egyptian experience were precognitive—the locality, houses, robe, hieroglyphs and the rest were all to be discovered by him—and it is no more strange that a dream should have launched him upon his quest, especially a dream so artifically produced, than that the reading of an illustrated book should inspire him to look for the objects pictured in it in museums and elsewhere. The literature of precognition shows that in the past it has occurred in brief spontaneous flashes or has been established by laboratory experiments which have little relevance to living. The new factors introduced by Christos precognition, if this is the true explanation of such experiences, are first that it can be produced by a novel technique; second that it can have such vividness, length and continuity; and third the intense subjectivity of the experience. Glaskin felt himself inside the Egyptian body with the same 'reality' that I experience of being inside my body as I write these words. Yet subjectivity, vividness, a sense of reality, continuity, etc, may equally be characteristics of an ASC brought about by drugs, which the taker subsequently understands to be unrelated to ordinary life.

Then there is the genetic memory theory; in some unknown way the individual tunes into an experience or mental process of an ancestor or a collective or racial memory. No comment can be made on this theory until far more is known about how and how much we inherit from our forebears. Glaskin asks pertinently 'if we do have subconscious memory from the lives of our ancestors, then why not reincarnated memory of one's own self?' Why not, indeed—*if* we have lived before?

In favour of reincarnation is the fact that the physical person one sees in past lives is often quite unlike the person in the present life, and that while the subject is experiencing the past, he is also conscious of the present and is not undergoing an hallucination like that inspired by drugs. Since he is conscious of present reality and in his right mind judges this simultaneous 'past' to be real, then real it must be. Though what 'reality' is will be debated by philosophers until the end of time.

A second argument in favour of reincarnation appeals to an individual experience rather than to intellect or reason. It is therefore only valid for the man who has the experience, though for him it may be the factor upon which he builds his life. Any wise psychical researcher, philosopher or theologian keeps his personal faith in a compartment of its own, while remaining open to new truth from whatever source it comes. He knows that although there are great bodies of evidence and argument for many points of view, for his own and equally for his opponents', there is no final proof of anything. His faith is at best a wager, a betting of his life and destiny on God or non-God or on whatever he has come through experience to believe. Yet this faith is essential if he is not to be a 'double-minded man, unstable in all his ways'.[216]

Such a faith is often produced by an overwhelming personal experience, such as a religious conversion or a lightning-flash of enlightment—or Glaskin's standing upon the spot of his vision gazing over a landscape he first saw six thousand years before. After it, the believer *knows*; all arguments are 'less than dust' to him. Even if many such experiences cancel each other out so that some at least must be untrue, paradoxically they all point to a truth. Glaskin describes his standing on the site of his dream as tremendously awesome, the most overwhelming experience of his life, convincing him that there is 'some part of us which is indeed truly immortal . . . some indication of what to expect at the end of it all'. For him an apparent reincarnation experience led him to 'Credo' (the title of the final chapter in his third book) and to his personal glimpse of truth.

9

THE WORK OF
DR IAN STEVENSON

A survey of reincarnation without a chapter devoted to the research of Dr Ian Stevenson and his associates at the University of Virginia would not be so much *Hamlet* without the Prince of Denmark as Shakespeare's plays without the Bard of Avon. The University of Virginia in something less than twenty years has accumulated approaching 2,000 cases of reincarnation in an international census, the first in history, showing that the alleged experience of having lived before is a universal human phenomenon. About a third of them have been extensively investigated, another third less thoroughly, and about one-sixth have been included on the strength of published reports or personal accounts in which Stevenson has confidence. All are accepted as authentic. There are several hundred others that are insufficiently authoritative. In a very few cases it has been possible for an investigator to be the first person to trace the previous family concerned.

These cases are being subjected both to individual and computerised analysis for the detection of all recurrent characteristics. Some of these features may be explained normally, some paranormally, but no single interpretation explains them all. Analysis establishes that standard cases can be shown in each culture containing both features that are similar the world over and cultural characteristics, the latter influencing paranormal as well as normal patterns. As some of the cultures have been isolated from each other for centuries and may never have had contact, the authenticity of these features seems likely: they transcend culture. On the other hand, mankind may share common mythopoeic tendencies and, possibly, archetypal experiences.

Their investigation is no ivory-tower study within ivy-clad university walls. Dr Stevenson has visited many countries himself and personally interviewed protagonists and witnesses sometimes several times over a period of years, in some cases eight to ten. Writing in 1975, he listed as his fields of operation India (mainly North), Sri Lanka, Thailand, Lebanon, Turkey and Alaska (Tlingit Indians), with a 'modest extension' to neighbouring groups of natives, Eskimos, Haidas and Tsimsyans, and has also researched in Burma. Preliminary information added expectation of many cases in Japan, while Nigeria and other countries of West Africa, especially Senegal, hold out promise, together with Vietnam, the Druses of Northern Israel, Nepal and Southern India. Increasing numbers of cases have been coming to light in the USA from children whose memories are similar to those of Asians, though they are not so detailed, and other instances have been collected from most countries in the western world. The phenomenon is so common that no one should dismiss a claim to have been reborn as a mere aberration.

Dr Stevenson has published his findings in over twenty books and articles in learned journals from 1960 to the present, marshalling his facts and arguments in as scholarly and objective a fashion as could be desired. What follows is a digest of some of this work, comments of the present author being placed in parenthesis to distinguish them from Stevenson's.

Characteristics recurring in all cultures are that many young children remember past lives, about which they begin speaking when they are two to five years old and stop from five to eight years. There could in some instances be unconscious influencing by parents or others where adults believed that the child was a former youngling who had died and been reborn to the same mother, for adults seldom realise how much a baby can absorb from the conversation and attitudes of those around it. Where reincarnation does not occur in the same family, it usually takes place in one completely unrelated and often of a different caste, about fifteen miles away. There are many exceptions but usually subjects are reborn near the locality in which they died. 'International' reincarnations exist, but they tend to be weak or totally lacking in verifiable details.

The typical case is of a child, usually between two and four years old, who tells those round him that he remembers another life before his birth, making statements proved later to be accurate about an existence often in a place far removed by difficulty of transport and communication, more rarely by distance. His behaviour is unusual in his family and is found to correspond with that of the former person with the same special interests in food, clothing and activities that may collectively constitute a skill of the kind that Ducasse considered to provide evidence of the survival of a personality after death—including in one instance the keeping of a pet cobra. The child usually asks to be taken to the place where he formerly lived, and, if distances and difficulties are not too great, the search for the former family is nearly always successful, and often many unprompted recognitions of former relatives and places are made, the child describing places as they *were* in his lifetime and pointing out changes made since his death. He is usually accurate in about ninety per cent of his statements about the previous family. The volume of detail reaches its maximum between the ages of three and five, and then memories seem to fade. Memories in all cultures come in a waking state. In one instance they came only in dreams, in another only under hypnosis.

Stevenson's first large work in this field was his *Twenty Cases Suggestive of Reincarnation*, drawn from India, Alaska, Lebanon, Sri Lanka and Brazil, published originally in 1966 and in a revised edition in 1974. In this he established a method of investigation which he has continued to use, with refinements learned from experience, in later volumes of cases from India, Sri Lanka, Thailand, Lebanon and Turkey. Among his later cases are more where investigators have been sent to the scene within a few months or even weeks of the main events, and he has sought more information about the *behaviour* of each subject with relation to the previous life. Only a reading of the books themselves can give a fair idea of the care with which Dr Stevenson marshals his facts and the objectivity with which he states his conclusions. He first gives a summary of the case, followed by a list of usually from a dozen to twenty witnesses interviewed by himself or his colleagues. The relevant facts of geography and the possibility of normal means of communication between the families of the dead subject (A) and his alleged reincarnation (B) are summarised, followed by notes on the life, death and character of A, statements and recognitions made by B, B's behaviour related to his previous life, his attitudes towards his former family, that of his family to him, any evidence of ESP on the part of B, comments on paranormal aspects of the case, and notes on B's later development. A table under the headings of 'item', 'informants', 'verification' and 'comments', occupying an average of some dozen pages, is included in each account, and there are frequently extra sections on such material as the evidence of birthmarks, and special skills and knowledge allegedly handed on from the previous life.

Emerging from the case studies and summarised in introductions to the sections dealing with each country and in independently published articles are the special cultural features mentioned above. These may be summarised under the headings of (1) sexual changes; (2) length of intermission; (3) familial connections; (4) birthmarks; (5) violent deaths; (6) dreams announcing rebirth; (7) incidence of reported cases.

1 In approximately 220 cases from the Alevis of South-central Turkey, the Druses of Lebanon and Syria, and the Tlingits of south-east Alaska, there was no change of sex. There were two cases of change among the Yakutant Tlingits farther north, fifty per cent of 44 cases studied among the Kutchin of North-west Canada, twenty per cent of about 250 Burmese and Thai cases and about five per cent in all other cultures. When it is believed that no change of sex is possible, no change occurs. Belief may therefore have an effect (but may it not be the result of observation and experience?).[217] Stevenson suggests that the belief held by a person before he dies may influence what actually happens to him after he dies, if and when he reincarnates. Where lives of the opposite sex are recalled, children may show traits characteristic of it which they usually but not always outgrow, a fact that may explain the gender confusion that is sometimes observable.

2 Among the Alevis the average intermission is 9 months (the human gestation period), in Sri Lanka 21 months, in India 45,

and among the Tlingits 48. There is no known reason for these differences. The Druses believe that a dead person's spirit is at once reborn in a new baby, and the Jains that the departed soul enters its new body at the moment of conception (which suggests that the Druse and Jain populations must be static).

3 85 per cent of Tlingit cases show a familial relationship, between 66 and 70 per cent on the maternal side, their society being a matrilineal one. The statistics of their neighbouring Eskimos, from a smaller sample, show 47 per cent familial connection, 27 per cent in the mother's line. The incidence of relationship is extremely low in other cultures, for example 2 per cent in South-east Asia and two from eighty-five cases among the Indians of the Ganges valley.

4 Birthmarks corresponding either to those borne by the previous individual or to the wounds by which he met his death are found among 51 per cent of the Tlingit cases and 47 per cent of the Eskimo. It is only numerically that the cases are culturally different, for birthmarks are to be found everywhere where reincarnation experiences are found. But where cultures have recently been savage, as among the Tlingits, birthmarks are more often than not associated with violent death, wounds from spears, knives, axes, bullets, burns and bites (both the latter in fights). Birthmarks have been predicted in dreams (suggestive of psychosomatic self-fulfilling prophecies).

In a very few cases where the personalities are related in direct descent, there is some evidence for the inheritance of acquired characteristics, such as birthmarks, but they usually occur in widely separated families, just a few years apart as to death and birth, and there is no time for the birthmarks to appear as acquired characteristics (although branches of the same family, descended from a common ancestor, could conceivably inherit similar birthmarks from him). Nor could there always be a PK effect by the parents, for in some cases neither had knowledge of the previous marks or wounds.

Birthmarks can be and have been predicted in some instances, but why do they appear on one part of a person's body and not on another? Dr Stevenson has examined two hundred purporting to have been stab and bullet wounds from previous lives and mentions seventeen cases in which medical documents equated the location of wounds or diseases (which may be 'reincarnation-ally' inherited) with birthmarks.

5 The incidence of violent deaths is also common to all cultures (from 29 to 78 per cent) but is more prevalent in some. The Tlingits think it preferable to be killed than to die naturally, as this ensures a better, quicker-returning life. Since previous deaths are often dramatic, violent and obviously the last impression of the prior life, the events connected with them would be impressed on the memory.

6 Another common feature is announcing dreams, and again it is one that is more prevalent in some cultures than in others. They are more frequent among the Burmese, natives of north-west North America and the Alevis, and occur among the Tlingits usually to women in the last stages of pregnancy. In 26 out of 29 dreams recorded the correct sex was foretold, and of 20 identifications of the returning person in dreams, 8 were made by the mothers-to-be, 12 by other women, and in one case by one of each. There could be pressure on a child to relive a former personality, and there could also be *post hoc* deception.

7 The incidence of cases in any culture will obviously always be greater than the number reported, and where there are societies that subscribe to a reincarnationist creed the investigator will expect a higher number of reported cases. Other factors, however, enter in. For a child of some eastern races to remember his past life is regarded as an indication of early death, and his reminiscences will therefore be checked. In other races there is no such fear, and children are encouraged to remember. So, among the Tlingits, Stevenson estimated that one in a thousand of the population had a rebirth memory, and in one village the proportion was one in sixty-five. In nearly a quarter of the Tlingit cases the personality predicted his return and in over a fifth selected the couple that should be his parents.

Much of Stevenson's work has been an expansion of principles laid down in a prize thesis, the evidence for survival from *Claimed Memories of Former Incarnations*, published in 1960. In this he discussed the pros and cons of reincarnation under the headings of the normal acquisition of knowledge, the paranormal acquisition of knowledge without survival of physical death, and survival. He looked forward to further investigation under the headings of hypnosis, dreams, revived memories, crises with emotional arousal, and further searches among children. Although elsewhere stating that he has little faith in hypnotic regression, he denied here that memories of a subject were necessarily put into his mind by the hypnotist or were offered to the hypnotist in an effort to please him. Some were perhaps memories of the present life or fictions invented to satisfy the hypnotist's requests or derived their source from paranormal perceptions. Regression under hypnosis could be partial and also fluctuate. In some cases it had been possible for the subject to understand English spoken to him while he had largely replied in a foreign tongue, unfamiliar in his waking state. The complex relationship of hypnotist and subject could influence the production of images. (My own experience is that the link between every hypnotist and every subject is unique; a hypnotist is continually surprised by the response of his subject.)

Dreams might prove an important additional source of material and something could be learned from drugs. Lysergic acid could induce the recall of forgotten memories of the present life, and certain subjects could create fantasies or images in which they seemed to be in some foreign land or earlier time. A study of Jungian archetypes could help here.

Yet another source of material ascribed to reincarnation experiences was revival memories. A visit to a boyhood home could recall events which took place there but, because of their distance, and perhaps paramnesia, seemed to belong to another existence. Crises with emotional arousal, such as severe illnesses, operations and approaching death could produce apparent memories of former lives, and information about all these alternate explanations of rebirth events needed to be collected, collated and evaluated.

There was need for a search for children with reincarnation memories in the West, where parents tended to ridicule such children into silence, and where, even if this did not happen, neither parents nor children had the climate of belief or vocabulary to enable them to express in words what had allegedly happened.

In his *Claimed Memories*, Stevenson listed nine principles of method which he enlarged upon in subsequent work. These were (i) that written records should be made of cases *prior to* checking; (ii) that further information about the dead person and possible sources of normally acquired information should be verified, for in this way much more might be learned about the circumstances favouring the occurrence of such memories; (iii) sources of conscious or unconscious fraud must be excluded; (iv) sources of information should be checked under hypnosis (this applies particularly to instances of hypnotic regression but can also be used in other cases); (v) plasticity in an apparent memory does not prove it a fantasy, nor does durability of the images prove them to be accurately recalled.

(vi) Attention to physical components of apparent memories may help. There may be physiological changes, even in the viscera and skin, such as bleeding wounds or rope marks round a once-bound man. Striking as such evidence may seem in some examples, it cannot be concluded that people exhibiting physical signs experienced them in a previous life. Stigmata on the bodies of religious people worshipping before a crucifix appear in the same places as the wounds in the image of Christ before which they worship (and it may be commented that all stigmatics exhibit the wounds in the palms of their hands and insteps of their feet, whereas modern research has shown that in crucifixion the nails were driven through the wrists and ankles). Stigmatics do not claim to have been crucified in a previous life nor to be reincarnations of Christ, but to identify with him in his sufferings. But if physical changes can be shown to be neither an experience that happened to the percipient nor an extremely strong identification, they could indicate the recall of a prior life experience. Dr Stevenson mentions a report by Dr Blanche Baker, who saw an area of erythema (patchy superficial inflammation of the skin) on the back of a patient the day after he recalled being stabbed in the back in a previous existence. A sensitivity to and phobia of feathers disappeared completely following the recall of a painful experience with vultures which had apparently occurred in another life. (Such characteristics could perhaps be psychosomatic in origin, produced in the one case by a very strongly envisioned previous existence that had not happened outside the imagination, and in the other by a 'mental antibody'—see page 189—produced to attack and destroy the phobia.)

(vii) Significantly similar marks should be taken into account. Birthmarks have already been mentioned, and there are instances where special features of particular children were accurately predicted by sensitives who claimed to be communicating with discarnate personalities about to be reborn (here again there could be psychosomatic effects making the prophecies self-fulfilling). Such small but possibly important similarities of physical appearances may show up more often than has been observed.

(viii) Word association tests might be adapted to investigate alleged reincarnated personalities.

(ix) Where possible (examples are extremely rare) memories of former incarnations in which the subject speaks a foreign language quite unfamiliar to him in his ordinary state should be collected. Such xenolalia or xenoglossy must be responsive if it is to be evidential; that is, the subject must converse naturally, answering questions and commenting intelligently on the topics raised in conversation. There are many examples of foreign languages being recited but not conversed in through cryptomnesia.

If survival after death is not the destiny of humans, supposed reincarnation experiences can at least be used therapeutically. Part of the value of Dr Stevenson's work is that he, a medical doctor, can communicate with doctors. In 1977 in an article in the *Journal of Nervous and Mental Disease* he summed up the features of typical cases of the reincarnation type, showing that these touched on the fields of psychology, psychiatry, biology and medicine, and while it was not a substitute for the contributions that genetic science and environmental influences made to the study of personality, the idea of reincarnation was a third, supplementary, factor. Whatever the true cause of these experiences, they must be recognised as existing by those responsible for healing the minds and bodies of patients. The memories of violent deaths have already been mentioned. There are also phobias and philias ascribed to prior lives and places. Phobias of water, automobiles, bladed weapons, particular foods are attributed to former existences ending in drowning, car accidents, stabbing and food poisoning. Philias of religion, engines, cars, alcohol, *bhang* (an intoxicant), cigarettes, hookah-smoking are similarly ascribed. Likewise play or unusual skills may indicate a hangover from other lifetimes, so that overmuch or sophisticated pretence at being a teacher, soldier or night-club owner, or a genius-like capacity to compose and play music, calculate mathematically or speak foreign languages should interest psychologists and possibly psychiatrists. No western child prodigy has, however, ever claimed to remember a previous life.

Genetics can help to explain the similarities in families but do not shed light on the differences. Handel's surgeon-father, for example, discouraged his music. Similarly, genetics help us to understand the likenesses between monozygotic twin pairs and conjoined twins, but reincarnation may explain their differences.

Supposed reincarnation memories can explain cases of nationality confusion as among Burmese children who recall that they were once American, British or Japanese soldiers killed in the Second World War Burmese campaigns. Craving for or aversion to certain foods by pregnant women may correspond to tastes attributed to the related previous personality.

Just touching on the complicated question of karma, Stevenson maintains that there is no evidence for retributive karma, but there is some for developmental karma.

Whatever his medical colleagues may think of Stevenson's findings, he has not been without his critics in the parapsychological field. C. T. K. Chari, by no means an unworthy opponent in terms of knowledge and scholarship, was of the opinion that the doctor had underestimated the range of paranormal cognition and its high degree of selectiveness, and that almost all reincarnationist knowledge could be explained in terms of super-ESP. Stevenson points out in reply that children who remember past lives show no other ESP ability. It is difficult to see how their pattern of inherited interests and skills, where these exist, could be communicated by ESP. They never claim to be reincarnations of living persons, and their behavioural similarity to and identification with the previous personality is very striking. If ESP is an agent, why is *one* personality selected, and how and why that personality (or those, where several are recalled), and how and from where does the information come? An adult could obtain by normal means whatever accurate information was available, but a small child, especially in the East, is under a surveillance that would prevent his acquisition of normal knowledge, even if adequate transport gave him access to the scene of his former life. Mingling of memories of children and parents could lead to false claims, but there are a few cases where a written record was made and in a considerable number investigators reached the scene within a few weeks of its main events, thus reducing errors of memory, though not errors of bias. As for ESP or super-ESP, the evidence is such at the moment that only guesses can be made of the range, strength and qualities of paranormal cognition, and one man's opinion is as good as another's.

Stevenson suggests a 'perfect case' of reincarnation, all of the features of which he feels could not be explained by ESP. The subject envisaged is a French village boy with several distinct birthmarks who, when he began to speak, indicated a previous life in which he had been killed by bullets hitting him at the sites of these marks. As his speech developed, he named his assassins and said that one of them had accused him of cheating at cards just before shooting him. He gave his own name, those of his parents, his siblings and a girl friend, stated where he had lived, where he had been shot, and many other particulars of his previous life.

He resisted learning French, talked a language incomprehensible to his parents, ate with his hands, rejected the family food, demanding rice and hot curries, wore a cloth like a Ceylonese sarong instead of trousers, showed agility in climbing trunks of tall trees and said that he used to pick coconuts. He wanted to play cards and asked for his favourite drink, *arack*. His parents made a written record of his statements and behaviour, and when the child had mentioned enough details, called in an experienced investigator. He identified the language as Sinhalese, found that the village existed in Sri Lanka, and that a coconut picker by the name given by the boy had existed and been murdered by shooting several years before the boy was born. The accusation of cheating, wounds, names, fondness for *arack* and playing cards all corresponded exactly.

Such a case, Stevenson maintains, fulfils three criteria: first, imaged memories of the events in the life of the dead person; secondly, behavioural traits including skills (language and climbing); thirdly, wounds and birthmarks.

The Sinhalese would have to be responsive and the boy tested in this way. If it were, the case would be almost too good, because so complete an identification would indicate possession rather than reincarnation,[218] for it is hard to visualise the French boy maintaining his own personality at all, if at the age of two or three he were to display all the characteristics listed. There would not be room for the child to assert himself against the man. And difficult though it might seem to be to uphold the super-ESP hypothesis in face of such a marshalling of evidence, it is still possible to explain each separate fact in this way.

One further type of fact is needed, one known to no one but the liver of the previous life, such as money that he has hidden in a certain place which can be shown to be still there, of which he can give exact details in, say, the total amount and the number and value of each coin.[218] Better still would be a reincarnated ancient Egyptian (though it would be quite impossible to check the details of his personal life) who could indicate a buried site of some kind utterly unsuspected by any archaeologist and describe it in detail together with its exact locality so that it could be excavated and the facts confirmed. For it is only knowledge revealed that no one in the world knows now that can escape the net of super-ESP. Even then it will be explained away in some fashion by the universal subconscious, the *akashic* records, topographical psychometry or a communication from outer space before reincarnation be admitted as the explanation.

Dr Stevenson's interests and learning are not confined to reincarnation. Studying his work, the reader is impressed by the breadth of his scholarship, which includes such disciplines as the nature and laws of evidence, seldom examined by many who use the words 'proof' and 'evidence' facilely enough. It is fortunate that the pioneer in the scientific study of reincarnation-type experiences should be the careful, methodical and objective scholar that he is, settling a standard and pattern for serious researchers; for the subject could so easily have been captured by the lunatic fringe and ruined.

10

THE ARTHUR GUIRDHAM STORY

Group reincarnation is a common belief among those who accept rebirth. Friends, acquaintances and enemies brought into close contact by association or by the circumstances of their era (for example, opponents in politics or war, or persecutors and persecuted) come together in subsequent centuries to work out the karma inherited from the relationships created in the previous existence or to carry on work begun together. Examples of such groups would include Edgar Cayce's entourage; and the recognition of each other by pairs of former lovers is almost a commonplace of reincarnationist literature. Yet the Guirdham story must surely be unique.

Arthur Guirdham, doctor of medicine and psychiatrist, by nature and training sceptic and scientist (his family nicknamed him 'Doubting Thomas') has described his experiences in three books, *The Cathars and Reincarnation, The Lake and the Castle* and *We Are One Another*. The story is complicated and there is no substitute for reading the books themselves open to the serious student of reincarnation. No summary can do justice to the books' revelation of an extraordinary series of interlocking circumstances and relationships; they are certainly paranormal in the strict sense of 'beyond normal experience'. If the reincarnation hypothesis is rejected, some other must be found.

The story begins with a Mrs Smith who was a patient of Dr Guirdham's. Long before she met him she had allegedly received a detailed knowledge of Catharism, the dualist heresy that flourished in southern France and northern Italy in the twelfth and thirteenth centuries. This had come to her in an uprush of 'far memory' in 1944, when she was in her early teens, though she did not know the name of the heresy. Poems were 'given' to her in medieval French with phrases in langue d'oc in what was surmised to be a mixture of clairaudience and memory. She had come to know and set down in writing certain details of which the historians who had written on the subject in any language in the seven centuries which have elapsed since Catharism existed were ignorant. An example of these was that Cathar priests wore dark blue robes. It was not until 1965, twenty-one years later, that this fact was found to be true by the experts, who until then had all believed that they were black. Many other obscure facts and names were strung together by Mrs Smith when she was thirteen, seemingly beyond all possibility of coincidence.

On her first visit to France in 1957 Mrs Smith had experienced a feeling of familiarity in Capvern in the Pyrenees. Similar sensations came to her on a holiday in 1964 in St Jean Pied de Port, round which she could find her way on her first visit as readily as she could her own town. She had a number of other *déjà vu* experiences, not least a feeling of horror of Toulouse and its cathedral, where the Cathar heretics were tried and condemned. Before he met Mrs Smith, Dr Guirdham had likewise found Provence 'strangely compelling' and had discovered an equally strong attraction in Languedoc and the Pyrenees, scenes that he was to discover had to do with his own previous life as a Cathar. This existence was revealed to him in 1962 when the first thought of reincarnation came to him in an interview with Mrs Smith, then in her early thirties. He was in his fifties, mature and experienced enough not to surrender his scepticism at a whim or in response to the groundless fantasy of a woman with whose revelations he was, as he confesses himself, at first impatient. She met him in an outpatients' department and recognised him at her first appointment with him as her lover of Cathar days, Roger Isarn, son of Bec de Fanjeaux and Aude de Tonnens, although she did not tell him this until much later. He called her Puerilia in that past life. Roger and Guirdham had a number of character traits that were identical, though they were unlike in general character.

Mrs Smith had suffered from a recurrent nightmare in which a man entered a room in which she was lying and approached her from her right-hand side. His coming filled her with terror. She was aware that he had murdered someone and was unrepentant of the crime. The dream corresponded to a similar nightmare of Guirdham's in which a tall man approached the place where he was sleeping but from his left, inspiring a similar apprehension. He felt that the same man and incident was 'remembered' in both dreams. Mrs Smith's nightmare never returned after her first interview with Dr Guirdham, and his dream ceased within a few weeks of his meeting her. Such dreams are said to be a form of psychic communication which cease when they have served their purpose. Mrs Smith was the agent who was to start the process of recall of his life as a Cathar for Dr Guirdham; from that beginning all else was to follow.

The following months saw a series of events that confirmed Dr Guirdham's growing conviction that he had lived before as a thirteenth-century dualist. In December 1963, he went to tea with a Mrs A. who told him that she had discovered he was a Cathar and must now prepare himself for his next incarnation. He felt that his former Catharism was confirmed by certain tendencies within himself; for example, a hatred of Roman Catholicism ('hate is always tinged with fear', he wrote),[219] of clericalism and of destroying anything living, and a temporary revulsion to flesh food: 'All this was the Cathar in me coming to the surface.'[220]

Later in the same month, another hostess out of the blue handed him a book, *Albigeois et Cathares*, and on 7 January 1964, Dr Guirdham's wife picked up at her hairdresser's an article on an order of *bonshommes* associated with Catharism which turned out to have been written by one of the doctor's patients. Five days later Guirdham visited Mrs Smith's house in snow, and they were both reminded by the circumstances of an occasion when he had taken refuge from a snowstorm in her home in the thirteenth century.

Following these revelations, there were several synchronisations of thought and action between Dr Guirdham and Mrs Smith. She was undoubtedly psychic and showed gifts of precognition. In February she asked the doctor if the name Fabrissa, which had come to her, of either a person or a place, meant anything to him. The name was found to be that of the aunt of Pierre de Mazarolles who was identified as the unrepentant murderer in both their dreams. Historical research discovered that Pierre had been one of the murderers of the Inquisitors whose slaying had been the cause of the campaign against Montségur.

Mrs Smith, whose learning of past events as a schoolgirl seems to have been by 'far memory', began to dream in 'fluent French' (would she not have dreamed in the langue d'oc?) about a number of people whom research in the records of the time showed to belong to the same circle of Cathar adherents. She dreamed that an 'Alice' lived in the same house as Roger, writing the name as *Alaïs*, of which an alternative spelling is *Hélis*. Hélis was Roger Isarn's sister, who made a deposition to the Inquisition on 5 August 1243; she was Fabrissa's sister-in-law. Hélis, Roger, Pierre de Mazarolles and Fabrissa, all mentioned widely in authoritative writers on Catharism, constantly appeared in Mrs Smith's dreams, visions and memories; her information and details of contemporary Cathar life when checked appeared true in almost every particular. In addition she dreamed of symbols, some of which were dreamed of by Guirdham and appeared independently in other testimony later, and one of which was drawn in his diary before she dreamed it.

The above summary of facts could be explained by a paranormal combination of psychic qualities on the parts of Guirdham and Mrs Smith, whose meetings sparked off reaction in each other. A reviewer of *The Cathars and Reincarnation* suggested as much when he wrote, 'Dr Guirdham ... tends to act as a "transmitter" of psi-type activity in those liable to it ... the received material could arise from telepathic and precognitive communication rather than retrocognition.'[221] There is also an allegation that Mrs Smith's father was interested in Provençal poetry and could have unknowingly influenced his daughter's taste and knowledge, but there is no evidence that he had any specific interest in the poetry's being medieval or Provençal, and his role was indefinable and minimal.

Dr Guirdham's case is not much strengthened by *The Lake and the Castle* (written after *We Are One Another*) which, as the author acknowledges, is an almost entirely subjective narrative of experiences of himself and his friends who had shared incarnations not only as dualists but as members of the Celtic Church in the seventh century and as French sailors, prisoners-of-war in England at the time of the Napoleonic wars. The account is given with little attempt to confirm its details by historical research and should not be condemned for failing to do what it specifically does not try to do. It does, however, widen the circle to include many more personalities than the doctor, Mrs Smith and the three or four other acquaintances. Its value for reincarnationists is in throwing much light on the psychic experiences, intuitions and relationships of individuals reborn several times within a group. The sceptic, while not doubting the genuineness of the feelings, will in the absence of evidence reject them as nothing more then communal self-hallucination.

We Are One Another produces a great deal more evidence of the 'Mrs Smith' type, supplied by a larger circle of witnesses, and both its quantity and quality are challenging. In this book the interlocking circumstances and relationships mentioned at the beginning of this chapter are to be found.

It begins with a Miss Clare Mills whose part in the account is that of a keystone: all the relationships are centred upon her. She was a casual visitor to the Guirdhams and mentioned two names running through her head, Raymond and Albigensian (a name popularly synonymous with Cathar). She also recounted two dreams, one of running away from a castle which held some horror for her, the second of walking barefoot to a stake on a pile of heaped faggots with others going to the same fate of being burned alive. On the way someone struck her on the back with a flaming torch. Since childhood, she had been terrified of fire and trumpets.

Corresponding to the blow with the torch, there was a line of protuberances from the skin on Miss Mills' back that looked like blisters from burns although there was no liquid in them and they were semisolid. As with Mrs Smith, the meeting with Dr Guirdham led to a cessation of the dreams, allegedly a sign of recognition from a previous incarnation; pain from which Miss Mills had been suffering also disappeared. Another curious physical effect was that both Miss Mills and Dr Guirdham experienced Menière's syndrome when psychic receptivity burst through or was about to manifest itself.

Before she met Dr Guirdham, Miss Mills was moved to visit Carcassone and was deeply affected by the city. Much later she was bombarded with voices which insisted that she must confide in Guirdham. Miss Mills was no pale psychic dressed in Liberty prints and amber beads and seeing the hand of some grand master or Tibetan adept in every trivial coincidence of daily life, but a practical, hard-working, normally ebullient woman, who did her utmost to keep her psychic experiences to herself. It was at first with extreme reluctance that she confided in Guirdham, and she would probably not have done so at all, had her voices not insisted.

While this was happening to Miss Mills, the doctor had occasion to visit a geriatric ward, where a ninety-nine-year-old lady talked spontaneously to him of Catharism, saying that it was urgent that the sects' theology again be disseminated. Shortly after, Miss Mills began to find messages in her home written in her hand but which she had no memory of writing. She asked Guirdham about Cathar sacraments and the terms *filius major* and *filius minor* which she had never heard until her voices spoke of them to her. A Cathar bishop was 'understudied' by a *filius major* who took his place when he died, and the *filius minor* moved up to become *filius major* to the new bishop. Knowledge of these Cathar ranks was confined to experts; Guirdham, seeking in reference books for answers to the questions prompted by communications from Miss Mills' voices, found that again and again, far beyond the reach of coincidence, he went instantly to the right line of the right paragraph of the right page—a classical sign that occult forces were at work.

Miss Mills asked the meaning of 'Make me a good Christian and bring me to a good end', words that had come to her. Guirdham replied that they were part of the *consolamentum*, the sacrament by which the lower-rank Cathar believer became a '*parfait[e]*' (perfect one). As a lapse into sin after the believer had become a *parfait* was regarded as serious, most Cathars took the *consolamentum* only on their death-beds. Soon after, Miss

Mills was given the words *apparellamentum* and *amelioramentum*, of which the former was a kind of monthly confession of sins. Guirdham was unfamiliar with the second, and was later informed by Miss Mills via her communicating entities that the words he thought came from the *consolamentum* were part of the *amelioramentum*. Here was the 'pupil' correcting the 'master' and the incident proved that telepathy from Guirdham to Mills was not always an explanation.

About the middle of 1971 a glut of Italian references, Vicenza, Sorano, Brescia, Desanzano, Treviso, Jean de Lugio, appeared on Miss Mills' writing pad. Guirdham once again found that the first book he consulted opened itself to him, as it were and he discovered that Jean de Lugio was the *filius major* of the bishop of Bellesmana. He had written the basic classic of Cathar theology, *Le Livre de Deux Principes*. Trogarium and Sorano appeared on the pad, and Nikolski on another piece of paper. The last name turned out to be that of the Slavonic gospel of the Bosnian heretics, including the Bogomils and Paulicians, usually regarded as the spiritual ancestors of Catharism. Trogarium was the centre of the heretic church on the Dalmatian and Istrian coasts, and Desenzano a focal point of Catharism in Italy, bishops of which lived in Sorano and Vicenza, and which sent missionaries to Languedoc. This and similar information communicated by Miss Mills' discarnate entity could be confirmed; Dr Guirdham commented, 'I could not realise that Miss Mills, utterly uninstructed in the subject, would make solid and fascinating contributions to our knowledge of the history and nature of Catharism.'[222]

Miss Mills was identified as having been Esclarmonde, daughter of Raymond de Perella, owner of the château of Montségur near the Pyrenees, destroyed in 1244, the home of a number of *parfaits*. Following the fall of the fortress she had been burned at the stake with many others. Anniversaries of past misfortunes such as the surrender of the castle and her burning affected her physically in this life even when she did not know them till later. (It is not clear if they affected her every year throughout her life or only after her 'far memories' were intensified by her meeting with Dr Guirdham, nor is it suggested that any allowance was made for the shifting of dates due to changes in the calendar since the thirteenth century.)

Whole strings of obscure names given to Miss Mills were confirmed in records of the Inquisition and given in the style of those records although she did not know modern French let alone that of the thirteenth century. (She was typical of those who learn languages at school and in adult life show no signs of remembering them. Her French and Latin were minimal.) One list of names was connected with another family and a link indicated between the former families of Mrs Smith and Miss Mills. Guirdham might well ask, 'What is my role in the grand strategy of this occult campaign?'[223] Events yet to happen rendered the question even more pertinent.

Extraordinary coincidences mounted in number. For instance, on 23 November, Miss Mills told Dr Guirdham by telephone that the words 'Termes' and 'water supply' had come to her. On 23 November 1209, the besieged Cathar castle of Termes had surrendered because of an outbreak of dysentery caused by contamination of the water supply.

Weeks of communication were devoted to scriptural references (the Cathars used the same New Testament as the orthodox but interpreted it differently), a key verse in Cathar theology, I Corinthians 15: 45, being given five times. Names were also given of dualist philosophers with Greek or Graeco-Roman backgrounds. Miss Mills developed speech in French, Latin and Occitan. She developed powers of healing, having been a healer in her Cathar existence, and she revealed that the *consolamentum* was not the final sacrament. There was a further stage which enabled the initiate to heal and gave him the power to withdraw into his spiritual body so as to be impermeable to physical agony. The *parfaits* were apparently able to do this when going to the stake and astounded onlookers by the composure, almost eagerness, with which they strode to execution.

Miss Mills' communications tapered off but were replaced by visions. Awakened one night by the barking of her dog, she saw an old lady at the foot of her bed. She felt no fear—on the contrary, a great peace—and the visits continued, the old lady's materialisation becoming denser and clearer as their number increased. The visitor was identified as Braïda de Montserver, a Cathar aristocrat, and two months after her first appearance she began to speak and was understood by Miss Mills. She communicated a knowledge of healing herbs and berries and there was a marked shift to an emphasis on healing ability at the end of December 1971. Guirdham himself had experience of Miss Mills' healing power which had, as it were, spilled over from her former ability to cure.

Conversations with Braïda confirmed that Guirdham had been Roger Isarn in the thirteenth century and had become 'something more than an ordinary *parfait*'. (His living with Puerilia had been before he had been a *parfait*, and men and women were allowed to live together as husband and wife until they were received; although, in Cathar practice, sexual intercourse was, ideally, forgone, and procreation regarded with distaste as the means of imprisoning more spirits in flesh.) Miss Mills found after a time that Braïda would appear on request, and she was accompanied once by a man who later appeared twice on his own. He was a chubby-faced man whom Guirdham identified as the most renowned of all the Cathar bishops, Guilhabert de Castres. Braïda appeared once as a young woman of thirty, to show what she had been like when de Castres began his mission. On another night, Miss Mills took down the names 'of the most cultured, articulate and like-minded of Guilhabert's entourage'.[224]

In January 1972, Guilhabert appeared with another man, identified as Bertrand Marty, a Cathar bishop, to whose care he entrusted Miss Mills as he had done in 1241 during their former lives. She was soon able to give Guirdham details of the capture of Montségur which did not agree with the information that he had collected in his reading; but further research proved her right and his information wrong.

Dr Guirdham's relationships with Mrs Smith and Miss Mills had been a one-to-one connection (though group reincarnation in which a wide circle of his acquaintances played their parts is the theme of *The Lake and the Castle*). Now there began an expansion of relationships. Betty, an old schoolfriend whom Miss Mills had not seen for years, began to ring her incessantly after her husband had died. He had gone on holiday to Langue-doc, leaving a journal indicating a knowledge of the Cathars, their healing powers and other details, suggesting that he was another of the group that was revealing itself. He died of a heart attack shortly after his return. Jane, Betty's seventy-year-old mother, then got into touch with Miss Mills, referring to drawing-books filled by Betty when she was seven years old and ill with scarlet fever. These, some of which are reproduced in *We Are One Another*, she had kept. They are notable for the frequent appearance of Cathar symbols and names of Cathar individuals. For example, a couple of pages in one drawing-book were headed 'Monréal 1204', and contained no fewer than nine names, coinciding closely with those made in the appropriate deposition in the Doat collection in the Bibliothèque Nationale in Paris. At this time, writes Guirdham, there were no books in English or French which could have supplied her with the obscure names written in her drawing-books.

On 16 March 1972 Guirdham, Miss Mills and Jane were all attacked by illness of various kinds. The doctor was seized by a fit of suffocating breathlessness at 3.30am. Miss Mills told him that she had vomited at the same time. Jane was wakened also in the small hours of 16 March by an agonising leg pain; she found that both her legs were fiery red and covered with blisters. Her doctor said that the appearance was exactly like that caused by burning, and if Jane had not been burned he could not account for it, for he had never seen anything like it; 16 March was the anniversary of the burning of the *parfaits* after the taking of Montségur.

Jane (whom Dr Guirdham never met) never studied Catharism, all that she knew coming to her through revelation. She told Miss Mills that she had been visited for some years by a man in blue robes whom she had taken to be a monk. The man appeared approximately every two months in seemingly much the same way as Braïda appeared to Miss Mills, and was later identified as the Cathar bishop, Raimon Agulher. Miss Mills, who was very reticent about her experiences, had told Jane nothing of them until Jane had disclosed her own and revealed the fact that she knew of Braïda's visits to Miss Mills—

presumably informed of them by Agulher. Living three hundred miles from her friend, Jane was completely aware of Miss Mills' physical condition. On a visit to her she described her help with the wounded at the siege of Montségur, and she confirmed the details Mrs Smith had given years before of the dress and ornaments, such as belt-buckles, worn by the *parfaits*.

Identifications emerged. Jane herself had been Bruna, married to a sergeant-at-arms at Montségur named Arnaud Domerq, with whom she had suffered death at the stake. Betty, her daughter in the twentieth century, had been Hélis, daughter of Bec de Fanjeaux and Guirdham's sister in his former life as Roger Isarn. Guirdham therefore bridged the gap between the Fanjeux and Mazerolles families and the Montserver and Perella clans in Miss Mills' 'far memories'. As already shown, she herself had been Esclarmonde de Perella. Jane identified Miss Mills' father as Bertrand Marty.

This was not the end of the enlarging circle. Another of Miss Mills' acquaintances, named Penelope, ill with cancer, who had been a business associate in the past and whom, like Betty, she had not seen for ten years, wrote to her asking her to visit her. Miss Mills was unable to do this and soon after was 'aware' that Penelope had died. A little later, Penelope's husband got into touch with her and told her that just before Penelope died she mentioned 'Brasiac', the phonetic pronunciation of Brasillac, which was the name of another sergeant-at-arms who had fought at Montségur. In a later letter the husband wrote that he must meet Miss Mills, for there were many things she could tell him. She mislaid the letter and consequently did not reply, but he appeared in person to tell her that among Penelope's effects were some pieces of paper with words written on them, including Pons Narbona, Arnaud Domerq, Brasillac and prayers to do with the *consolamentum*. Further writings among her papers clearly referred to the massacre of the Inquisitors. He added that for years Penelope had dreamed of a castle on a hill containing blue-robed men, and that she was terrified of fire and had an irrational fear of stones being thrown at her which presumably resulted from the horror of bombardment by stones from the *ballistae, trebuchets* and *manganelles* that had inflicted terrible injuries at Montségur.

He himself then had two dreams repeatedly, one of men and women in dark blue kissing as part of a ceremony (men kissing only men and women women) with fragments of prayers, the other of fighting in a castle on a hill. He had been wounded and cared for by the girl who was Miss Mills in this life, remembered a girl named Silla (Penelope in her Cathar life?) and was identified himself as Brasillac.

Yet another link was forged in the chain. Miss Mills unaccountably suffered for several days from what seemed to be a coronary condition which caused her considerable pain. She was telephoned soon after by Kathleen, another school acquaintance whom she had not seen for ten years. She had been in hospital with coronary spasm—this had somehow been transmitted to Miss Mills, for part of the healing ministry that the latter had undertaken under the guidance of Braïda included taking on herself the pains of the illnesses of others. Kathleen said she had phoned because of a compulsion to do so. She believed in reincarnation, her faith being confirmed by a *déjà vu* experience in which she felt complete familiarity with the town of Foix in which she knew she had lived before.

Later Kathleen visited Miss Mills unheralded, told her dreams she had had of Betty in dark blue robes and of others similarly attired. She rang Guirdham, also without warning, and made some astonishing references to Cathar names and customs (although it is acknowledged that she had read most of his books though not *We Are One Another*). Revelations had been coming to her for about six months. She was identified as yet another of the Cathar circle, Arsendis, who had been burned at the stake with Bruna at Montségur.

No summary can do justice to the interweaving of revelations and relationships which is to be found in Guirdham's books. We are presented with a doubting Thomas of a doctor in his middle age being confronted with a woman who recalls to him his Cathar past in such a manner that he begins to be convinced in spite of innate scepticism. If the reincarnation theory is accepted, Mrs Smith's father, with his interest in medieval Provençal poetry, may himself have been one of the Cathar group reborn without the full realisation coming to his consciousness. Belonging to his generation is Jane, Betty's mother, whose contact with the spirits of Cathar personalities seems to have been as vivid as that of Miss Mills. (I asked Dr Guirdham, who came to see Braïda almost as clearly as Miss Mills, *how* he saw and heard her, to which he replied, 'Exactly as I hear you; seeing was less clear'—experience which is rare in psychical research where entities are seldom heard to speak, still less to communicate on the scale recorded in Guirdham's books, however clearly they may be seen.) Jane's daughter, Betty, as a child of seven, produces information about the Cathars and shares her reincarnation experiences in the twentieth century with two schoolfellows, though their former lives and relationships do not become explicit until comparatively late in their lives. Did they have any awareness at school? Or did the experience of all this group come to the surface only when Dr Guirdham and Miss Mills acted as catalysts, precipitating people's 'far memories' which before that time had been latent? Finally, Penelope and her husband are linked to the group via Miss Mills, and Miss Mills' group is linked to Mrs Smith via Dr Guirdham.

If group reincarnation is not acceptable as an explanation, some other must be found. It is difficult to see what normal psychological interpretation can be suggested. The string of coincidences and relationships is too bizarre to be explained by chance, yet the recorded facts will fit no ordinary hypothesis. Guirdham wrote, 'The whole experience has become so oceanic that I can now do little more than record it.'[225]

If no normal explanation can be found, there remain fraud and various paranormal hypotheses. Dr Guirdham, whose writing includes novels and poetry, could have constructed a clever fiction and, indeed, the anonymity of most of the characters, sheltered behind Christian names or ambiguous surnames only, together with the fact that a number of them have died, would make it impossible for anyone to establish the truth or falsehood of many of the stated facts. The materialist who believes in no form of survival or paranormality will reject the whole story as group hysteria produced by a number of credulous folk overemphasising their dreams and exaggerating a few strange coincidences, with regret that a sensible man of science should have let himself be led astray. Or the materialist may say that the affair is a tissue of lies put together for such motives as exhibitionism, making money, practical jokery, the spreading of a particular gospel or because of some psychological quirk in the brain of the author. Having met Dr Guirdham, I am sure he is no exhibitionist. As for making money, every author knows that there are easier ways of making it than by writing books—especially volumes of psychic experience about medieval heresy. Dr Guirdham does not strike me as a literary confidence-trickster. (Although, if he were, he would doubtless conceal the fact from someone whom he knew to be devoting a chapter to him in a book about reincarnation.) Still less is he a fanatic who would use what he would regard as the good end of preaching the dualist gospel, which its upholders believe to be true and original Christianity, to justify the deceitful means of fiction disguised as fact. The literature of psychical research is full of examples of trusted investigators who were later discovered to have been deceivers ever, perhaps with the best of motives: but if an accusation of fraud is made, the onus of proof lies on the accuser.

If the non-reincarnationist accepts paranormal explanations, he may see in the phenomena some examples of telepathy including a kind of group telepathic hallucination. Guirdham argues powerfully against telepathy, but there are some phenomena of which it could be the explanation, as there are many instances where it could not. An example of the former is that the doctor probably knew of the *filius major* and *filius minor* before Miss Mills asked him about them and could have sent his knowledge to her telepathically. On the other hand he was corrected in misconceptions by members of his group with facts that research showed later to be accurate. Clairvoyance, precognition mistaken for retrocognition and super-ESP on the part of several individuals complementing each other—a mingling of all these in a more than usually psychic circle brought together by chance—could have resulted in Guirdham's 'detailed mechanism'. Such an hypothesis of mixed causes of the phenomena is as

strange as that of reincarnation, and a good deal more complicated.

Alternatively, the non-reincarnationist might evolve the following theory. There seem to be individuals to whom psychic
events occur if the circumstances are right. Perhaps, if chance
brings several of these together, they form a kind of battery of
psychic power which increases the number of such events. If the
interest of several individuals is aroused in the same subject
(could there, for example, have been a history teacher at the
school where Betty, Kathleen and Clare Mills studied who
sparked off in them all, perhaps subconsciously, a concern with
Catharism?), it may be that their psychism adapts itself to this
subject and influences more neutral members of the group to
move in the same direction. There is a snowball effect as more
and more psychic power is directed towards the same object. So
here Mrs Smith as a child is fascinated by Catharism, for whatever reason; when she meets Guirdham, and psychic deep calls
to psychic deep, arousing in him qualities which had been latent
all his life until then, it is 'Catharwards' that she influences him
to move. Meanwhile Jane, obviously psychic, has similarly and
perhaps merely coincidentally guided her daughter, Betty.
Betty the schoolgirl interacts psychically with her schoolfellows,
Clare Mills and Kathleen, also unwitting sensitives. As the ini-
tiator in the psychic chain of cause and effect, she guides them,
too, into the subject that she has made her own. By chance Miss
Mills meets Dr Guirdham after he has set out on the Cathar trail,
and they react upon and reinforce each other. And so the process
continues, the psychic snowball gathering speed and power. It
must be remembered that such power seems capable of working
at a distance without obeying the law of inverse proportions, and
the attraction of Penelope to the group could again have been due
to Miss Mills' psychic sensors feeling their way towards any of
her past acquaintances whose sensitivity matched hers—the
attraction of like to like.

Of course the thesis is far-fetched, but some might say no
more extreme than a belief in group reincarnation. There is also
a philosophical question that has to be answered if group reincarnation is accepted. The reappearance of the Cathar brotherhood

in the twentieth century with its belief that Catharism was the true and primitive Christianity and its mission to disseminate the truth of dualism suggests that the Power that guides the universe has brought this about to conduct the world back to truth. Are we to expect reincarnated groups of Bogomils, Paulicians, other Christian gnostics and neo-Platonists to appear? Will they be opposed by reborn clusters of orthodox Christians, maybe of Inquisitors? Or is Guirdham's group the only one that may be expected, and will its message die with it? Through Jane the claim was made that many groups all over the world will be joined by psychic communication; but the Guirdham group and its experience remain unique so far, with their special niche in any survey of the subject of rebirth.

11

SUMMARY OF
THE ARGUMENTS

In considering the pros and cons of reincarnation there are two divisions of activity and thought to be considered; the empirical and the ethical. That there are many human phenomena suggestive of reincarnation has been shown by the contents of this book; that almost all of them can be given other explanations, normal or paranormal, is equally demonstrable; but that, after all explanations have been given, there is a residue inexplicable in our present state of knowledge, except by theories that are more far-fetched than reincarnation, is indubitable.

There remains also the ethical issue as to whether the belief in rebirth is one that can satisfy the highest ideals of human morality at least as much as those of other faiths.

Fraud is the first explanation. Instances of deliberate fraud appear very little in the literature, and Dr Stevenson writes that he has known only one case of deliberate fraud. To perpetrate a fraud good enough to deceive the world at large would take much time and trouble and would be purposeless except for a paranoiac exhibitionist or a fanatic: it would not be worth the effort. Any superficially prepared fraud would be exposed by the first serious researcher who enquired into it.

Unconscious deception, in the shape of subjective conviction on false premises and supposed existences built on such factors as parental attitudes, conscious or unconscious, absorbed in infancy, is usually so insubstantial as to be easily exposed. In many cases its origin can be shown by hypnosis, a useful technique for discovering personal truths unknown to the subject.

Cryptomnesia, hidden memory, explains a very wide range of phenomena, and has remarkable capabilities, such as the proven ability to recall a whole page of an unknown language seen once in a library many years before, if the subject goes into induced or spontaneous trance. If cryptomnesia is allied with fantasies incubated in the subconscious mind, a very convincing scenario can be built up, especially if the subject is well educated and can supply information from many sources.

Paramnesia, false memory, is another source of fictional past experience that often has a reincarnationist tinge. Here memories of this life are misinterpreted and coloured by other factors, creating the illusion of an existence in a historical past that convinces the subject he has lived before. Strong emotion often increases his certainty.

Altered states of consciousness, induced 'naturally' by meditation or mind-training techniques or artificially by drugs, are sometimes accompanied by phenomena so close to experiences of past lives that, if they are not what they appear to be, they cast doubt on all such experiences.

The existence of dissociated personalities, sometimes so many in a single individual that he might say with the Gadarene demoniac, 'My name is Legion', is a fact of abnormal psychology. Personalities of this kind, though often dramatising the needs and problems of the present life, may symbolise them by dressing them up in the trappings of a life of long ago. Very close to these is subconscious role-playing, which may be extremely vivid.

Inherited memories, folk, racial, ancestral, familial or genetic, may exist. The general opinion seems to be that although humans do inherit certain memories expressed in survival instincts and, possibly, readier ability to learn certain skills (we 'remember' to suckle, and perhaps a modern child learns to ride a bicycle more quickly than his great-grandfather did), these are very narrow in scope. If an exceptional case of apparent genetic memory comes along, another explanation is usually found. But if every case of seemingly inherited memory were collected from all the literature of abnormal psychology, parapsychology and psychical research, it might appear that the faculty is commoner than has hitherto been thought; and if inherited memory should be proved to exist, it could explain many reincarnationist experiences.

Memory crosses the border from normal to paranormal explanations, for another source of memory could be the universal subconsciousness envisaged by Jung, which verges upon the conception of cosmic memory and even of the *akashic* records. If some human minds can draw upon the storehouse of memories in any of these repositories through some psychological quirk, accepting them as their own, this could explain experiences of the reincarnation type. There would still need to be answered the question as to how and why a particular life or series of lives should be selected.

If the validity of paranormal phenomena be admitted, a whole range of explanations other than the reincarnationist can explain rebirth experiences. There is precognition, possibly arising from forgotten dreams, masquerading as memory. There is retrogression, a seeming stepping-back into a past existence of which the subject feels himself to have been a part. There is telepathy from parents, relatives or friends, and there could be telepathic paramnesia. A psychometry of places may exist, whereby atmospheric and other conditions impinging at the right moment on human sensitives may recall events fired with drama and emotion, and this may explain particularly veridical experiences of *déjà vu*. The mention of sensitives leads on to the explanation that extrasensory perception brings back false memories of previous lives, the information conveyed in this way being true but its application to the person receiving it being false. Super-ESP or general ESP is an extension of this which sets no limit to the sources of information the mind can tap nor the use it makes of them. There is no reason given as to why and how it selects the information it uses; and a powerful argument against it is that a very large number of those who have strong reincarnationist memories show no sign at all of other ESP experiences.

There is a range of phenomena that could be psychosomatically self-fulfilling. Dreams in which former individuals announce that they will return and will be recognised by birthmarks or other physical characteristics and which are duly fulfilled could belong to this category. So could birthmarks resembling former wounds when the mother is convinced that the man who died from these wounds is to be reborn of her. If such dreams and fulfilments were very common, their psychosomatic origin would be easily accepted by the medical profession, especially if the alternative were reincarnation. Because they are rare, coincidence or almost any other normal explanation is preferred to psychosomatism. The same is true of birthmarks; here the reincarnationist will add his contention that wound-corresponding birthmarks, some documented, have been known where the parents were ignorant of the correspondence.

The rare instances of possession, such as the Watseka Wonder case, can be used both to strengthen and weaken the belief in rebirth. It is strengthened in that possession is so self-evidently different from reincarnation experiences. In the former the possessing personality *becomes* the person possessed; in the latter the former life is remembered by the individual in much the same way as he remembers his own past. It is weakened in that if the phenomenon of possession is only a mental sickness, then a reincarnationist experience is simply another mental sickness of the same family, not so acute.

Responsive xenoglossy, especially when allied with accurate information, is a very powerful argument in favour of reincarnation. Cases are, however, extremely rare, and those that are known are not so strong as to be completely convincing.

Memories of past lives, including those delved from the minds of hypnotic patients, may be therapeutic romances, created as mental antibodies to cure phobias and neuroses of the present life, or perhaps escapist in some instances. The insight of sensitives like Cayce into the previous lives of others might also be a kind of telepathic romancing, healing in the same way. Yet a reincarnationist would be right in thinking this a more extravagant interpretation than his own belief.

He would be correct also in pointing out that if the recognitions of people and places shown to be accurate by many of Stevenson's subjects—they are the best examples in all the literature, the most closely and objectively investigated—had applied to this life, they would not have been doubted for a moment. That is to say, that if a man of twenty had gone back to the scenes of his childhood after a separation of fifteen years from it and anyone connected with it, and had pointed out changes and recognised the former home and relatives, and close catechism had proved him substantially right, the only reaction would be, 'What a good memory!' There would be no seeking for alternative explanations. It is only because the idea of reincarnation is so unacceptable to a materialistic age that other interpretations of the phenomena are sought.

The argument that reincarnation explains childhood geniuses is countered by the contention that when we know more of genetics we shall understand how genes affect human development and may one day be able to produce geniuses to order. To which reincarnationists may reply that genetics are an agent of karma.

Ethical arguments against rebirth are that faith in it leads to fatalism, passivity and depression. Yet any faith may have negative results, from smugness and self-righteousness, to fanaticism and cruelty. To many, reincarnation brings a message of hope, confidence in the ultimate rightness of things and inspiration to work for continuous advance to a future of union with God or the inexpressible bliss of nirvana.

Surprisingly, the opponents of the creed assert that it is against the law of nature and the rule of progress; to which the reincarnationist would reply by the direct assertion that it is precisely natural development and progress that rebirth effects.

The belief justifies cruelty, pain and wretchedness, say its enemies, all of which are agents of karma inflicting punishment for past evil which is not remembered and for which only unconscious and therefore useless retribution is made. We cannot acknowledge that there is justice in punishment for sins of which we are unaware. Against this is the argument that karma is an unalterable law of the universe which says that as a man sows, sooner or later he shall reap; and all the lessons from our past lives live in our subconscious minds (as, for example, learning to walk lives on in the minds of adults) or are known in the intermissions, when we see the whole panorama of our past lives and choose the next life so as to influence our karmic entail aright.

That reincarnation is a subtle form of materialsim is a more subtle form of argument. This might well be true of primitive forms of the belief, but can scarcely be levied at the higher, where increasing spirituality is looked upon as a condition of progress. Hence the next attack, that reincarnationist concern with individual advance is a selfishness that disregards one's fellow-man and leaves no room for self-sacrifice, forgiveness or vicarious suffering. Again, this is not true of higher forms of the belief, except possibly in the instance of some die-hard theosophists, the Calvinists of their creed, who insist on the utter immutability of karma. The stories of Buddha show how often he sacrificed himself. Bodhisattvas, though qualified to enter nirvana, refrain from doing so to help mankind. And we have seen that in all the major religions there may be found a doctrine of grace, not least in those of which rebirth is a fundamental dogma.

A certain archetypal theme runs through many creeds, for all their differences. We originate in some way from God; we descend into matter; we progress back to God. The purpose of the process is completely ethical and educational, to lead us by experience from innocence to so triumphantly victorious a morality that we are able and worthy to rejoin our Maker on—dare it be said?—equal terms. Reincarnation is the tool by which our destiny is shaped.

12

A THEOLOGY OF
REINCARNATION
FOR MODERN MAN

'A rational man, if he wants, can believe in reincarnation on the basis of evidence', wrote Stevenson.[226] But in what kind of rebirth? While there are varieties of reincarnation theory, there are basic agreements. These should make it possible to evolve a doctrine of rebirth which it is possible for modern man to accept and to reconcile with such knowledge as he has of the nature of the universe. Let it be assumed that the materialists have had their say in the never-ending debate as to whether or not man survives death. Unconvinced, they have gone their way. Let it also be assumed that all the survivalists who reject reincarnation as a possible mode of life after death have departed with them. Reincarnationists alone remain, but with their ideas as yet unclear in face of the many differences in detail. Perhaps these can be clarified.

Little is said by the religions that preach reincarnation about the nature of time, beyond the assumption that there is an unlimited amount of it. Whether one thinks of time as lineal, like an infinite carpet-roll being unwound for ever, as is perhaps the western concept, or as circular, so that all things end as they began prior to beginning again, as is the eastern way, it is plain that any philosophy of rebirth must take time into account. Time is subjectively unreal—the same hour goes like a minute to a happy or a concentrating man and is an eternity to a bored or tortured one. So it is conceivable that an intermission of a thousand years might be a few seconds of spiritual life, or the reverse—a few seconds seem like a thousand years.

There can be added to this quality of time the knowledge of its nature that has come from the theory of relativity. A man travelling at a certain speed faster than light for fifteen years by his watch in a straight line from the earth's surface and returning, making a total of thirty years, would find on his arrival on the planet that three hundred years had elapsed since his starting date and would meet his posterity of a dozen generations on.

Add to these two concepts a third. Theologically, eternity is far more than a very long time followed by another very long time followed by another very long time for ever and ever. It is a state quite other than that of time. The difference has been likened to a football team first walking in single file along a passage and then scattered at random throughout Hyde Park.[227] In the passage one can say who is in front of whom, who is before and after another. In Hyde Park the relationships are no longer before and after but are different. So it is with men who are at one and the same time, if religious teachers are to be believed, creatures of time and of another state called eternity. Since 'eternity' implies everlastingness, perhaps the term 'futurity' is a better one—at least until it is established that futurity *is* eternal.

The idea of reincarnation can be embraced equally by theistic or nontheistic religions. I must confess that, perhaps because of my western, Christian upbringing, I find the term 'nontheistic religion' to be self-contradictory. Such religions seem compelled to bring God in by the back door in concepts like the *life force*, the *first principle*, the *supreme oversoul* and the *adibuddha*, which are simply attempts by finite man to give a name to an indefinable numinous. God is a shorter and simpler word and everyone knows what and who the word means though no one knows what or who he is in his plenitude of being.

The primary choice of the philosopher of religion is between theism and atheism. If he chooses theism his next choice is between what might be described as a static perfected God, 'the same yesterday, today and for ever',[228] or an evolving God, who though always perfect (else he would not be God) moves from perfection to perfection in something of the way that a perfect baby could develop into a perfect child, a perfect adolescent and a perfect adult. Within the present perfect is always the seed of the future. The two concepts are not irreconcilable because the omniscient Continuing-to-be-perfected Perfect One must know to what he is being perfected, but this reconciliation is beyond human conception. The great theistic religions of the world all preach in their various vocabularies the self-sufficiency of God. He, the Creator, did not need to create, though it is difficult to envisage an uncreative Creator, and creation must surely be an essential activity arising from the nature of God. He created us for his beneficent purposes, in short, out of love for us, and that we might know him, love him and enjoy him for ever. His creative love sets the stage for the drama of his universe's destiny, of which man's is the part with which we are concerned.

The existence of human entities could have come about in three ways. They could have coexisted always as a part of God, emanating from him in the beginning like a shower of sparks from a fire. Or God could have created all the human entities there are at a point in time, not necessarily to take up residence simultaneously on the earth but ready to be fed into terrestrial existence as occasion demanded. Or God could be continuously creating souls to inhabit the human bodies being continuously born, which is the orthodox Christian viewpoint. It would seem on the surface that these alternatives are mutually exclusive. They are so only if there really is a corridor of time and not a Hyde Park of eternity. For if present, past and future *are* in the being whom the Hebrews by a stroke of genius called the 'I Am', then the alternatives can be reconciled, albeit mystically. Preexistence and special creation of souls cease to be a problem of time because they take place in another state, that of eternity, where events and relationships cease to be 'before' and 'after' and simply 'are'. This concept cannot be understood except at rare moments by the mystic. It can be taken only on faith.

So, basically, there is God, who is evolving perfection, a being of eternity which includes time but is quite different from it, from whose nature as Creator creation springs, including the creation of the souls of men. 'Soul' is an ambiguous word with many shades of meaning. For some reincarnationists it is an entity, like the Hindu *atman*, existing in the heavenlies, that projects part of itself into a succession of lives, each of which enriches the entity until it is sufficiently experienced, wise and purified to realise its oneness with the supreme being. For others it is a germ which begins as the most material, least spiritual, particle imaginable and evolves over aeons from unconsciousness to consciousness to self-consciousness to superconsciousness to God-consciousness. Several reincarnationist systems believe that the evolution of mankind is from mineral to vegetable, insect, lower animal, higher animal, man, and beyond, systems of faith that on the surface seem absurd. Yet modern knowledge makes them less ridiculous. If a rock, a table, an animal and a man all consist of certain basic particles of electricity whirling around in galaxies between which there is space proportionally as extensive as that between the constellations in the heavens, and if the basic *material* difference between a rock and a man is simply that the particles of electricity are very much more densely packed in the former, the concept of mineral evolving into man is not so absurd as might first appear. But we cannot know nor do the mechanics of our spiritual evolution really matter. What does matter is an understanding of its purpose.

The purpose is that we shall become co-creators with God. God as perfection moving towards not more but other perfection does this through his creation. Each creature transmigrating from life to life adds its quota of experience to its total stored away in eternity. During its intermissions, having absorbed the lessons of its past life, it sees what it needs to create in its next existence, but is, of course, able only to learn what its development allows it to learn—a creature who has just mastered its alphabet cannot at once proceed to an honours degree.

So at death, the soul adds to its stock collected from previous lives, is enlarged by it, and in the next incarnation advances a little further until it attains the self-consciousness of man which is the highest that man can know though not the highest form of consciousness that is to be. At this stage, speculation about the process and about such parts of it as the length of intermission can take place, and this can be based partly on experience. The ideas of the length vary, for example, from the immediate rebirth of the Druses to the millennia that spiritually advanced entities spend between lives according to the theosophists. Perhaps relativity can help here. There seems little doubt that belief affects performance, which may mean either that the believer deceives himself by seeing data to support his faith where none exist, or that the data are true but appear differently to observers of different outlooks. A Druse may spend a few seconds between death and rebirth in earth time which will be ten thousand years in futurity existence, while an intermission of several decades may be as seconds to the experiencing soul. The fact that the length of intermissions varies so greatly from reincarnationist culture to culture may argue that the whole business is mistaken; or it may be realised that A born in 1930 and last died in 1897, has spent a shorter time in futurity than B who was born in September 1930 and died in December 1929. Earth time bears no relation to futurity time—it relates only to other earth times and may be, as we have seen, largely illusory and deceptive, stretching and contracting for men experiencing different things.

Whatever the length of its intermissions, when a soul evolves to a certain level, it begins to realise its creative ability in many ways. One of the most important of these, if not the most important, is the building of relationships between itself as a self-conscious entity and other self-conscious entities together with the evolving of a primitive idea of God and its relationship to him. It is at about this point that the 'fall upward' takes place, for relationships at once involve moral choices, 'I want' being challenged by 'They need'. So we enter on the process that God the Creator has created a moral universe, that man must become morally perfect as God is perfect if he is to enter into full communion with him, that moral perfection results from opportunities for moral growth, and that these can only be given by real choices between good and evil. The concept of karma has its part to play here, and a modern reincarnationist has a choice of two views of karma—the theosophist's view that God must bow to karma (it is perhaps fairer to say that karma is an expression of the nature of God who cannot be other than he is) and that all good and bad entail must be worked out till its last ripple has ceased to move the mirror surface of eternity; or the Christian's view and that of some sections of other great religions that God uses karma as a tool but is free to replace it with grace that freely forgives and welcomes the believer into full communion with him without the necessity of further living.

This concept does not contradict the teaching of any of the great religions of the world (with the possible exception of Buddhism) though it is not necessarily upheld by them. Hinduism has its doctrine of grace, as has been seen. Judaism's God yearns for his people to accept his forgiveness and to embrace them with his love as a husband his wife. Even Buddhism says that *now* is the moment when a man can step off and upwards from the top rung of the ladder of existence towards nirvana. Christianity inherited the Jewish concept and added the forgiveness of sins through the atonement of Christ on the cross. To Mohammedans, Allah is the compassionate, the all-merciful.

If among all the religions of the world there is one whose claim to be the only or the best way to God is true, then, as we have seen, it is only a matter of time before every progressing soul will reach a life in which he finds himself a member of that supreme faith. He will have arrived.

And when he has arrived, he will enter into full communion with God, and will add to God the sum of his experience perfected by the grace of God, causing the perfection that is God to evolve towards the perfection that God is going to be. There are philosophical problems here that are insoluble—how can the supreme being be added to and remain supreme; how can the Creator and his creatures coexist as 'individuals' without the creatures being absorbed into the Creator; how can there be one and many? It is only in brief scintillas of mystical experiences that mankind can glimpse for a moment an understanding of these problems, such as the lightning-flash of unity with the whole of creation, or the beatific vision when the mystic is entirely lost in the contemplation of God yet never so much his complete self as when he is so lost.

This is the individual entity's destiny. It is often a criticism of reincarnationists that they are concerned only with their own spiritual evolution. This is not a just judgement, and even if it were, a modern reincarnationist would not want to nor need to be tarred with that brush. Two ways are open to him to escape it. He may realise that the more experience he has of living lives of both sexes and of many faiths and races, the greater his understanding of and sympathy with others. The lack of memory may trouble him here, but if it is true that we are what we are because of all the past experience from former lives that has gone into the making of us, then the result may be a Mother Teresa or a Yehudi Menuhin and will be for all of us in time. It may not be on this earth, for in the innumerable possible habitable worlds that astronomy has revealed to exist, there may be other opportunities to evolve.

The second way is the way of the post-mortem Myers' 'group-soul'[229] where evolved humans would conglomerate in eternity into groups which share their experiences. This may appear a little too much of a beehive for some people's tastes; but when one thinks of the joy that friendship, love and comprehension between two human beings bring and the way in which the lover longs to enter into ever completer understanding of the beloved, and if one adds to this the greater efficiency in creatorship that such a concept suggests, the concept is not without attractions. Loss of individuality need not be feared; a man or woman, losing the self in love for another human being, fulfils the self. It is a common experience of the lover that he wants to share the being of the beloved. To be able to have such a relationship with many other souls when they have simultaneously reached their own ideal selves and to be aware of it and to know that one is communicating with the others on the same level must be bliss indeed.

Do *I* believe this? Dr Stevenson once wrote, 'I don't think my belief is important'.[230] What is important is that a rational man may know something of the beliefs, evidence and both sides of the discussion of a matter of faith. What he does with the information is his own business.

BIBLIOGRAPHY

Addison, J. T., *Life Beyond Death in the Beliefs of Mankind*, London, Allen & Unwin, 1933

Alger, W. R., *A Critical History of the Doctrine of a Future Life*, New York, reissue, Greenwood Press, 1968

Allen, Eula, *The River of Time*, Virginia Beach, USA, ARE Press, 1965

——, *Before the Beginning*, Virginia Beach, USA, ARE Press, 1965

Anderson, J. A., *Reincarnation, A Study of the Human Soul*, San Francisco, 2nd ed, 1894

Aurobindo, Sri, *The Problem of Rebirth*, Pondicherry, Sri Aurobindo Ashram, 1952

Barker, Dianne, *An Investigation into the Role of Hypnosis in Imaginative Role-Playing and Personality Changes*, unpublished BA (Hons) thesis, 1979

Bendit, Laurence J., *The Mirror of Life and Death*, Wheaton, Illinois, The Theosophical Publishing House, 1965

Bernstein, Morey, *The Search for Bridey Murphy*, New York, Doubleday, 1965

Besant, Annie, *The Ancient Wisdom*, Madras, India, The Theosophical Publishing House, 7th ed, 1966

——, *Karma*, Madras, India, The Theosophical Publishing House, 1971

——, *Reincarnation*, London, The Theosophical Publishing House, 1898

Bjerregaard, C. H. A., 'Sufism', *The Path*, I, New York, 1886–7

Blakiston, Patrick, *The Pre-Existence and Transmigration of Souls*, London, Regency Press, 1970

Blavatsky, H. P., *The Key to Theosophy*, London, The Theosophical Publishing House, 1968

Bloxham, A., *Who Was Ann Ockenden?* London, Neville Spearman, 1958

Bonwick, James, *Egyptian Belief in Modern Thought*, London, Kegan Paul, 1878 reissued, 1956

Bowen, Francis, 'Christian Metempsychosis', *Princeton Review*, May 1881

Bukowski, A., 'La Réincarnation selon les Pères de l'Eglise', *Gregoria-num*, IX, 65–91

Bunsen, C. C. J. (Baron), *Egypt's Place in Universal History*, IV, 638–53, 'Metempsychosis', London, Longman, 1848–67

Cannon, Dr Sir Alexander, *Power Within*, New York, Dutton, 1953

Cerminara, Gina, *Many Lives, Many Loves*, New York, William Sloane Associates, 1963

—— *The World Within*, New York, William Morrow & Co, 1957

——, *Many Mansions*, New York, New American Library, 1967

Challoner, H. K., *The Wheel of Rebirth*, London, The Theosophical Publishing House, 1969

Chari, C. T. K., 'Can We Prove Reincarnation?', *Spiritual Frontiers*, X, 1, fall 1978, 17–27

——, 'Parapsychology and Reincarnation', *Indian Journal of Parapsychology*, 3, 1961–2, 32–8

——, 'Buried Memories in Survivalist Research', *International Journal of Parapsychology*, 4, 3, 1962, 40–65

——, 'Paranormal Cognition, Survival and Reincarnation', *Journal of the American Society for Psychical Research*, 56, 1962, 158–63

——, Foreword 1 to Dr Ruth Reyna's *Reincarnation and Science*, New Delhi, India, Sterling Publishers (private), 1973

Christy, Arthur, *The Orient in American Transcendentalism*, New York University Press, 1932

Cooper, Irving, S., *Reincarnation, The Hope of the World*, Wheaton, Illinois, The Theosophical Publishing House, rev ed, 1972

Cragg, Gerald R., *The Cambridge Platonists*, New York, Oxford University Press, 1968

Cummins, Geraldine, *The Road to Immortality*, London, Nicholson, 1932

——, *Beyond Human Personality*, London, Nicholson, 1935

Davy, John, *Work Arising from the Life of Rudolf Steiner*, London, Rudolf Steiner Press, 1975

Delanne, G., *Documents pour servir à l'étude de la réincarnation*, Paris, Editions de la BPS, 1924

Delarrey, M., 'Une Réincarnation Annoncée et Verifiée', *Revue Metaphysique*, I, 1955, 4

De Silva, Lynn A., *Reincarnation in Buddhist and Christian Thought*, Colombo, Sri Lanka, Christian Literature Society of Ceylon, 1968

Dickinson, G. L., 'A Case of Emergence of a Latent Memory under Hypnosis', *Proceedings of the Society for Psychical Research*, 25, 1911, 455–67

Dooley, Anne, *Every Wall a Door*, London, Transworld Publishers, 1973

Ducasse, C. W., *A Critical Examination of the Belief in Life after*

Death, Springfield, Illinois, C. C. Thomas, 1960

——, *Nature, Mind and Death*, Paul Carus Lectures, eighth series, La Salle, Illinois, Open Court, 1951

——, *Is a Life after Death Possible?*, Berkeley, California, University of California Press, 1948

——, 'Doctrines of Reincarnation in the History of Thought', *International Journal of Parapsychology*, autumn 1960

Ebon, Martin, *Reincarnation in the Twentieth Century*, New York, Signet Books, New American Library, 1970

——, *Evidence for Life after Death*, New York, Signet Books, New American Library, 1977

Edgerton, F. trans and ed, *The Bhagavad Gita*, New York, Harper & Row, 1964

Encyclopaedia Britannica, articles on Australian Aborigines, Buddhism, druidism, head hunting, Hinduism, Jainism, karma, lycanthropy, metempsychosis (ie reincarnation), Mithras, mysticism, Orphic doctrine, Philo, Plato, priscillianism, Pythagoras, Sanskrit literature, Sikhism, theosophy, Tibetan Buddhism, Unitarians, universalists

Evans, W. H., *Reincarnation, Fact or Fallacy*, London, Psychic Press

Evans-Wentz, W. Y. ed, *The Tibetan Book of the Dead*, London and New York, Oxford University Press, 3rd ed, 1957

Figuier, Louis, *Le Lendemain de la Mort ou la Vie Future Selon la Science*, Paris, NR 1871; also translated by S. R. Crocker, *The Tomorrow of Death*, Boston, 1872

Fillmore, Charles, *Talks on Truth*, Lee's Summit, Missouri, Unity School of Christianity, 1965

Fletcher, J. G., 'Reincarnation in the West, the Need for Belief', *The Aryan Path*, October 1935, 625–8

Flournoy, T., *From India to the Planet Mars*, New York and London, Harper & Bros, 1900

Fox, Emmet, *Reincarnation*, New York and London, Harper & Row, 1967

Frieling, *Christianity and Reincarnation*, Edinburgh, Floris Books, 1977

Glaskin, G. M., *Windows of the Mind*, London, Arrow Books, 1974

——, *Worlds Within*, London, Arrow Books, 1978

——, *A Door to Eternity*, Australia, Wildwood House, Book Wise (Australia), 1979

Goudey, R. F., *Reincarnation: A Universal Truth*, Los Angeles, The Aloha Press, 1928

Grant, Joan, *Winged Pharaoh*, London, Methuen, 1939

——, *Life as Carola*, London, Methuen, 1939

——, *Far Memories*, New York, Harper & Bros, 1956

——, and Kelsey, D., *Many Lives,* London, Gollancz, 1967

Grant, R. M., *Gnosticism and Early Christianity,* New York and London, Columbia University Press, 1966

Guirdham, Arthur, *The Cathars and Reincarnation,* London, Neville Spearman, 1970

——, *We Are One Another,* London, Neville Spearman, 1974

——, *The Lake and the Castle,* London, Neville Spearman, 1976

Gupta, L. D., Sharma, N. R. and Mathur, T. C., *An Enquiry into the Case of Shanti Devi,* Delhi, International Aryan League, 1936

Haggard, Sir H. Rider, *The Days of My Life,* London, Longman, 1926, see chapter on religion

Hall, Manley P., *Reincarnation, The Cycle of Necessity,* Los Angeles, The Philosophical Research Society, 1967

Hartley, Christine, *A Case for Reincarnation,* London, Robert Hale & Co, 1972

Head, Joseph and Cranston, S. L., *Reincarnation: An East–West Anthology,* New York, The Julian Press, 1961

—— and ——, *Reincarnation in World Thought,* New York, The Julian Press, 1967

—— and ——, *The Phoenix Fire Mystery,* New York, The Julian Press, 1979

Hearn, Lafcanio, *Gleanings in Buddha Fields*, Tokyo, Tuttle, new ed, 1972

Henderson, A., *The Wheel of Life,* London, Rider & Co, 1935

Herodotus, A. D. Godley trans, *The Histories,* London, William Heinemann, 1960

Hick, John, *Death and Eternal Life,* London, Collins, 1976

Holzer, Hans, *Born Again,* Folkestone, Bailey Bros. & Swinfen Ltd, 1975

Howe, Quincey, Jr, *Reincarnation for the Christian,* Philadelphia, Westminster Press, 1974

Hughes, Thea Stanley, *Reincarnation—The Twentieith Century Question,* Australia, T. S. Hughes, 1977

Humphries, Christmas, *Karma and Rebirth,* London, Murray, 1959

Hurnscot, Loren, *A Prison, A Paradise,* New York, The Viking Press,

Iverson, J., *More Lives than One?,* London, Souvenir Press, 1976

Johnson, Raynor C., *The Imprisoned Splendour,* London, Hodder & Stoughton, 1955

——, *A Religious Outlook for Modern Man,* London, Hodder & Stoughton, 1963

——, *The Light and the Gate,* London, Hodder & Stoughton, 1965

Johnston, Charles, *The Memory of Past Births,* New York, The Theosophical Society, 4th ed, 1900

Jung, C. G., Anna Blackwell trans, *Concerning Rebirth, Collected*

Works, 9, 1, New York, Pantheon, 1959

Kardec, Allan, *The Spirits' Book,* London, Psychic Press, 1898 and 1975

King, C. W., *The Gnostics and Their Remains, Ancient and Mediaeval,* London and New York, David Nutt, 1887

Kline, Milton V. ed, *A Scientific Report on the Search for Bridey Murphy,* New York, The Julian Pess, 1956

Knight, Marcus, *Spiritualism, Reincarnation and Immortality,* London, Gerald Duckworth & Co, 1950

Kolisko, Eugen, *Reincarnation and other Essays,* London, King, Littlewood & King, 1940

Krutch, Joseph Wood, *More Lives Than One,* New York, William Morrow & Co, 1962

Langley, Noel, *Edgar Cayce on Reincarnation,* New York, Paperback Library, 1967

Leek, Sybil, *Reincarnation, The Second Chance,* Briarcliff Manor, New York, Stein & Day, 1974

Lewis, H. Spencer, *Rosicrucian Questions and Answers,* San José, California, The Rosicrucian Press, and Kingsport, Tennessee, Kingsport Press, 1975

—— *Mansions of the Soul,* San José, California, The Rosicrucian Press, 17th ed, 1975

Livingston, Marjorie, 'Reincarnation, A Historical and Critical Review', *The Aryan Path,* June 1938, 95–299

Lutoslawski, W., *Pre-existence and Reincarnation,* London, Allen & Unwin, 1928

McIntosh, Alastair I., *The Christos Phenomenon,* unpublished typescript

McTaggart, J. M. E., *The Nature of Existence,* Cambridge, Cambridge University Press, 1927

——, *Human Immortality and Pre-Existence,* New York, Kraus Reprint, 1970

——, *Some Dogmas of Religion,* London, E. Arnold & Co, 2nd ed, 1930

Martin, A. R., *Researches in Reincarnation and Beyond,* Sharon, Pennsylvania, Martin (privately printed), 1942

Martin, Eva, *The Ring of Return,* London, Philip Allan, 1927

Meyer, Louis E., *Reincarnation,* Unity Village, Missouri, Unity School of Christianity, nd

Millard, Joseph, *Edgar Cayce, Man of Miracles,* London, Neville Spearman, 1961

Mirza, N. K., *Reincarnation in Islam,* Adyar, Madras, India, The Theosophical Publishing House,

Montgomery, Ruth, *Here and Hereafter,* Greenwich, Connecticut, Fawcett Publications, 1968

Moore, George Foot, *Metempsychosis,* Cambridge, Harvard University Press, 1914

Moss, Peter and Keeton, Joe, *Encounters With the Past,* London, Sidgwick & Jackson, 1979

Muller, Dr Karl E., *Reincarnation Based on Facts,* London, Psychic Press, 1970

Murry, John Middleton, 'The Reasonableness and Practicality of Reincarnation', *The Aryan Path,* June 1938, 271–6

Parrinder, E. G., 'Varieties of Belief in Reincarnation', *The Hibbert Journal,* April 1957

Pearce-Higgins, Canon J. D. and Whitby, Rev G. S., *Life, Death and Psychical Research,* London, Rider & Co, 1973

Pezzani, André, *La Pluralité des Existences de l'Ame,* Paris, Didier, 1865

Raymond, A. Moody, *Life After Life,* New York, Mockingbird, Bantam, 1975

Reyna, Ruth, *Reincarnation and Science,* New Delhi, Sterling Publishers, 1975

Rittlemeyer, Friedrich, *Reincarnation in the Light of Thought, Religion and Ethics,* London, Christian Community Bookshop, 1940

Rochas, A. de, *Les Vies Successives,* Paris, Chacornac Frères, 1924

Rodney, J., *Explorations of a Hypnotist,* London, Elek, 1959

Ryall, E. W., *Second Time Round,* London, Neville Spearman, 1974

Seton, Julia M., *The Gospel of the Red Man,* London, Psychic Press, 1937

Sewell, Homer Belk, *An Assessment of Ideological Conflict Between Reincarnation and Karma Notions and Fundamental Notions in Christian Doctrine,* unpublished PhD dissertation, University of Lancaster, May, 1978

Sharma, I. C., *Cayce, Karma and Reincarnation,* New York, Harper & Row, 1975

Shirley, Ralph, *The Problem of Rebirth,* London, Rider & Co, 1938

Stearn, Jess, *The Sleeping Prophet. The Life and Work of Edgar Cayce,* London, Frederick Muller, 1967

——, *The Second Life of Susan Ganier,* London, Leslie Frewin, 1969

Steiner, Rudolph, *Reincarnation and Karma, Their Significance in Modern Culture,* London, Anthroposophical Publishing Co

—— *Reincarnation and Immortality,* Blauvelt, New York, Multimedia Publishing Corporation, 1974

——, *Reincarnation and Karma; How Karma Works,* New York, Anthroposophical Press

Stevenson, Ian, 'The Evidence for survival from claimed memories of former incarnations', *Journal of the American Society for Psychical Research,* 54, 1960, 51–71, 95–117

——, 'Cultural patterns in cases suggestive of reincarnation among the Tlingit Indians of Southeastern Alaska', *Journal of the American Society for Psychical Research*, 60, 1966, 229–43

——, 'Characteristics of cases of the reincarnation type in Turkey and their comparison with cases in two other cultures', *International Journal of Comparative Sociology*, 11, 1970, 1–17

——, 'Characteristics of cases of the reincarnation type in Ceylon', *Contributions to Asian Studies*, 3, 1973, 26–39

——, 'The "perfect" reincarnation case', *Research in Parapsychology*, W. G. Roll, R. L. Morris and J. D. Morris eds, Metuchen, New York, Scarecrow Press, 1973, 185–7

——, *Twenty Cases Suggestive of Reincarnation*, Charlottesville, University Press of Virginia, 1966, 2nd rev ed, 1974

——, *Xenoglossy. A Review and Report of a Case*, Charlottesville, University Press of Virginia, and Bristol, John Wright & Sons, 1974

——, 'Some questions related to cases of the reincarnation type', *Journal of the American Society for Psychical Research*, 68, 1974, 395–416

——, *Cases of the Reincarnation Type, Vol I Ten Cases in India*, Charlottesville, University Press of Virginia, 1975

——, 'A preliminary report on a new case of responsive xenoglossy: the case of Gretchen', *Journal of the American Society for Psychical Research*, 70, 1976, 65–77

——, *Cases of the Reincarnation Type, Vol 2 Ten Cases in Sri Lanka*, Charlottesville, University Press of Virginia, 1977

——, *Cases of the Reincarnation Type, Vol 3 Fifteen Cases in Thailand, Lebanon and Turkey*, Charlottesville, University Press of Virginia, 1978

——, 'Reincarnation: Field Studies and Theoretical Issues', *Handbook of Parapsychology*, Benjamin B. Wolman ed, New York, London, etc, Van Nostrand Reinhold Co, 1977, 631–63

Stewart, A. J., *Falcon*, London, Davies, 1970

Story, Francis, *Rebirth as Doctrine and Experience*, Kandy, Sri Lanka, Buddhist Publication Society, 1975

Sugrue Thomas, *There is a River (The Story of Edgar Cayce)*, New York, Dell Publishing Co, 1970

Toynbee, Arnold ed, *Life After Death*, London, Weidenfeld & Nicolson, 1976

Underwood, Peter and Wilder, Leonard, *Lives to Remember*, London, Robert Hale, 1975

Walker, E. D., *Reincarnation, A Study of Forgotten Truth*, London, William Rider & Son, 1913

Wambach, Helen, *Recalling Past Lives: The Evidence from Hypnosis*, London, Hutchinson, 1978

Weatherhead, Leslie, *The Case for Reincarnation*, Burgh Heath, Tad-
worth, M. C. Peto, 2nd ed, 1960
——, *The Christian Agnostic*, London, Hodder & Stoughton, 1965,
and Nashville, Tennessee, Abingdon Press, 1972
Wood, F. H., *After Thirty Centuries*, London, Rider, 1953
——, *Ancient Egypt Speaks*, London, Rider, 1937
——, *This Egyptian Miracle*, London, Rider, 2nd ed, 1955
Zolik, E. S., '"Reincarnation" phenomena in hypnotic states', *Inter-
national Journal of Parapsychology*, 4, 3, 1962, 66–78
——, 'Case Study of the origins and psychodynamics of an "other life"
experience', *Journal of Clinical Psychology*, 14, 1958, 179–83

NOTES

An author's name followed by a page or chapter number indicates that the reference is to the book under that name in the Bibliography. A name followed by a date shows that two or more books are listed under the author's name in the Bibliography and the date is that of the book containing the reference. Books not in the Bibliography are listed in full in the notes.

Chapter 1

1 *Haunted Britain*, A. D. Hippisley Coxe, London, Hutchinson, 1973, p. 26
2 E. D. Walker, p. 5
3 Head and Cranston, 1979, p. 190
4 Manley P. Hall, pp. 10–11
5 e.g. Walker, p. 295
6 *News Letter* of the *American S.P.R.* Vol. 5, No. 3, July, 1979
7 Ibid
8 J. T. Addison, p. 75
9 Walker, p. 336
10 Marcus Knight, p. 57
11 Head and Cranston, 1967, p. 72
12 Walker, p. 270
13 Head and Cranston, 1967, p. 41
14 *News Letter* of the *American S.P.R.* ibid
15 Head and Cranston, 1967, pp. 44–5
16 Ibid, p. 85
17 Ibid, p. 92
18 Ibid
19 Ibid
20 *The Dhammapada*, Path of Discipline
21 *Sammannaphala Sutta*, tr. T. W. Rhys Davids
22 Head and Cranston, 1967, p. 65
23 Ibid, p. 147
24 Ibid, p. 50

Chapter 2

25 Book III, Section 123

26 *Jewish War*, Book 3, Ch. 8, No. 5

27 *Ante-Nicene Library*, Edinburgh, Clark 1867, pp. 92–3

28 *Encyclopaedia Britannica*, 'Pre-Existence', 1959 ed.

29 *Eclogae ex Scripturis Propheticis, Ante-Nicene Library*, Edinburgh, Clark 1867, II, 92–3

30 *Stromata*, IV, 12

31 English Version by G. R. S. Mead, quoted Eva Martin, pp. 81–5

32 *De Principiis*, IV, Cap 3, 10; 26, 23.

33 *On the Soul and Resurrection*, Ch. 32. *A Select Library of Nicene and Post-Nicene Fathers*, 2nd. Series, VII, Edinburgh, Clark pp 453–4

34 Head and Cranston, 1967, p. 106

35 Ignatius Donnelley, *Atlantis, the Antediluvian World*, New York, Harper, 1882

36 Private letter to the author

37 Eva Martin, p. 107

38 *Lux Orientalis*, 1662

39 *Ethics*, Book V, Prop. 23

40 Head and Cranston, 1967, p. 255

41 *The Philosophical Principles of Natural and Revealed Religion*, II, 236–246, Edinburgh, 1748

42 *Philosophical Dictionary*, Section X, 'Soul', London, 1770, 3rd. ed. p. 288

43 'The Immortality of the Soul' in *Essays, Moral, Political and Literary*, London, 1875, II, 404

44 *Miscellaneous Pieces in Verse and Prose*, London, 1770, 3rd. ed., p. 288

45 Head and Cranston, 1967, pp. 258–9

46 *Miscellaneous Philosophical Writings*, New York, Harper and Row, 1909, p. 103

47 Head and Cranston, 1967, p. 260

48 Ibid, p. 263

49 Ibid, pp. 264–5

50 Ibid, pp. 271–2

51 Ibid, pp. 125–6

52 Kolner Vorlesungen (Cologne Lectures), ed. von Windischmann, Bonn, 1837, pp. 202–3, 206

53 *The World as Will and Idea*, trans. R. B. Haldane and J. Kemp, London, Kegan Paul, 1906, III, pp. 299–300

54 *Parerga and Paralipomena*, Vol. II, Ch. 15

55 *Three Philosophical Poets*, (Goethe's Faust), Harvard University, 1910

56 A. Bertholet, *The Transmigration of Souls*, London, Harper, 1909, p. 104 (Letter to Christoph Wieland)

57 *Memoirs of Johannes Falk*, Leipzig, 1832, reprinted in Goethe-Bibliothek, Berlin; Head and Cranston, 1967, p. 269.

58 Head and Cranston, 1967, p. 125

59 E. D. Walker, 1913, p. 94

60 *Consolations in Travel* (Dialogue IV)

61 Introduction to *The Works of Plato*

62 Head and Cranston, 1967, pp. 277–8

63 *De l'Humanité*, Vol. 17, 1872, p. 330

64 *Seraphita*, Ch. 6

65 *Human Immortality*, Ingersoll Lecture, Harvard University, 1893, pp. v – ix

66 *The Soul of the Universe*, New York, David McKay, 1940, Chapter 11 on 'The Soul'.

67 *The Self in Transformation*, New York, Basic Books, 1963; Harper Torchbook, 1965

68 *San Francisco Examiner*, August 28th, 1928. Interview with Ford reported by G. S. Viereck

69 *Diary and Sundry Observations of Thomas Alva Edison*, New York, Philosophical Library, 1948, p. 236

70 *Victor Hugo's Intellectual Autobiography*, trans Lorenzo O'Rourke, New York, Funk and Wagnalls, 1907, pp. 260, 269

71 *The Philosophy of Life*, A. M. Baten, Hammond, Indiana, 1930, p. 163

72 Eva Martin, pp. 279–80

73 Ibid, pp. 268–9

74 Ibid, p. 189

75 Ibid, p. 222

76 Ibid, p. 244

77 *The Perennial Philosophy* (Ch. 14)

78 Raynor C. Johnson, 1963, Introduction and pp. 178–80

79 Head and Cranston, 1967, p. 327

80 Ibid, p. 348

81 *Philosophie Religieuse Terre et Ciel, Paris,* 1854, pp. 305–8

82 *Le Personnalisme,* Paris, Felix Alcan, 1903, pp. 125–6

83 Head and Cranston, 1967, p. 314

84 Lutoslawski, W., 1928, pp. 28–9

85 *The Philosophy of Mysticism*, trans. C. C. Massey, London, 1889, II, pp. 230–2

86 *Collected Works,* New York, Pantheon, 1959, Part I includes lecture 'Concerning Rebirth'

87 New York, Pantheon, 1963, pp 321–2

88 *The Realm of Ends,* Gifford Lectures, 1907–1910, Cambridge

University Press, 1911, pp. 402–5

89 *Value and Destiny of the Individual*, Gifford Lectures, 1912, London, Macmillan, 1913, pp. 267–8

90 II, pp. 396–7

91 *From Religion to Philosophy*, London, Edward Arnold, 1912, p. 229

92 *Christ and the Modern Man*, London, Churches' Fellowship for Psychical Study, 1961, pp. 8–9

93 Weatherhead, 1965 and 1972, Chapter on 'Reincarnation and Renewed Chances'

94 *A Psychological and Poetical Approach to the Study of Christ in the Fourth Gospel*, quoted by Eva Martin, p. 265

95 Quoted by Eva Martin, pp. 293–4

96 *Transmigration of Souls*, Essay on 'The Teaching of Reincarnation and the Problem of Man', Paris, YMCA Press, undated

97 *Indian Thought and Its Development*, Boston, Beacon Press, 1952, pp. 222–3

98 *Symbols of Eternal Life*, Harvard Divinity Bulletin, April, 1962

99 *Pythagoras and the Delphic Mysteries*, trans. Fred Rothwell

100 *An Idealistic View of Life*, London, Allen and Unwin, 1929, Ch. 3

101 *Letter to Mathilde Wesendonck*, quoted by Head and Cranston, 1967, p. 313

102 *Gustave Mahler*, Richard Specht, Berlin, Schuster and Loeffler, 1913, p. 39

103 Head and Cranston, 1967, p. 350

104 Ibid, p. 411

105 Quotation supplied by correspondent, source unknown

106 *From the Conscious to the Unconscious*, trans. Stanley de Brath, New York, Harper and Row, 1920

107 Quoted by Eva Martin, pp. 227f

108 *The American Weekly* ('Did You Live Before?'), April 8th, 1956

Chapter 3

109 See Bibliography

110 A good summary of Kardec's reincarnationist teaching is to be found in Manley P. Hall. See Bibliography

111 St Matthew's Gospel, Ch. 13, v. 11

112 St Luke's Gospel, Ch. 1, vv. 52–3

113 'Reincarnation and Christianity' *Christian Parapsychologist*, Vol. 3, No. 4, Sept. 1979

114 Marcus Knight, 1950, pp. 66–7

115 John Hick, p. 370

116 *On the Soul,* Chs. 23–4, 28–35
117 *Refutation of All Heresies,* Book VII, Ch. 20
118 *On First Principles,* Book III, Ch. 9, 6–8
119 *On the Making of Man,* Ch. 28
120 Confessions I: 6
121 *Against the Heathen,* II, 16
122 *Christian Parapsychologist* (see Note 113)
123 Ibid

Chapter 4

124 Pamphlet, Baluja Press, Delhi, 1936
125 Manley P. Hall, p. 136, and other sources
126 Martin Ebon, 19, quoting *The American Magazine*, July, 1915
127 'Credo'—Television Programme, notes made by author
128 Frances Story, 1975, p. 252
129 Lionel Oliphant, *The Land of Gilead,* London, 1880
130 Karl E. Muller, p. 43
131 Ibid, p. 51
132 Ibid, p. 55
133 Head and Cranston, 1979, p. 401f
134 Ruth Montgomery, p. 32
135 Jess Stearn, 1970, p. 290
136 Karl E. Muller, p. 208
137 See Bibliography
138 Hans Holzer, pp. 82–4
139 Ibid, p. 88
140 Ibid, pp. 98–9
141 Karl E. Muller, p. 161
142 Ibid, p. 87
143 Ibid, p. 47
144 Ibid, p. 178
145 Ibid, p. 95
146 Hans Holzer, Ch. 6
147 Martin Ebon, 1970, pp. 13–14
148 Karl E. Muller, p. 100
149 Underwood and Wilder, p. 182
150 *Sunday Express*, May 26th, 1935, quoted by Head and Cranston, 1979, pp. 413–14
151 Hans Holzer, p. 222
152 Ralph Shirley, Ch. 5
153 Raynor C. Johnson, 1965, p. 59
154 Karl E. Muller, pp. 214–15
155 Thomas Flournoy *From India to the Planet Mars,* New York and

London, Harper and Bros., 1900
156 See Bibliography for Wood's three books
157 'The Watseka Wonder', *Journal of the Society for Psychical Research* Vol. X, pp. 98–104
158 C. T. K. Chari, 1962
159 *Psychic News*, Aug. 27th, 1960
160 A.R. Martin

Chapter 5

161 C. T. K. Chari, 'Paramnesia and Reincarnation' in *Journal of the Society for Psychical Research*, Vol 40, 1960, p.278
162 Ibid.
163 E. D. Walker, pp. 41–2
164 pp. 15–16
165 *Nineteenth Century*, June, 1906
166 Karl E. Muller, p. 167
167 Raynor C. Johnson, 1965, pp. 185–6
168 Ibid, pp. 58–9; Weatherhead, 1960, pp. 11–12
169 C. T. K. Chari, op. cit., p. 277
170 W. B. Seabrook, *Adventures in Arabia*, 1927
171 Karl E. Muller, pp. 111f, 122–3f
172 Ibid, pp. 112f
173 Weatherhead, 1960, p. 14
174 Martin Ebon, 1970, Ch. 17
175 Karl E. Muller, pp. 60f
176 Proceedings Society for Psychical Research, Vol. XI, 1895, pp. 351–2
177 C. T. K. Chari, 1962 (*Buried Memories*)
178 Podolsky, ed. *Encyclopedia of Aberrations*, London, Arcon Publishers, 1953, p. 267
179 Karl E. Muller, p. 104

Chapter 6

180 Gina Cerminara, 1967, p. 29
181 Noel Langley, p. 77
182 Ruth Montgomery, p. 86
183 Ibid, pp. 135f
184 C. W. Ducasse, 1960
185 Gina Cerminara, 1963, pp. 46–7
186 Gina Cerminara, 1967, p. 41
187 Ibid, p. 143
188 Jess Stearn, 1967, Ch. 14
189 Gina Cerminara, p. 131

190 Ibid, p. 44
191 Gina Cerminara, 1957, p. 197
192 Noel Langley, p. 168
193 Gina Cerminara, 1967, p. 50
194 Ibid, p. 71
195 Ibid, p. 43
196 Ibid, p. 102

Chapter 7

197 Karl E. Muller, p. 26
198 Vol. 25, pp. 455–67
199 Morey Bernstein, p. 222
200 Gina Cerminara, 1957, p. 36
201 Hans Holzer, Ch. 5
202 Ruth Montgomery, pp. 57ff
203 J. Rodney, pp. 76–86
204 p. 47
205 Peter Underwood and Leonard Wilder, *passim*.
206 Peter Moss and Joe Keeton, pp. 7–9
207 Ibid, p. 157
208 E. S. Zolik, 1962

Chapter 8

209 G. M. Glaskin, 1979, p. 180
210 Ibid, p. 14 (unnumbered)
211 Ibid, p. 54
212 G. M. Glaskin, 1978, p. 177
213 G. M. Glaskin, 1979, p. 59
214 G. M. Glaskin, 1974, Ch. 20
215 G. M. Glaskin, 1978, p. 238
216 *Epistle of James*, Ch. 1, v. 8

Chapter 9

217 Stevenson comments that if a child talked of a previous life as a
     person of the opposite sex in a culture that regarded sex change as
     impossible, his remarks might be suppressed. 'We should inter-
     pret cautiously the relationship between beliefs about reincarna-
     tion and data of cases.' (Letter to author)
218 He further comments, 'You may not have given sufficient weight
     to xenoglossy as a phenomenon not suitable of explanation by the
     super-ESP hypothesis' and 'The finding of the hidden object
     could be attributed to clairvoyance'. (Ibid)

Chapter 10

219 Arthur Guirdham, 1970, p. 23
220 Ibid, p. 24
221 *Journal of the Society for Psychical Research*, Vol. 45, 1969–70, p. 424
222 Arthur Guirdham, 1974, p. 35
223 Ibid, p. 56
224 Ibid, p. 122
225 Ibid, p. 186

Chapter 12

226 Head and Cranston, 1979, p. 440
227 Dom Bernard Clements, *What Happens When We Die*, London, S.C.M. Press, 1939
228 *Epistle to the Hebrews*, Ch. 13, v. 8
229 Geraldine Cummins, 1932, quoted by Karl E. Muller, p. 219
230 Head and Cranston, 1979, p. 440

INDEX